I SEE
Thrones!

IGNITING & INCREASING
YOUR INFLUENCE

IN THE SEVEN MOUNTAINS OF CULTURE

DR. GORDON E. BRADSHAW
FOREWORD BY DR. BRUCE COOK

I SEE THRONES!
IGNITING & INCREASING YOUR INFLUENCE IN THE SEVEN MOUNTAINS OF CULTURE

Printed in the USA | First Printing Sept. 2015

ISBN (print): 978-1-939944-31-3
ISBN (kindle): 978-1-939944-32-0
ISBN (other format): 978-939944-33-7

Library of Congress Control Number: 2015951286

Cover Design: James Nesbit | Interior Formatting: Wendy K. Walters

Published By Kingdom House Publishing
LAKEBAY, WASHINGTON | USA

To Contact the Author:
WWW.GEMSNETWORK.ORG
DRGEBRADSHAW@GMAIL.COM

DEDICATION

This book is dedicated to all of the "kings" who serve the needs of humanity and community, give of themselves for the plight of nations, contribute to enhancing the quality of life for others, shape and re-shape the context and contents of this world and to those who love and serve the King of kings and Lord of lords, Jesus Christ and who endeavor with all that is within them to see that *"The kingdoms of this world have become the kingdoms of our Lord and of His Christ, and He shall reign forever and ever!" (Rev. 11:15, NKJV)*

It is dedicated to the countless believers who have impacted their homes, communities, businesses, social circles, corporations, organizations, jobs, families, friends, and the world, but may have had no title, no official recognition and no accolades, but did it for the love of God and humanity. We celebrate you and encourage you to press toward new marks for prizes that are beyond your dreams! It is also dedicated to those who may have been fortunate enough to be recognized, appreciated and supported for their impactful deeds. We celebrate you and encourage you to continue growing and to enlighten and encourage others. Pass on the power of your influence in positive ways.

I say to you, your future is bright, and that it shines with the light of God from a throne that is brilliant and glorious!

"But the people who know their God shall be strong, and carry out great exploits."

(Dan. 11:28, NKJV)

ACKNOWLEDGEMENTS

I would like to begin by thanking the greatest King of all time... the Lord Jesus Christ – King of kings and Lord of lords! Without His magnificent life, teachings, and dedication to the purpose and mission of redemption for our lives and our planet, there would be no thrones and no hope of reclaiming our lost world. I thank God, the Father, who has such love for us as to allow us to share in this incredible mission, and the Holy Spirit who has so kindly shared the wisdom, gifting and revelations that makes this book possible. Lord, I am forever yours.

I have a wonderful cadre of "kings" in my spiritual family circle. They provide the constant fellowship, faith, fortitude, function, friendship and "fire" that I need. Life at this level is impossible without people like this! I love and appreciate you all. I thank my network - Global Effect Movers & Shakers (GEMS), a group of kingdom-level leaders who are determined to be God's "vibrating voices" to the world; the Voice of God Ministries family, who stands in support of me without wavering; the 3M Project Global Initiative team; Dr. Bruce Cook (CEO) and the Kingdom Congressional International Alliance (KCIA) family who are valuable beyond words. Dr. Cook is my friend, covenant brother, publisher, editor, compass, apostolic/prophetic colleague and a stellar example of a "king!" Dr. Francis Myles, my covenant brother... I appreciate your great revelation of the Order of Melchizedek and your friendship..."*Bayete!*" I acknowledge and thank Dr. Sylvester Brinson III, my good friend, apostolic colleague and brother and a "scholar of scholars," and my friend and brother Dr. Carl White – who has always believed in me and in my message.

I'd like to thank Dr. Curtis Gillespie, Beverly Harbour, Dr. James Brewton, Matthew Fleming, Dr. Bill Manduca, Belinda Taylor, John McClain, Alex McCaskill, Jeanette Williams, Wanda Anderson, Manessa Williams, James Hatten, Charlie Fisher, Dr. Glories Powell, Russell and Glenisaah Stauffer, Charles "Chuck" Hughes, John Anderson, Wende Jones, Dr. Mark Kauffman, Dr. Ethel Williams, Priscilla Brown-RN, Cheryl Scott-Fields, and Ambassador Dr. Clyde Rivers and iChange Nations. I thank Chief Dennis Gault, Chief Rudy Rinas and Chief Cary Darnell for their trust in my abilities as a public safety leader. The names of those who have had impact upon me and on this message for over the years are too numerous to list, but they are embedded in the history that helped shape this moment. I give special thanks to my lovely daughter, Kaylyn Joelle Bradshaw for her unending love, for her trust in me as her father and for encouraging me in all that I do. I appreciate the prophetic support and prayers of each and every person who stood by me in this vision and mission and those who were true examples of the kingdom of God. I thank the churches, ministries, organizations, boards, networks, teams, committees and departments who have trusted me in leadership over the years. For all of you... **I SEE THRONES!**

ENDORSEMENTS

D r. Gordon E. Bradshaw is one of the leading pioneers in the occupation of the Seven Mountain Movement. The underlying gift Dr. Bradshaw possesses is his ability to be in step with times and seasons. He has a revelation of the king and priest that is a needed revelation in this day and hour. This book *I See Thrones!* is creating the paradigm that will cause the kings to occupy the mountains. As the Ambassador of a nation I would recommend this book as a training model for any government of the world that wants to see biblical transformation in their country.

Amb. Dr. Clyde Rivers

World Peace Ambassador and Special Representative from
Interfaith Peace-Building Initiative to the United Nations
Victorville, California

D r. Bradshaw has done it again. *I See Thrones!* is a direct message from
God delivered through one of his very accomplished messengers.
We all want to be successful in business. Dr. Bradshaw has very adeptly
given us the blueprint to achieve positive results in business and in life.
Like when you take a math exam, sometimes you are given the answer
but the successful, accomplished individual has the ability to show you
their work. The road to failure is in trying to please everyone. The secret
to success is pleasing God. If you are uncovered or insecure, it is because
you are a bystander. Be an "Upstander" and know through God that you
will be blessed and all of your needs will be met. My vision is clear... *I
See Thrones!*

Charles "Chuck" Hughes, MPA

Executive Director – Gary, Indiana Chamber of Commerce

Goodwill Ambassador – Golden Rule International

Recipient – iChange Nations Distinguished Leadership Medal

Gary, Indiana

I *See Thrones!* is an incredible resource for the times we are in and the call
for all of God's children to step into their assignments, to pick up their
crowns, to sit on their thrones and be the answers to the world's problems
we are called to be. Dr. Bradshaw is a masterful storyteller as he brings
forth the incredible truths of God and His promises for His children
today. Just as his book *Authority for Assignment* gave me the language and
confirmation for my assignment, *I See Thrones!* breaks through additional
barriers and mindsets to set us free to move fully into our assignment and
see our thrones God has set before us since the beginning of time.

ENDORSEMENTS

I am honored and blessed to call Dr. Bradshaw my friend and comrade in arms. The revelation he carries and releases regarding our kingdom mandate here on earth and our kingly authority and responsibility to carry out our assignments is truly transformational. *I See Thrones!* will encourage you, challenge you and provide you the wisdom and knowledge of God's word to be empowered to take full authority in your assignment and see your thrones!

Wende Jones
CEO, Agile Labs
Board Chair, Christian Chamber of Commerce of the Northwest
Author, The God Port
Beaverton, Oregon

God has given Dr. Gordon Bradshaw keys to unlocking dimensions of the kingdom, essential for our reigning and being seated as kings and priests in the Seven Mountains of Influence. The early church turned the world upside down; this revelatory teaching of Apostle Bradshaw is about to turn the world right side up!

Charlie Fisher
CEO, Guiding Business Transitions
President, Kingdom Economic Yearly Summit (KEYS)
Grande Prairie, Alberta, Canada

D r. Bradshaw has a firm grasp of what is required to defeat the Kingdom of Babylon that has dominated the marketplace for thousands of years, and replace it with the Kingdom of God. If we cannot oust or overcome this despicable culture of greed, fear, and corruption, we will never ascend any of the 7 Mountains and we will never see the Kingdom of God manifest on the earth. *I See Thrones!* introduces this concept on the first page of the first chapter – Thrones That Move Mountains... *"it has always been the intention of God for His people to have the highest seats of influence and not for any contrary forces to rule there. History has proven this to be a difficult task, not because of the weakness of God, but of men with their proclivity toward greed, lust, covetousness, pride, unrighteousness and ungodliness and because of the demonically-engineered strategies of dark forces. However, the situation is turning around, even as you read this chapter."*

It is immensely refreshing to find a work that addresses the reality of the marketplace and I commend Dr. Bradshaw for the great job he has done with *I See Thrones!*

Dave Hodgson

CEO, Paladin Corporation

Founder and Leader of Kingdom Investors

Mooloolaba, QLD, Australia

A s I started to read *I See Thrones!* I went from chapter to chapter with great revelation and anticipation of what the next chapter would reveal. Deep in my heart I have been seeking out the matter of Thrones and how does it apply to our life in Christ. In Matthew 28:18 Jesus says: *"All authority has been given to me in heaven and on earth."* All is a very inclusive word. What does this mean to his followers? Then Jesus says in John 15:15, *"No longer do I call you slaves, for the slave does not know what his master is doing; but I have called you friends, for all things that I have heard from My Father I have made known to you."* In *I See Thrones!* Dr Gordon Bradshaw's deep practical revelation on walking out our God-given authority and responsibility in the Kingdom is clearly explained. If you want to see the Kingdom come on Earth as it is in heaven, as many do, then I recommend making this book your friend.

Al Caperna
Chairman, CMC Group
Director of Call2Business
Bowling Green, Ohio

D r. Bradshaw promotes awareness of the need for this generation to take their position and begin to affect, transform and influence the seven cultural mountains of society. All creation, especially in these cultural mountains, waits expectantly and earnestly for God's sons to be made known and to be bold enough to bring the Holy Spirit led solutions that will impact the world!

Dr. Ed Turose
President, The Focus Institute and Global Innovation Group
National Account Executive, Coca-Cola Refreshments
Volant, Pennsylvania

I n the past, the subject of sovereignty was often sequestered…" Dr. Bradshaw has unmasked one of Satan's most dastardly schemes: relegating promises meant for the present as only accessible in some future state, be it in the Millenium or even Heaven. In falling for this lie, the Church has tolerated powerlessness and accepted weaknesses and subservience to earthly "rulers" over the Seven Mountains of Culture. When you open this book, your eyes will be opened to see the throne for which you have been uniquely prepared to sit and accept your destiny as a co-regent with Christ in fulfillment of the scriptures, *"If we endure, we shall also reign with Him"* (2 Tim. 2:12). Do you hear the groan of creation as it awaits the sons of God to be revealed and take their place? Are you groaning like I am to see the day when we rise up to exercise dominion as we were commanded from the beginning? Yes, Lord Jesus, help us to SEE THRONES!

Rev. Kevin A. Graves

President, Target Ministries

Singapore, Singapore

I n *I See Thrones!*, Dr. Bradshaw shows us a room of empty thrones waiting for us to take our God-given places of authority. He then takes us on a journey that not only leads to our ascension to these "thrones" by the King of kings, but also gives us our assignments of "lordship" by the Lord of lords. Dr. Bradshaw describes "lordship" as a term describing our spheres of influence within Seven Mountain territory. As God gives us authority to rule and reign in our assignments, we are led into ever expanding and increasing responsibilities. Then we are "called," "chosen," and "faithful" in respective areas of assignment. Dr. Bradshaw declares that we are about to see phenomenal advances in breakthrough technology and ideas that will rattle and shake "status quo" environments and normalcy. Unusual and uncommon things are about to happen. So read *I See Thrones!* and take courage because your increase is closer than you think!

Timothy Hamon, Ph.D.
CEO, Christian International Ministries Network
Santa Rosa Beach, Florida

As pioneers who contend for 7 Mountain dominion, we remain alert for the road map that will provide the straightest ascent. Bushwhacking is hard work, and many of us have grown weary along the way. As a businesswoman, I want to know how I've impacted the transfer of wealth in my time here on earth. As a philanthropist, I want to understand the ways in which God is calling me to shape society. As one with the heart of a public servant, I yearn to witness a righteous government that is restored with judgment and justice. *I See Thrones!* cuts through cobwebs and confusion and delivers a shakeup to the mind and heart while ushering in encouragement and strength to the spirit. Practical yet powerful applications are delivered through case studies and divinely-delivered decrees that accompany each chapter. Brilliantly written, Dr. Bradshaw captures the 7 Mountain sound and language that reach to the heavens; the result is a "throne song" that will be harmonized by those who quest for fresh revelation. May each sojourner who holds this book in his or her hand connect to the image of Jesus, fist pump in the air in triumph at the revelation and renaissance it releases as each declares, "I see thrones!"

Sher Valenzuela
Vice President, First State Manufacturing
Author, The World's Best Customer
Milford, Delaware

I n his latest book, *I See Thrones!*, Dr. Gordon Bradshaw has masterfully shown the importance of recognizing and embracing our Kingdom of God call to royal service, some to thrones, others on thrones, but all to the majesty of sons or daughters of the Most High King. In the classic story of "The Prince and the Pauper", the Prince, having been accidentally forced to live the mean life of the pauper, is abused and used, ridiculed, attacked, robbed and finally arrested. The Pauper, likewise living in the palace, is trained in the ways of royalty. Through all the Prince endured, he never forgot who he was and that he was destined to sit on the throne. This drove his every decision and action. The Pauper grew in wisdom, never grasping for personal gain, in his integrity restoring the prince to his royal place on the throne, also lived out his life in the royal courts. From this place of royalty, they changed the world. Please read this extremely important book and embrace your high calling to royalty. It will change your life and change the world.

Dr. Greg Linnebach

Apostle and Serial Entrepreneur

Arizona Prior – Knights of Malta, Sovereign Order of St John of Jerusalem

Peoria, Arizona

D r. Bradshaw is a diligent student of the Word of God, and through his diligence in diving deeper and deeper into the Word, this time he has resurfaced with an absolutely remarkable clarity of understanding about some deep truths regarding Kingdom Authority and its application in today's society which is brilliantly displayed throughout the pages of this book.

This book describes in detail God's plan to fully utilize the eternal purpose of each human life, repair our thinking, adjust our posture, restore our authority as kings and priests and mend the rift between earth and mankind. It also generously provides practical keys for us to engage in this vital process of transformation.

I believe that *I See Thrones!* will be a catalyst in the lives of many believers to step into their true Kingdom assignments and thus help usher in the "Glory of the Lord" upon the church as prophesied through Isaiah with the consequence that "Gentiles shall come to thy light, and kings to the brightness of thy rising" (Isa. 60:3, KJV).

Karl O. Bandlien, MD

Co-Founder & President of Global Compassion Network

Co-Founder & Vice President of Transformation Health Network

Co-Chair of KCIA Science, Technology and Healthcare Committee

Highland, Michigan

Dr. G. E. Bradshaw has successfully captured the essence of true Kingdom citizenship. *I See Thrones!* is a double-edged sword that has cut through the mediocrity of religiosity and exposed the true meaning of being a 'royal priesthood'. You hold in your hands an instruction manual for both "Ruler and Worshipper." With its broad range of relevance to our social, economic and spiritual conditions, *I See Thrones!* inspires us to take our position in the Seven Mountains and exercise our divinely-appointed sphere of influence and depth of authority as both King and Priest.

Dr. Glories Powell

Senior Pastor—CODA Ministries

President – Glories Powell Ministries

Executive Director – REVIVE Prison Re-Entry Program

Las Vegas, Nevada

Since the birth of the American experiment, men and women have been loath to properly regard royalty. Believers, especially, have too often spiritualized the reign of King Jesus, and have put aside any notion that we will reign with him until the Millennial Age. But, in this vital work, Dr. Gordon Bradshaw has shed new light on the clear meaning of Holy Scripture that depicts the role of kings in bringing the Kingdom of God into manifestation in our communities and nations. This book should be part of every saint's training in learning to function as both "priests and kings" [Rev 1.5-6].

John Anderson, MBA
Executive Chairman, Global Development Partners (GDP)
Gig Harbor, Washington

Spiritual forefathers of your city of Chicago like Dowie and Moody never passed their mantles; therefore men like Capone held a seat (throne) and released and exercised a spirit of corruption that has ruled your city to this day. But, what you've written you will NOW experience! You shall occupy a place in the spirit and influence your city in a redemptive way! Take your governorship mantle and reign!

Dr. Mark Kauffman
Overseer – Kingdom Regency Alliance
President – International Coalition of Marketplace Leaders (ICML)
President – Kingdom Congressional International Alliance (KCIA)
New Castle, Pennsylvania

ENDORSEMENTS

In 1975, Dr. Bill Bright of Campus Crusade for Christ and Loren Cunningham of Youth With a Mission blessed the body of Christ with the Seven Cultural Mountains model. This metaphor was popularized in the early 2000's by Dr. Lance Wallnau. As with every prophetic revelation, it takes time for the power of the word to realize its full effect. We may understand the times and seasons as a result of a prophetic word, but not have the clearest understanding of what to do. Dr. Bradshaw's book, *I See Thrones!*, changes all that. His latest book ensures that the revelation of what we have been given will continue to impact the Church's advancement on Earth well into the 21st Century. From his first chapter on Thrones That Move Mountains to the last on Restoring Souls, Systems, and Societies, he gives us the means to see sustained transformation and accomplish what the prophetic word revealed over 30 years ago.

This is a meaty book filled with rich revelation and wisdom on how to receive our heavenly inheritance that comes with a personal relationship with Jesus the Messiah, the King of kings and Lord of lords. With this deeper revelation of our identity in Christ, now we can walk humbly in our godly authority as sons and daughters in His Kingdom here on earth. Because of this book, the world is one major step closer to seeing what can happen when there are people who are totally sold out to God.

I have known Apostle Bradshaw for some time now and all I can say is that through his friendship and professional collaboration, my life has changed forever. Read and apply the principles he presents and you too, will be a force the gates of hell will not be able to prevail against. Misrah!!!

Dr. Bill Manduca, MBA, DSL

Business Visionary, Strategist, and Coach

The Vantage Point Group

Ocean Springs, Mississippi

D r. Bradshaw challenges each member in the Body of Christ to identify God's purpose/destiny/assignment for His kingdom implementation in the earth. As believers, we are called to govern in a sphere of influence in the earth. There must be an understanding of our roles of influence from the "culture of authority as managers of people, places and things." All of humanity, through the work of the cross, has received an invitation to be restored to fellowship with God and given back "authority to reign on the earth as its lawful and legal guardians." This book will help you to identify and celebrate as you discover and recover God's plan for your life and how to function on your throne in your sphere of influence within "the Seven Mountains of Culture."

Dr. Sylvester Paul Brinson III

Governing Apostle – Hope Outreach Ministries Inc.

President – The Brinson Institute

Chicago, Illinois

I *See Thrones!* is an explosive, masterful work of cutting-edge revelatory gems of Scripture, which indeed have been hidden from the saints of this age but are now revealed through the uniquely expressed language of Dr. Gordon E. Bradshaw. He is a person whom I, as well as others, take in strong consideration as being among the very chiefest apostles of the 21st Century age and beyond, and as a spiritual father and mentor to many. *I See Thrones!* is a must read, and helpful as becoming a navigational blueprint for the cause of developing the spiritual state of the believer and equipping them toward the processes of inheriting the thrones within the kingdom of God.

John McClain

Founder and Apostle of Judahlionz Kingdom Ministry

Minneapolis/St. Paul, Minnesota

ENDORSEMENTS

Over the years I have learned that the Lord is extremely intentional regarding the vessels He chooses to bring forth specific revelation into the earth. In Dr. G.E. Bradshaw, the Lord has raised up a conduit of rare revelation that results in practical implementation, personal transformation and systemic restoration. He is a man of This Hour and this *I See Thrones!* message is an invitation; an open door for people to enter into their temporal and eternal destinies. This book is for everyone who can hear the Call of His Voice.

Matthew Fleming
Chief Solutions Officer of Omega ProVision
Charlotte, North Carolina

It happened again! God has connected with Dr. Gordon E. Bradshaw and has revealed to him one of the most "Ultimate" purposes of God's heart - thrones that will be occupied by sons/daughters – kings with total fulfillment of God's purposes on their lives. Thrones that move mountains reveal the original mandate that God put in Adam and Eve concerning the purity of the kingdom. Dr. Bradshaw's writings give us divine clarity that causes one to function and operate with excellence fulfilling the Kingly-Governmental purpose of God in the earth. God through Dr. Bradshaw connects the reader with the very dynamics of His God's Purity, Nature, Passion-Zeal, Strong Momentum, and Love for His Purpose.

Dr. Bobby Orange
CEO and Apostle of Christ Kingdom People Ministries/Marketplace International
Jacksonville, Florida

D r. Gordon E. Bradshaw sees the thrones of God clearly and better than most. His insight opens up the "heavenly" realm and dimension so that others can see what he sees and act accordingly. I thank God for vision and insight that supersedes the natural sight through the eyes of faith and spiritual gifting. Now, let us enter in and take our seat on the thrones that God has prepared for His sons and daughters.

Dr. Carl L. White, Jr.

Senior Pastor – Victory Christian Int'l Ministries

President – Southland Ministerial Health Network

Markham, Illinois

I n his latest book, *I See Thrones!*, Dr. Gordon Bradshaw brings to us a fresh revelation from the heart and mind of God. *I See Thrones!* sheds light on the single most astonishing revelation given to man from God; that for the first time throughout the history of eternity, there is a physical man (Jesus Christ) sitting on the throne of God; and that we too, as believers by faith in our ascended Lord as our head and representative, are also seated upon the throne of God. It is from the throne position that the believer, according to the will of God, is supposed to rule and govern the Seven Mountains of Culture.

There were kings who have abdicated their thrones and walked away from them because they didn't have the ability to govern correctly. This book will be used by God as the vehicle to restore hope to those kings who have left their thrones. It is also a manual for kings to rule correctly from the 8th mountain. This is actually leading to the fact that we are becoming the "race of God," which is a race of kings and priests. This has been the plan of God all along and will bring light and revelations of this new order. The ability to walk in this power and govern it was inadequate when we walked simply as "believers," but walking as kings we are more than able to demonstrate the power of God.

I See Thrones! is a must read for the mature and kingdom-minded believer, who is ready to claim his or her rightful seat by faith upon the highest seat in the universe, the Throne of God. This book shares with us the importance of thrones and how, according to the plan of God, we are to reign in this lifetime as kings. It is upon Mount Zion, the 8th and highest mountain, where the believer is to rest and rule from.

Dr. Curtis Gillespie
Vice President of Training/Development – The SCOPE Vision Group
Dean of Education – The Misrah Academy Governmental Empowerment Center –
Global Effect Movers & Shakers Network (GEMS)
Michigan City, Indiana

This book is a must read for those who seek to restore God's Kingdom on Earth. Dr. Bradshaw has decreed that the Body of Christ is foreordained to be kings over God's Heavenly Thrones on Earth. He reveals how we, as kings, are to restore souls, systems and society back to God's original creation. As kings, we will restore the provision of sustainability and resourcefulness for the well-being of humanity on the Seven Mountains of Culture. This book equips us to operate as kings.

Cam McConnell
CEO, MGLLC
Author, Build to Prosper
Palos Verdes Estates, CA

I See Thrones! is a depiction of our true identity in Christ, being demonstrated and enacted in the earth today as Sons and Daughters, but more importantly as Kings and Priests. Embracing true identity, coupled with appropriating our rightful and appointed position in the earth realm, has often been a struggle simply because many Christian leaders have not had a keen discernment or understanding of true identity or rightful position. Dr. Bradshaw presents a profound, yet simple and easily comprehensible storyline, if in fact you are a revelatory receiver, ready to grasp hold of truth released in the council room of God.

It is obvious Dr. Bradshaw has spent long hours on the mountaintop seated at the feet of the teacher. He eloquently states: we are called to reinstate the balanced, civil, righteous, and wise influence that Jesus would, if He were in our place. The only way we can respond to this call is to know the position to which we are called. To take our position on the throne to which we are called, we must expand our thinking to first seeing ourselves there. Thank you Dr. Bradshaw – I've heard your teaching on this subject, but reading it, swishing the words around in my mouth, meditating on it, takes it to a whole new level. BRAVO, my friend.

Dr. Gayle Rogers

President/Founder, Forever Free, Inc.

Network Leader, Apostolic Coaching for Empowerment

Author, Healing the Traumatized Soul, and The Whole Soul

Dana Point, California

ENDORSEMENTS

Rarely does a book reach out and touch your heart and life within the first few pages; *I See Thrones!* does exactly that. Each page stands as a gateway into Kingdom realities. The words leap from the pages with anointing and placement within Kingdom of God for this generation of leaders. Dr. Bradshaw has set a banner upon a hill calling us to rise to the call of our Lord to occupy the thrones prepared for each of us until He returns. In that hour we will bow and cast our crowns at His feet.

Danny J Dean
Chief Operating Officer, SunTracker North West LLC
Founder and Apostle of Oregon School of the Prophets D.B.A. West Gate Gathering
Yakima, Washington

We are living in one of the most pivotal times of shifting in all of recorded history. In *I See Thrones!*, Dr. Gordon Bradshaw has written a timeless masterpiece of revelatory literature that will dramatically transform your understanding of the governmental rule of Christ in us. Within these gilded pages, Dr. Bradshaw gives us a majestic panorama of the Thrones of Heaven within us and how we can operate at our maximum capacity.

I believe it's through this fresh lens of clarity that your eternal mandate will begin to crystalize before your eyes and move you into your destiny with greater acceleration. *I See Thrones!* will impart a new and dynamic "Re-formation" of your Kingdom perspective, both personally and corporately.

We, as Christ's Body on earth, have now moved from the Church age to the Kingdom age. One can only receive this level of revelation by having an incredible walk of intimacy in the Spirit with the Lord. The keys of true stewardship and authority are only entrusted to those who have been qualified through many years of faithfulness, forged from the fires of adversity and the staircase of promotion. Dr. Bradshaw has my greatest respect.

I See Thrones! will take you to new levels of maturity and position you to begin operating at new thresholds of the Spirit to impact the spheres of influence you walk in. Rarely are we given such rich "Manna" from Heaven, especially when it is needed most in our culture. We are all the true benefactors of Dr. Bradshaw's uncompromising walk of integrity and honor. I believe your life will be enriched in unparalleled ways as you begin to rule from your Throne of Authority.

Gary Beaton
President, Transformation Glory Ministries
Award-winning documentary and media producer
Apostle & Prophet
Maryville, Tennessee

I See Thrones! describes a panoramic view of the body of Christ in relationship to all aspects of society, walking in the fullness of their priestly and kingly inheritance. It ignites the reader with fire and passion to reach for higher heights and deeper depths. It certainly reiterated to me that I am seated in heavenly places with God and rule in dominion, power and authority. It reemphasizes that each believer chosen by God has a mandate on their life to make a kingdom impact in all levels of society. Kudos to Dr. Bradshaw for obeying God's voice in writing this treasure.

Apostle Sharon Billins
Overseer-Palm Tree International Ministries, Inc.
President-The SAMUEL School of the Prophets
President-Palm Tree International Ministerial Alliance (P.T.I.M.A.)
Columbus, Georgia

ENDORSEMENTS

I See Thrones! is an important piece of relevant revelation in this hour, being well researched and articulated for the most exacting of scholars. I believe this is the finest hour for the Church of Jesus Christ. I also believe it is the finest hour for America in which she will rise to her place and position in these last days to be a Kingdom Nation and a light shining in the darkness. The clash between two kingdoms is NOT a fair fight. We have a guaranteed outcome and WE have unlimited resources as we are living from Heaven to Earth. The enemy does have a budget and does not have the luxury of TIME being on his side. We live in eternity. We are seated with Christ in the Heavenly realm already and in addition to all this, we also have our own measure of rule, or metron. As we are faithful to rule our measure well, our metron is expanded ... since the Kingdom is ever expanding under the rule of the ONE who created all things to bring pleasure to Himself.

In the year 2000 I had an open vision in which God's signet ring was deposited into my upturned right hand and the Lord spoke audibly to me. Since that divine encounter I have been continually aware that positionally, I am in Christ! My prayers are more often declarations and decrees, reinforcing the Victory of Christ in earthly situations and circumstances. This book is a HOW TO diagram for access and a must read for every intentional believer. In all my Christian walk I have never read a book that impacted me as much as this book. *I See Thrones!* is a must have for every intentional Kingdom citizen in this hour. For too long, the Body of Christ has lived below her privilege and right to rule on earth as it is in Heaven.

Pamela Ferguson

President, Kingdom Ready Equipping Ministries

Director, Full Gospel Fellowship of Churches and Ministers of Oregon

International Prophet, Teacher, Revivalist, Church Planter

Coeur D'Alene, Idaho

There are those who have prophetic eyes to see the trajectory of the Kingdom and discern the "new thing" God is doing in the earth in each season and generation. They have Issachar understanding of the times and know how the Ekklesia must successfully navigate them in order to see powerful advances of God's Kingdom in the nations. They are a new breed 21st century apostolic leader skillfully breaking open the scrolls of present-truth revelation from Scripture that will ignite fresh fires of reformation in a hungry remnant ready to run with wild abandon into their destiny as kings in the earth.

Dr. Gordon Bradshaw is that kind of apostolic vanguard leader whose incredible book, *I See Thrones! Igniting and Increasing Your Influence in The Seven Mountains of Culture*, powerfully takes the Seven Mountain Mandate message to a new place of revelation and understanding that will greatly contribute to the movement's growth in wisdom and stature, while also unpacking the apostolic in a fresh and new way for a new generation. I highly recommend *I See Thrones!* as a book that I believe will cause you to see through the lens of revelation your true identity as kings, and your true Kingdom purpose more clearly than you ever have before.

Axel Sippach
Founder & Presiding Apostle
EPIC Global Network
Seabeck, Washington

ENDORSEMENTS

I See Thrones! is a much-needed resource and valuable revelation for the body of Christ and an invitation to take our rightful position as kings and priests in the kingdom of Jesus by being seated on our God-given thrones with Christ. From there we can have an increased perspective and influence. The Bible says *"when the enemy shall come in like a flood, the Spirit of the Lord shall lift up a standard against him"* (Isa. 59:19, KJV). Often that standard is you and me. May the Lord bless us to be His standard bearers in the earth—wise as serpents but harmless as doves. *"Darkness now covers the earth, and total darkness the peoples; but the Lord will shine over you, and his glory will appear over you"* (Isa. 60:2, HCS). God's light is shining upon us and His glory is available to appear over us anywhere, anytime. Let's don't hide our light under a bushel, but rather be a city set upon a hill to bring His light into the darkness.

Philip Tan, CEO
Phil Tan Productions Inc.
Member, Directors Guild of America (DGA), Screen Actors Guild-American Federation of Television & Radio Artists (SAG-AFTRA)
West Hills, California

The season of presumptuous activity around the throne of God and the misunderstanding of His governmental responsibility to His saints and their authority is over. *I See Thrones!* is a curtain raiser ushering God's people into a new era of engagement and a new level of influence with culture, and faithful partnership with God to manifest His glory through humble vessels in the Earth. It's a must read.

Dr. Emmanuel Ziga
President, Grace for All Nations Ministries International & Grace Business Forum
Senior Leader, Sunshine Church
Bellevue, Washington

I just put Dr. Gordon Bradshaw's new book down. We are in completely different ministry circles and I was so glad to be brought into his through this book. I See Thrones! is a very well thought out and researched book. The biblical understanding that went into this was astounding, as Dr. Bradshaw took some of the best of thinking on our royalty and authority and helps believers relate to the Hebrew mindset of God. Ephesians 1: 20-23 says that Jesus was raised up far above all rule and authority, power and dominion, and every name that is invoked, not only in the present age but also in the one to come. And God placed all things under his feet and appointed him to be head over everything for the church, which is his body, the fullness of him who fills everything in every way. Ephesians 2 then goes into how we are seated with Christ in heavenly places. Dr. Gordon Bradshaw's book helps us to occupy our heavenly seats now through this book. I agreed with so much of his approach and loved how I was learning through his fascinating approach. He definitely has a revelation in this book along with a powerful teaching gift to bring you into a full throttle pursuit of your Kingdom authority.

Shawn Bolz

Author of Translating God, Keys to Heaven's Economy, & Throne Room Company

Senior Pastor of Expression58 Church

Los Angeles, California

I See Thrones! is a great blueprint showing us biblical patterns and placing us on an exponential path of becoming confident and effective in our assignments. It is empowering and truly revolutionary, pointing out clearly the pitfalls of responding to needs and opportunities. Understanding and applying the technology of thrones will enable us to see and function in the authority available for fulfilling our assignments.

Cristian Voaides
Founder and President, Quantickum Ltd.
Co-founder, ProVision Global Capital
Tirgu Mures, Romania
Kansas City, Missouri

I See Thrones! by Dr. Gordon E. Bradshaw is a book that will ignite and increase our influence as the Body of Christ in the historic nations, institutions and societal spheres of Europe, and the globe! I have seldom read a book that has given me such practical insights into the spiritual authority that we have within the actual spheres of society. It is no longer "just" about "church" in Rome and Constantinople, but about our influence in the real life of Brussels, Paris, Frankfurt, London and Moscow.

Jan-Aage Torp
Director of Transformational
Pastor of Restoration Oslochurch
Convening Apostle of European Coalition of Apostolic Leaders
Oslo, Norway

I See Thrones! by Dr. Gordon Bradshaw is more than just another in a series of books by a very astute and gifted author. It is a mandate from the "King of Kings" to each of us as "His kings" on this earth to step into our destinies. The powerful pages of this book will powerfully reverberate in your spirit as it did in mine. You will know that you are hearing from the Throne of God Himself. You will hear the Words of the Creator once again saying to you: "Let them have dominion!"

You will see yourself boldly advancing the Kingdom of God and His Kingdom Culture on this earth. As a "king" you will be making kingly decrees from the mountain(s) of influence that God has given you on this earth. These decrees will reverberate with the very heart of God Himself. You will find yourself forcibly advancing the Kingdom of God from the authoritative position of "the throne" that God has given you on earth at this strategic time. You will hear and decree God's will on earth with a new authority, knowing the decree of a king is the law and cannot be changed and "the word of the king has power!"

Dr. A.L. "Papa" Gill
President, Gill Ministries
Bestselling author, including Supernatural Living and Authority of the Believer
Big Bear Lake, California

SPECIAL ENDORSEMENTS

Once in a while there comes a book, containing a revelation so combustible that it changes forever how we see the person of God and our stature in Him...in a radical and dramatic fashion! *I See Thrones!* is such a book. Its content is revolutionary and reformatory. It challenges and slices to pieces long-held religious beliefs that place constraints on the extent of believers' authority in heaven, on earth and under the earth. Like cattle forever branded by the white-hot branding instrument of a seasoned cattle rancher, you will forever be branded with an unwavering sense of dominion over your God-given domain. You will be supercharged to embrace your purpose with a renewed vigor.

I See Thrones! is a book about first "seeing" before "becoming!" We must first "SEE" that we have already been "ENTHRONED" with Christ in Heavenly Places (Eph. 2:6) to rule in God's stead and overthrow despot demonic kings that are ruling industries that control the destinies and livelihoods of millions of people on planet Earth. The rapid moral decline in many nations and the rise of Satanism necessitates a radical and swift response from the greatest government in the Universe: the Government of God! The future that the Kingdom of God wants to establish here on earth does not lie in the hands of Christians with protest placards; reformers and revivalists who have SEEN their THRONES of POWER and INFLUENCE are the ones God is going to use to shape the future!

I See Thrones! is an apostolic and prophetic blueprint, a roadmap so to speak for Kingdom citizens who are tired of "Powerless and man-centered" Christianity! *I See Thrones!* is for overcomers who desire to overcome in this life even as Christ Jesus overcame during His earthly pilgrimage. "I See Thrones" is a wake-up call to a life marked by genuine spiritual authority. *I See Thrones!* is a global call to the saints of the Most High God to attend their own "ASCENSION!" Can you imagine how ridiculous it would have been for Jesus Christ to be resurrected and then MISS the MOMENT of His own "ASCENSION?"

"CHRIST'S ASCENSION" was the final mark on Christ's total victory over the fallen demonic powers. But as in Christ's case, every "ASCENSION" culminates in the "SEATING ON A THRONE!!!" Inside *I See Thrones!* is clarion "CALL" to your own "ASCENSION... are you READY to HEED the CALL? I sure hope you are tired of "talking the talk" without "walking the walk!" My dear covenant brother Dr. Gordon Bradshaw has once again done the Body of Christ worldwide a great service. I prayerfully ask you to consider telling as many people as you can about buying this book for their own library. Truly, *"Evil can only Triumph when good men choose to do nothing!"*

Dr. Francis Myles

Bestselling Author: The Order of Melchizedek

Senior Pastor: Royal Priesthood Church International

www.francismyles.com

Tempe, Arizona

ENDORSEMENTS

It is vitally important to the Body of Christ that we understand our position in Christ as "kings and priests unto God" who serve as gods (see Ps. 82:6), making righteous decrees on God's behalf concerning people, places and things; and who make requests to God on behalf of people, places and things. As we do so in Jesus' name, we exercise the authority of Jesus from His heavenly throne where we are seated together with Him and where He employs and deploys all power in heaven and earth. Thrones represent the seat of power. As we exercise this right being citizens of the Kingdom of Heaven, we literally take on the image of our heavenly identity on earth. It makes sense, then, that if we have been given a heavenly throne *with* Christ, we have also been given an earthly throne *in* Christ.

In *I See Thrones!*, Dr. Gordon E. Bradshaw remains true to His God-identity as a revelator of revelators, as he so eloquently takes the Body of Christ to new heights of supernatural awareness and expression. He confidently affirms, biblically, that God has equipped us with supernatural tools to stand in our official earthly assignments (our thrones) which reflect the "government" or Misrah of God – the power, force and prevailing grace that defends the constitution of the Kingdom of Heaven and defends believers against the onslaught of the spirit of Babylon, the demonic force that exalts itself against the knowledge of God.

I See Thrones! is about the reformation of life, restoring the orderly format of all creation as God originally intended, which includes bringing His rightful sons and daughters to their position of purpose where we all know beyond the shadow of a doubt that God has ordained that each of His children sit on his or her rightful earthly throne – the place of our assignments, having dominion over the social order of the Seven Mountains of Culture.

Dr. Bradshaw masterfully leads us into a discovery of how "sovereignty" overpowers the natural, carnal and earthly systems of life, how we walk in a new-found authority for assignment, how to leverage the influence of your throne, how to redeem earthly systems, how to rule and reign as the Body of Christ and how to unseat illegitimate rulership and regain lost destinies.

Once again, Dr. Bradshaw raises the standard for the Body of Christ, inviting us into God's open door where we "become" commissioned kingdom leaders who reflect the pattern of heaven, living it here on earth. This is a must read for the spiritually hungry and those who are thirsty for revelation knowledge (present truth). It will infuse your life with a new sense of excitement and purpose!

Dr. James Brewton

Bishop, Apostle, Goodwill Ambassador
Author of "Back Porch Meditations, Holy Spirit Revelations"
Co-founder of ACT (Allendale County Transformers)
Founder and Senior Pastor of Community Empowerment Ministries, Inc.
Allendale, South Carolina

PREFACE -
PREPARING FOR
YOUR PURPOSE

"Then I saw thrones and people sitting on them..."

(Rev. 20:4, ERV)

This is one of the most powerful statements ever spoken on earth, yet it has been largely overlooked and ignored until now, and in fact, this is the first book-length treatment of the subject of thrones from a spiritual perspective of which I am aware. This statement originated not on earth, but in the heavens, and it reflects a powerful revelation of the reality of authority, assignment, accomplishment, glory, governance and grace in the supernaturally-enhanced lives of kingdom citizens in the Earth realm. Not only is the statement filled with historical context regarding the fabric of past history and a glimpse into the victorious days ahead, but it reflects a present and powerful truth about where we are today. These words aren't designed just to celebrate an idealistic and utopian notion of Christianity and its power in "the sweet by and by" but to ignite a revelation and a revolution in our hearts and minds now, and to reveal a spiritual technology that is readily available and can be utilized and applied by the followers of Jesus to maximize and optimize their influence, effectiveness and authority on planet Earth.

"But because of his great love for us, God, who is rich in mercy, made us alive with Christ even when we were dead in transgressions—it is by grace you have been saved. ***And God raised us up with Christ and seated us with him in the heavenly realms in Christ Jesus,*** *in order that in the coming ages he might show the incomparable riches of his grace, expressed in his kindness to us in Christ Jesus."*

(Eph. 2:4-7, NIV, emphasis added)

What do you think it means when the Bible says we are seated above in heavenly places or heavenly realms with Christ Jesus? It means we are seated on thrones, as we will explain and expound upon in greater detail throughout this book. The word **seated** in the Greek is *synekathisen,* meaning "to cause or make to sit down together, place together" (Strong's Concordance, 4776).

A further inspection and unpacking of the revelation within the noble phrase, *"I saw thrones..."* will yield a more glorious sense of purpose and identity in our hearts. It's about the enhancement of our faith and thinking and about shifting our perspectives on fulfilling the great commission and making the kingdoms of this world merge into the greater sphere of the kingdom of our Lord and of His Christ (Rev. 11:15). It's about experiencing a new reality that activates a greater measure of courage and boldness than we've known before. It's a new season that will serve as the backdrop for some of the most powerful expressions of kingdom manifestation ever to be seen in the earth!

PREFACE

I have been assigned to do something important for you as a reader. It was my responsibility to do the research, examinations of texts, cross examination of concepts, unpacking of revelations and establishing of conceptual bridges to bring you a "packaged portfolio" of kingdom references and practical, real-life contexts and examples that allow you to *"spend more time learning, than looking"* for ways to discover the power and purpose of thrones. It is certainly my honor to do so.

I received the revelation of *I See Thrones! Igniting and Increasing Your Influence on the Seven Mountains of Culture* a few years ago and I've spoken on the subject in seminars and conferences, but now it is time for this to be shared with many others globally. I have written this book with a varied background as a theologian, church planter, former faculty member of a state college, former naval petty officer, a chief officer with a 30-year fire service career, board member of health organizations, consultant, governmental training instructor, chamber of commerce board member, network president, published author, public policy committee chairman and other positions and roles over a 42-year span in the Body of Christ.

In my life, and after serving in various capacities in the Seven Mountains of Culture, I found one common thread of experience… a need for the presence of God and the ability to proficiently and providentially manage the resources and responsibilities that come with our assignments. This book is not written to "oversaturate" you with biblical references but rather to give you a thorough and comprehensive biblical and faith-based foundation for accomplishing all that you can in your places of assignment. The language used herein is not specific to each of the Seven Mountains nor is it a glossary of terms that you are necessarily to use publicly, but it's a **"library of truth for empowerment."** It's designed to increase your faith so that you can increase your pace and enlarge your space! It's a new day for citizens of the kingdom of God!

"'Sing, O barren, you who have not been borne! Break forth into singing, and cry aloud, you who have not labored with child! For more are the children of the desolate than the children of the married woman,' says the Lord. 'Enlarge the place of your tent, and let them stretch out the curtains of your dwellings; do not spare; lengthen your cords, and strengthen your stakes. For you shall expand to the right and to the left, and your descendants will inherit the nations, and make the desolate cities inhabited.'"

(Isa. 54:1-3, NKJV)

This book is designed to increase your capacity for **"Star Quality!"** That's why there is a **"fiery throne"** in a starry sky on the cover of this book! But, notice the "cushion" that sits on the throne. It signifies that God wants us to be **"at rest as we rule!"** When we are confident in our capacity as kings, we can rest better as we rule and reign. This "star quality" isn't for the purpose of exalting one's ego or for competing with one another. Rather, it's for the purpose of emphasizing the power and the results that come with the exercise of godly wisdom.

"The wise leaders will shine with all the brightness of the sky. AND THOSE WHO HAVE TAUGHT MANY PEOPLE WILL SHINE LIKE THE STARS FOR EVER."

(Dan. 12:3, GNB, emphasis added)

The throne illustrated on the cover of this book is a type or representation of the fiery throne of God. There are flames with fire on the armrests of the throne to signify that we have a powerful "ignition source" that activates our authority and the power of influence in our assigned spheres.

"While I was looking, thrones were put in place. One who had been living for ever sat down on one of the thrones. His clothes were

white as snow, and his hair was like pure wool. HIS THRONE, MOUNTED ON FIERY WHEELS, WAS BLAZING WITH FIRE, AND A STREAM OF FIRE WAS POURING OUT FROM IT. There were many thousands of people there to serve him, and millions of people stood before him. The court began its session, and the books were opened."

(Dan. 7:9-10, GNB, emphasis added)

The word **"Fire"** or **"Nuwr,"** in Hebrew means - To shine, fiery, bright. It also corresponds to the Hebrew term "Nerah," meaning – To glisten; a lamp (i.e. the burner) or the light, candle or lamp.

"Clouds and darkness are round about him: RIGHTEOUSNESS AND JUSTICE ARE THE FOUNDATION OF HIS THRONE. A FIRE GOETH BEFORE HIM, AND BURNETH UP HIS ADVERSARIES ROUND ABOUT. His lightnings lightened the world: The earth saw, and trembled. THE MOUNTAINS MELTED LIKE WAX AT THE PRESENCE OF JEHOVAH, at the presence of the Lord of the whole earth."

(Ps. 97:2-5, ASV, emphasis added)

The "mountains" of culture that are out of alignment with kingdom order will begin to melt like wax when they are exposed to the fire of God. Any despotic forces that are exposed to this fire are subject to the sovereign authority of God Himself. The fire, light, and burners of God have the ability to reveal, expose, cleanse, purify, and separate the elements. Kingdom components remain unscathed while lesser carnal elements are trapped, subjugated, reduced or destroyed. We may not witness complete transformations all at once, but the process is well on its way each day that believers see their assigned thrones and exercise the influence of kingdom culture!

I SEE *Thrones!*

"Your word is a lamp to guide me and a light for my path."

(Ps. 119:105, GNB)

The fire of God produces enlightenment, wisdom, truth, knowledge, purification, wit, ingenuity, solutions, resourcefulness, courage, victory and other virtues of the kingdom of God. Just as streams of fire issue from the throne of God, these virtues will issue from our places of influence as believers are ignited and increased by the fire of God!

This book can't address each and every possible scripture verse or subject on "thrones," influence, authority or government, but it can serve to activate your core identity and motivate the inherently powerful destiny assigned to each and every one of you. Along the way we have to perform our own due diligence in consecration to God, the study of His Word, right living and the show of civility to each and every human being on this planet. We are, after all, laborers together with God for the fulfillment of the destiny of the Earth.

As believers, we often talk about ruling and reigning, but it's sometimes no more than formless conversation, powerless religion (2 Tim. 3:5) and empty rhetoric that doesn't necessarily reflect or impact on real-time events, people, places or things. It seems to be more of a statement of hope for a time to come: a dream of one day coming into our place of victory, and sometimes being unable to attach that dream to the reality that we so badly need. Often, we just wait for heaven or our "chariot" to "appear" out of nowhere or thin air and take us out of our misery.

In this season, heaven does appear, but maybe not in the way that many expect it to! Indeed, these are **"The days of heaven on earth!"** (Deut. 11:14) and the days when heaven is making a powerful and practical appearance in the earth realm and on the platforms of everyday life. The

Kingdom of God is manifesting now! *"Do not be afraid little flock, for your Father is pleased to give you the Kingdom." (Luke 12:32, GNB)*

I want to take you on a journey while you read this book and I want you to discover and appropriate for yourself the technology of thrones and the tremendous texts and principles of the Bible that show a very clear and distinct pattern and pathway for restoring the glory of God to people, places and things in the earth and for the reversal of *"Ichabod,"* (the glory has departed) that we've experienced on Earth. It is the restoration of the glory of God in His people that serves as an antidote for the misfortune that we've experienced on this planet and in its systematic and societal structures. *"The nations you conquered wore themselves out in useless labor, and all they have built goes up in flames. The Lord Almighty has done this. But the earth will be as full of the knowledge of the Lord's glory as the seas are full of water." (Hab. 2:13-14, GNB).* The glory of God upon His restored "kings" will play a major role in the transformation process.

I have searched the scriptures, and tried to be thorough, if not altogether exhaustive, in placing them in relevant locations in this book so you can see a pattern that is restorative, reformational and revolutionary! There is a generous amount of biblical texts, with the respective Hebrew, Aramaic, and Greek translations on hand to give readers the benefit of powerful explanations and reinforcements of kingdom principles that the ancient languages provide. There is an advantage to having this kind of information at our disposal, especially if we intend to be confident and effective in our kingdom assignments. The more we know about God's original ingenious design for **"kings,"** the more we'll be able to saturate the earth with His sovereign purpose and power, bringing about the long-awaited transformations that we need in our own lives and in the culture around us. We'll have stronger reinforcements of the wonderful identity called "kings and priests" that Jesus modeled and purchased for us.

This book isn't about a simple formula of quoting verses and watching things "magically" appear, nor is it an attempt to change you into theologians or Bible scholars, but it's about the hope of being transformed by the renewing of our minds so that we can prove the good and acceptable and perfect will of God on the earth (Rom. 12:2). Our understanding will increase, and so will our faith, giving us the courage and kingdom mentality to step forward onto the thrones that God has prepared and reserved for us and to make us more confident and capable through the idea of "becoming" what we read about and developing the kingdom level mindset that positions us above and beyond the obstacles that challenge our destiny, purpose and assignments on earth, and putting us in Christ, *"Far above all principality, and power, and might, and dominion..." (Eph. 1:21, KJV)*

"...For the earth shall be full of the knowledge of the Lord, as the waters cover the sea."

(Isa. 11:9, AMP)

We know that no matter how great the knowledge of mankind is, the knowledge of God far exceeds it in quantity and quality! The knowledge of God is about to be poured out in powerful tidal waves of truth that will forever change how we function on earth as kingdom citizens. My purpose is to stir your faith, increase your knowledge and spark a new sense of destiny, purpose and assignment as you read this book!

John the Apostle wrote the powerful words of Revelation 20:4 based on what he saw at the time. This book is not an exegesis on the millennial reign of the saints nor about the discussion of timelines or eschatology. It is, however, the extraction and exegesis of a powerful statement about thrones and the accompanying principles that amplify how we are to rule and reign in life. He opened the door for a new statement of power and victory, not only for his own time but beyond. And while John's experience was extraordinary, as one who visited heaven "in the Spirit" (Rev. 4:1-2), we are all challenged to see more, and that same Spirit is also available to each of us. John saw thrones and he saw the "judgment" that was given to the believers who sat on them. He saw their assignments to stand in a place of jurisprudence and governance and to affect the outcome of the history of planet Earth.

The type of "judgment" that we'll explore in this book is associated with the governmental mantle of Jesus Christ and His "justice" that accompanies the restoration of all things on planet Earth as God would have it. This isn't about brutal attacks on nations nor the disruption of peaceful societies, nor the shedding of innocent blood, nor the disruption of valuable and important cultural or ethnic foundations. Rather, it's about the sovereign and superior kingdom of God bringing the loving and powerful reign of Jesus Christ as King of kings and Lord of lords to the planet that He made. It's about restoring all things according to God's plan by equipping and placing believers in key strategic and tactical places within the Seven Mountains of Culture to impact the world.

We'll make a number of references to my previous book *Authority for Assignment: Releasing the Mantle of God's Government in the Marketplace* (Kingdom House Publishing, 2011). The text of Isaiah 9:6-7 is the foundational basis for the message of that book which helps to reveal the governmental mantle of Christ known as **"The Mantle of Misrah."** It gives ample support to the template and technology of "thrones," as you will read in this book.

"For unto us a child is born, unto us a son is given: and THE GOVERNMENT SHALL BE UPON HIS SHOULDER: and his name shall be called Wonderful, Counsellor, The mighty God, The everlasting Father, The prince of Peace. Of the increase of his government and peace there shall be no end, upon the THRONE of

David, and upon his kingdom, to order it, and to establish it with judgment and with justice from henceforth even for ever. THE ZEAL OF THE LORD OF HOSTS WILL PERFORM THIS."

(Isa. 9:6-7, KJV, emphasis added)

The portrait and profile of planet Earth will certainly look very different after the saints fully deploy **"The Mantle of Misrah."** *"Misrah"* is the Hebrew word for "Empire, Government, Authority and the Power to Prevail." The government is on the "shoulder" of Christ, signifying that it's a "mantle" which is the symbol of authority worn on one's shoulders in certain cultures and in Biblical history among prophets and priests and the stole which is worn by kings. "Mantle" is also the word used to describe the posture of a bird of prey as it spreads its wings over its conquered and captured prey. As we advance in our knowledge, experience and application of *"Misrah,"* we'll ascend to higher levels of responsibility in our assignments of governance and the restoration of God's glory on Earth.

As "birds of prey" we will watch the issues of life from greater heights and with more accuracy and focus. We'll be able to descend from the high places back to the natural levels where we can apply *"glory on ground level"* and affect the changes that are needed. The judgment and justice of Christ and the zeal of the Lord of Hosts will be manifested in us, making way for the restoration of all things. A great reversal of circumstances is taking place! Now, we'll find ourselves re-examining battles that we seceded to our enemies in the past. If you gave up hope, now you can return to the place of discovery and recovery! In fact, I believe there are angels who accompany us while we wear the Mantle of Misrah to help us discover and recover lost thrones of influence. There are empty thrones on the horizon, waiting on us to take our rightful places.

PREFACE

*"And all of us, as with unveiled face, [because we] continued to behold
[in the Word of God] as in a mirror the glory of the Lord, are constantly
being transfigured into His very own image in ever increasing splendor
and from one degree of glory to another; [for this comes] from the Lord
[Who is] the Spirit."*

(2 Cor. 3:18, AMP, emphasis added)

You'll be re-introduced to the power of God's glory on your life, the
glory of a throne that He assigned to you before time began! You'll take
another look at yourself in the mirror of revelation truth that transforms
you into the glorified image of yourself; the image that God intended
you to be all along! Take a good look and see who you really are. As
a matter of fact... **YOU LOOK BETTER ALREADY, BECAUSE
WHAT YOU LOOK AT WILL DETERMINE WHAT YOU LOOK
LIKE!** This is the principle of Behold and Become (2 Cor. 3:16-18).
Since you read this preface, you are already being transformed! It's an
exciting journey! I invite you right now to re-aim your line of sight, re-
sharpen your focus, take your crown out of storage and begin to say...
"I SEE THRONES!"

MISRAH!

Dr. Gordon E. Bradshaw

President – Global Effect Movers & Shakers Network (GEMS)
Founder/Director of the 3M Project Global Initiative – Merging Ministries,
Marketplace & Municipalities for Community Transformation
Vice President – Kingdom Congressional International Alliance (KCIA)

I SEE *Thrones!*

CONTENTS

FOREWORD

My close friend, covenant brother, kingdom ambassador, and fellow network leader Dr. Gordon Bradshaw has done it again. *I See Thrones!* is a call to spiritual arms, to maturity and wisdom, and to cultural relevance, engagement and leadership for the modern church and all kingdom citizens globally in the 7 Mountains of Culture. It is a call to shift not just attitudinally or behaviorally into a more alert and aggressive and proactive posture and mindset, but *positionally* as well. As a theological treatise, it is revelatory and scholarly. As a roadmap and blueprint for change in tactics and engagement with culture, it is strategic and masterful. This is an important, vital and essential **"missing piece"** to the kingdom model that God has released to Dr. G.E. Bradshaw for the benefit of and use by the entire body of Christ.

This summer as we have watched the foundations of America and Western culture shake and veer further to the left before our very eyes, and continue to erode and disengage from their Judeo-Christian origins and heritage, the phrase "Everything that Can Be Shaken Will Be Shaken" comes to mind and seems applicable and relevant in light of current events. Thus, the question is posed: How can we become unshakeable in a shaking world?

Heb. 12:27-28 (AMP, emphasis added) says, *"Now this expression, Yet once more, **indicates the final removal and transformation of all [that can be] shaken**—that is, of that which has been created—in order that what cannot be shaken may remain and continue. **Let us therefore, receiving a kingdom that is firm and stable and cannot be shaken**, offer to God pleasing service and acceptable worship, with modesty and pious care and godly fear and awe;…"*

The word "shaken" in the Greek comes from the root *saleuó*, meaning "to agitate, shake, by extension to cast down, to excite, disturb in mind, stir up, drive away." Strong's Concordance, 4531, says there are 15 occurrences of this in the New Testament, including derivatives such as *asaleuton, Saleuomenōn, saleuomena, saleuthō,* or *Saleuthēsontai.*

Jesus warns us in Luke 21:26 (AMP, emphasis added) of a time coming where we will see *"Men swooning away or expiring with fear and dread and apprehension and expectation of the things that are coming on the world; **for the [very] powers of the heavens will be shaken and caused to totter.**"* In addition, Luke in Acts 2:25 (AMP, emphasis added) says, *"For David says in regard to Him, **I saw the Lord constantly before me, for He is at my right hand that I may not be shaken or overthrown or cast down** [from my secure and happy state]."* This is no idle statement but a proven reality tested in the heat of battle and the crucible of life of one of history's greatest leaders, a man after God's own heart. We must learn from the life of David and others to be seated on our throne so that we are not overthrown.

As one of many examples we could cite, when David and his men returned from a raid to their base in Ziklag and saw their homes and city burned with fire and their wives and children and animals and possessions missing, his men "wept until they could weep no more" and were "bitter of soul," and "threatened to stone" him. David quickly called for the ephod to be brought to him and went to inquire of the Lord. In his flesh he was tired, heartsick, "greatly distressed" and in "great danger," but "David found strength in the Lord his God" and in his spirit He was seated with the Lord on a throne in heavenly places when he heard the words, *"Yes, go after them. You will surely recover everything that was taken from you!"* (1 Sam. 30:1-8, NLT). The NAS translation says, *"Pursue, for you will surely overtake them, and you will surely rescue all."* The rest is history and David and his men won a great victory with the Lord's help and recovered their families and property plus spoils and plunder from the Amalekites.

We see the Lord constantly before us and at our right hand when we are seated with Him in heavenly places. That can only happen when our spirit rules our flesh, and not the other way around, so there is a price we must pay to follow Jesus and be His disciples, and to access our throne. We must be willing to take up our cross daily and to die daily, as the Scriptures teach, exhort and admonish us. Jesus must become Lord of our lives in every area, and not just our Savior. This is part of what it means to rule and reign with Christ, not just in the age to come, in the sweet bye and bye, but also in the here and now, in the nitty gritty of life on planet Earth. The kingdom of God cannot be shaken; neither should we.

Scripture tells us that the foundations of God's throne are righteousness and justice and love (Ps. 89:14; Isa. 9:7, 16:5, 28:16-17), and that the foundations of earthly thrones of kings are built on righteousness also (Prov. 16:12-13; Prov. 25:5). Neither God nor His throne nor His word nor His plans nor His kingdom can be shaken or defeated (Matt. 24:35; Mark 13:31; Luke 21:33; John 1:1-5; Ps. 119:89, 160; Isa. 55:8-11; James 1:13; Heb. 12:28). This is an example for us, since our lives and our thrones must also have godly foundations to endure and prosper.

How does this work? Quite simply, we must internalize, incubate and incarnate the DNA of heaven and the word of God in our own lives and character before we can influence or transform others. Psalm 37:5-6 (NIV) says, *"Commit your way to the Lord; trust in him and he will do this: He will make your righteousness shine like the dawn, the justice of your cause like the noonday sun."* When our foundations are the same as God's, we will be properly aligned and will start seeing His affirmation, favor and blessing in our lives on a regular basis. Others will notice, too.

Like David of old, we must learn to fix our eyes upon Jesus and see or set the Lord constantly before us, rather than giving too much of our precious, valuable time and attention and hope to secular sages, political pundits, media moguls, cultural icons, reporters, analysts, fearmongers, racial agitators, economic doomsayers, color commentators, "spin doctors," "talking heads," and "conspiracy theorists," realizing that as Jesus is seated at the right hand of the Father in heaven, as an eternal high priest who ever intercedes for us (Heb. 7:1-8:6), so is He seated at our right hands also (a place and position of strength and stability and permanence) since we are **"seated (raised up) in heavenly places in Christ Jesus."** (Eph. 2:6, emphasis added)

Therefore, we can be confident that as we adopt a renewed mindset and assume our rightful positions, that we also will "not be shaken or overthrown or cast down," but rather, as those who know God in an intimate, personal way, we "will participate in the divine nature" (2 Pet. 1:4), "will do mighty deeds and exploits" (Dan. 11:32), "be wise as serpents and harmless as doves" (Matt. 10:16), "pray for kings and all who have authority" (1 Tim. 2:2), "take the kingdom by force" (Matt. 11:12), be "rooted and grounded and built up in Christ Jesus and His love" (Col. 1:23, 2:7; Eph. 3:17), be "steadfast, immovable and always abounding in the work of the Lord" (1 Cor. 15:58) and "occupy until He comes" (Luke 19:13).

Rom. 8:18-19 (AMP, emphasis added) tells us, *"For I consider that the suffering of this present time (this present life) are not worth being compared with the glory that is about to be revealed to us and in us and [a]for us and [b]conferred on us!* **For [even the whole] creation (all nature) waits expectantly and longs earnestly for God's sons to be made known [waits for the revealing, the disclosing of their sonship].***"* It is time, and past time, for the sons and daughters of God to be revealed and made manifest in the Earth and to the 7 Mountains of Culture—some overtly and some covertly—and be seated on their thrones. From there we can rule and reign and exercise influence dominion in our respective spheres of society.

The tactics and strategies of the church over the last several decades have largely been ineffective in slowing or stopping cultural and moral decay, decline, deterioration and degradation. We have not been positioned properly, either in the natural or heavenly realms. Dr. Bradshaw's new book *I See Thrones!* is a seasoned and well-reasoned and -articulated antidote, remedy and prescription for this cultural cancer, and a blueprint and roadmap for God's plan for the future and way forward. It infuses and imparts fresh revelation, strategy, tactics, wisdom, order and hope for us in a world that is spiraling out of control. Thank you Dr. Bradshaw for your faithful service and sacrifice to fulfill this assignment in a timely and effective manner. History, and generations, will be changed and impacted because of this book. Buy it, read it, share it, and put it into practice as soon as possible…and the sooner the better.

Dr. Bruce Cook
Chair, KCIA, KEYS, Kingdom House, VentureAdvisers
www.kcialliance.org
www.keysnetwork.org
www.kingdomhouse.net
www.ventureadvisers.com

I SEE *Thrones!*

THRONES THAT
MOVE MOUNTAINS

"...I will ascend into heaven, I will exalt my throne above the stars of God; I will also sit on the mount of the congregation on the farthest sides of the north."

(Isa. 14: 13, NKJV)

Lucifer desired to be like God and planned to place his throne on *"the mount* (mountain) *of the congregation on the farthest sides of the north,"* where the kingdom of God made its symbolic abode (Ps. 48:2). Here is a template that Lucifer and other spirits driven by Babylonian impulses desire to follow. The Babylonians built a tower to exalt their identity in the Earth and planned on reaching even to "heaven" (Gen. 11:4). It is a common practice of government that thrones, or captured territories, should be placed upon mountains as a symbol of authority over a particular sphere or over all that can be surveyed from that mountaintop. It suggests the possession of territory and influence.

In the Seven Mountains of Culture, it has always been the intention of God for His people to have the highest seats of influence and not for any contrary forces to rule there. History has proven this to be a difficult task, not because of the weakness of God, but of men with their proclivity toward greed, lust, covetousness, pride, unrighteousness and ungodliness and because of the demonically-engineered strategies of dark forces. However, the situation is turning around, even as you read this chapter.

"Praise is awaiting You, O God, in Zion; And to You the vow shall be performed. O You who hear prayer, To You all flesh will come. Iniquities prevail against me; As for our transgressions, You will provide for them. Blessed is the man You choose, And cause to approach You, That he may dwell in Your courts. We shall be satisfied with the goodness of Your house, Of Your holy temple. By awesome deeds in righteousness You will answer us, O God of our salvation, You who are the confidence of all the ends of the earth, And of the far-off seas; WHO ESTABLISHED THE MOUNTAINS BY HIS STRENGTH, being clothed with power." (Ps. 65:1-6, NKJV, emphasis added)

The Seven Mountains of Culture or Influence are the spheres that shape how the various categories of society operate in the earth. Virtually every people group on the planet is influenced by, or is influencing, these spheres. In this book, *I See Thrones! Igniting and Increasing Your Influence in the Seven Mountains of Culture,* you'll be enlightened about thrones and what they mean to the kingdom of God and its citizens.

Thrones are not simply historical hardware for bygone eras, and they are not only symbolic, but they are realistic models with a tangible technology for today's kingdom citizens.

THRONES ARE STRATEGIC

Powerful principles are locked within the subject of thrones. To Jesus Christ, thrones represent the providentially-assigned places of governance that kingdom citizens operate from, and where His Body exercises the Great Commission and expands the kingdom of God. Thrones are not always visible in a physical sense but the influence and effect that they have on people, places and things is becoming increasingly evident as we move further through the kingdom age. Answers will come through the godly authority of God's sons and daughters who look toward the mountains and see their assigned seats at the top. Thrones are waiting for us! We are indeed **kings and priests** according to Rev. 1:6, KJV... *"And hath made us kings and priests unto God and his father; to him be glory and dominion for ever and ever. Amen."* We are both kings and priests. As **"priests,"** we petition God but as **"kings"** we command the forces of God!

"Thus saith the Lord, the Holy One of Israel, and his Maker, ASK ME of things to come concerning my sons, and concerning the work of my hands COMMAND YE ME."

(Isa. 45:11, KJV, emphasis added)

The technologies of "priests" and "kings" are visible in this text. The priest is the **"petitioner"** whereas the king is the **"commander."** There are situations that we face as kingdom citizens that implore us to act with authority over the forces that try to take dominion over a planet that Christ has given His life to restore. At times we are passive when we should be possessive. His blood was shed for us to restore us to our place as the rightful custodians of planet Earth. Forces are resisting this but His work will not be in vain.

"Having disarmed principalities and powers, He made a public spectacle of them, triumphing over them in it."

(Col. 2:15, NKJV)

3

The Seven Mountains, as we see and understand them, are not the same Seven Mountains as God providentially knows them. We are entering God's sovereign **"situation room"** to discover how these mountains and their influences in the earth should look through the lenses of the Creator Himself. God *"Established the mountains by his strength,"* and that means more than it appears to mean. I believe this is a revelation of the foreknowledge of God and His intent to reform and restore the mountains to their original purposes prior to the fall of mankind. Now that sin is subdued by the sacrifice and redemptive work of Christ, we can resume the journey of God's purpose.

In Psalm 65:6 the Hebrew text suggests that the words *"established"* (NKJV) or *"sets fast"* (KJV) comes from the terms **"Set"** or **"Kuwm,"** meaning: To set up, establish, fix, appoint, make proper, order and ordain. The second term is "Tsuwm" or "Fast," meaning: To cover the mouth, or fast. This literally means, "Establish a fast!" It suggests that God wants to put the Seven Mountains on a new diet! I believe that the mountains can only be healthy with a diet of input from God Himself and they are not allowed to continue *"eating"* from demonically-engineered *"menus"* fed by people who dishonor and disregard the purposes and power of God. The mountains of influence are about to get *"a taste of their own medicine"* and become influenced themselves by the strongest force in all of creation.

The foreknowledge of God created the historical move that we've been experiencing since the 1970's when Bill Bright and Loren Cunningham began teaching on the Seven Mountains of Influence in Culture. This initiated the time of restoration, and the time that I believe shifted the **"diet"** of the mountains. True kingdom messages began to emerge and the language of sermons started to progressively change. More and more believers started to embrace the fact that the practice of simple preaching wasn't enough to convert the attitudes of the world. The kingdom had to "come" and it had to acknowledge the existence of every kingdom in the world and not just the sphere of religion.

A DYNAMIC NEW DIET

"And the king appointed for them a daily provision of the king's delicacies and of the wine which he drank..."

(Dan. 1:5, NKJV)

In this scenario, Daniel and his associates had been taken captive to Babylon and were being indoctrinated into their culture. While doing so, they were offered the *"king's meat,"* a diet that the king had chosen for them. They refused this diet, believing that God would sustain them without it and they were correct. Today, the same spirit of Babylon feeds the Seven Mountains of Culture and has done so throughout history, making the climates and cultures of the mountains adversarial to the kingdom of God. This has begun to change. Throughout this book I will make many references to Babylon and God's plans and processes for melting the Babylonian influence. Moreover, the negative influences of the spirit of Babylon are losing potency because they are being supernaturally displaced by "new kings."

> **Every mountain of culture or influence has "thrones" assigned to it and it's the influential power of the entities who sit upon thrones that gives them the ability to affect culture as they do.**

The results are becoming clear. The installation of new "kings" who promote the diet of righteous kingdom order are in position now, and more are coming. We won't stand at a distance pointing to the mountains, complaining about their negative impact; we'll establish our thrones on the tops of the mountains and the purposes of God will be fulfilled! The new **"diet"** of information being fed to the mountains is actually the same information that's being fed to believers who recognize their place as kingdom citizens, and more specifically, as kings.

We enter the mountains of our assignments and we become **"digested"** by the culture of the mountains.

Our influence, through the demonstration of God-assigned skill sets, anointing, grace, and providence, leaves an effect on every mountain. The kings are the **"virus"** that, although small, affects the culture of millions of people. Our influence is born from a source far greater than ourselves. It is God that "sets fast the mountains" and calls a "fast" against the contaminating diets of the past. The mountains are **"hungering"** for new things.

> **The Seven Mountains are on a fresh new "diet" of Kingdom Culture! It is said, "You are what you eat ..." ... so the Mountains are coming forward with kingdom energy and power!**

"For we know that THE WHOLE CREATION groans and labors with birth pangs together until now. Not only that, but we also who have the first-fruits of the Spirit, even we ourselves groan within ourselves, eagerly waiting for the adoption, the redemption of our body."

(Rom. 8:22-23, NKJV, emphasis added)

Aren't the Seven Mountains part of "The Whole Creation?" Yes, they are, meaning that the identity of the Seven Mountains contains DNA that is crying out for the Creator's redemptive power to manifest! The Mountains want their Maker again! This reconnection will manifest through believers who rise as **"kings"** and establish their thrones of influence. The mountains will feed sumptuously on new "meat!" And, this is truly "the King's meat!"

TRAINED TO TREAD

"...Now therefore, arise, go over this Jordan, you and all this people, to the land which I am giving to them – the children of Israel. EVERY PLACE THAT THE SOLE OF YOUR FOOT WILL TREAD UPON I HAVE GIVEN YOU, as I said to Moses."

(Josh. 1:2-3, NKJV, emphasis added)

"Obey faithfully all the laws that I have given you; Love the Lord your God, do everything he commands, and be faithful to him. Then he will drive out all those nations as you advance, and you will occupy the land belonging to nations greater and more powerful than you. All the ground that you march over will be yours..."

(Deut. 11:22-24, GNB)

The thrones that we're to possess are not impossible to obtain, when it is the will of God. The predominant technology that we'll use to do it is our surrender to God and a consistent dependence on His foreknowledge, grace and purpose. Our quest is not unlike that of the children of Israel, who were providentially positioned to take the land. We are being **"trained to tread!"**

*"Behold, I give unto you power to tread on serpents and scorpions
and over all the power of the enemy: and nothing shall by any means
hurt you."*

(Luke 10:19, KJV)

We can't take the land or the mountains from outside their sphere of
influence. This has to be an "inside job." We have to actually have our
"feet" on the ground somewhere. The word **"feet"** in the texts in Josh.
1:2-3 and Deut. 11:22-24 is from the Hebrew term **"Regel,"** meaning: A
foot as in walking, but it also means: According as, which suggests that
the victory is relative or according to how the people walk in the enemy's
territory. If we walk timidly and without authority, our victory will be
small, but if we walk boldly as "kings," our victory will be greater. This
is the purpose of this book – to encourage believers in the principles of
thrones as a supernatural technology, so that you may boldly stand on the
territories of the Seven Mountains of Culture in your assigned sphere of
influence, on a throne of God's choosing!

LIFE-GIVING LANGUAGE

*"The Lord God has given me THE TONGUE OF THE LEARNED,
that I should know how to speak a word in season to him that is weary.
He awakens me morning by morning, he awakens my ear to hear as the
learned. The Lord God has opened my ear; and I was not rebellious, nor
did I turn away."*

(Isa. 5:4-5, NKJV, emphasis added)

Everything on the Earth has suffered from "weariness," which simply
means that things are worn down, exhausted, fatigued and sometimes void
of life. There will come a refreshing from the presence of the Lord through

our supernatural voices. When "kings" speak, there is a transformation of atmospheres and the presentation of divine "re-balancing."

"The royal line of David is like a tree that has been cut down; but just as new branches sprout from a stump, so A NEW KING WILL ARISE FROM DAVID'S DESCENDANTS. The Spirit of the Lord will give him wisdom, and the knowledge and skill to rule his people. He will know the Lord's will and honour him, and find pleasure in obeying him. He will not judge by appearance or hearsay; he will judge the poor fairly and defend the rights of the helpless. At his command the people will be punished, and evil persons will die. He will rule his people with justice and integrity."

(Isa. 11:1-5, GNB, emphasis added)

As we take our places of majesty on our thrones, we will not *"stick out like a sore thumb,"* so to speak, and be so obviously "religious" that our impact is diminished. The Lord is preparing us with the word of the King of kings and the power of the Holy Spirit and the Bible, but that word will run parallel in perspective and purpose with the languages and words of earthly rulers and people of influence in the Seven Mountain Culture. We will have the language that is respective of and relevant to the assignments we fill and we will have wisdom, knowledge and skill to articulate God's plans in the Earth.

Christ is the "New King" who arose from David's lineage and we are the "Body" of that new King. We will *"know the Lord's will and honor Him,"* and our sensitivity to root causes, hidden demonic agendas, dark influences, human frailties, cultural anomalies, historical experiences, territorial trends and other embedded nuances will become clear to us because we are assigned as kings with a higher level of awareness of our surroundings. We are assigned to be more than casual observers in the process of transformation – we are kings, and *"Where the word of a king*

9

is, there is power; And who may say to him, 'What are you doing?'" (Eccl. 8:4, NKJV)

Oftentimes, we'll operate in "stealth mode," but the "sovereign sound" of God's words can be felt in our voices, even when we don't quote a scripture and verse. We will truly speak with "new tongues."

"And they were all filled with the Holy Spirit, and began to speak with other tongues, as the Spirit gave them utterance. And there were dwelling in Jerusalem Jews, devout men, from every nation under heaven. And when this sound occurred, the multitude came together, and were confused, because EVERYONE HEARD THEM SPEAK IN HIS OWN LANGUAGE. "

(Acts 2:4-6, NKJV, emphasis added)

Although the history of this text is about the introduction of tongues of fire through the baptism of the Holy Spirit, it has a parallel meaning to the message of Seven Mountain transformation. Those who spoke in tongues supernaturally spoke in the native languages of the people who were assembled in the upper room. This was a powerful phenomenon, and **it still happens through us today.** But, we also note that we speak with the anointed language of kings for specific places of dominion or territory, where the result is… *"Everyone heard them speak in his own language."*

In this case, it isn't based on our speaking supernatural languages openly before everyone, but it certainly helps to do it in private and watch the downpour of supernatural results! When people hear our language today, it isn't necessarily based on the languages of ethnicity but on the shared ideologies, cultures, behaviors, mannerisms, points of interest, technologies, trends, and nuances of people within certain spheres of assignment. It simply means that people will hear the wisdom of the kingdom, covertly or overtly, in a way they comprehend.

"And these signs will follow those who believe: In my name they will cast out demons; THEY WILL SPEAK WITH NEW TONGUES; they will take up serpents; and if they drink anything deadly, it will by no means hurt them; they will lay hands on the sick and they will recover."

(Mark 16:17-18, NKJV, emphasis added)

> **Every "mountain" or sphere has its own nomenclature, jargon and verbiage, and we'll find ourselves being able to communicate the message of transformation using the language that's appropriate to the sphere.**

However, that language will not be "gibberish" or superficial babble; it will be the "sovereign sound" of God using the wisdom of His Spirit upon our tongues. We will virtually "echo" the purposes of God and transfer the will of God from heaven to Earth without a loss in translation. Truly, we will have a supernaturally-enhanced language that transforms the Seven Mountain Culture of the world. I believe that praying in our supernatural language of unknown tongues helps to prepare us to have the **"tongue of the learned"** or supernatural knowledge of God's plans to transform nations. Our ears are truly turned toward the Holy Spirit, so that we can have the clear and effective words that will help transform souls, systems and societies throughout the world.

11

"For assuredly, I say to you, WHOEVER SAYS TO THIS MOUNTAIN, 'BE REMOVED AND BE CAST INTO THE SEA,' and does not doubt in his heart, but believes that those things he says will be done, he will have whatever he says. Therefore I say to you, whatever things you ask when you pray, believe that you receive them, and you will have them."

(Mark 11:23-24, NKJV, emphasis added)

THRONE SOUNDS AND THRONE SONGS

There is a sound that a moving or movable throne makes, as recorded in Ezekiel with the beating of the angel wings and the turning of the wheels within a wheel. Ezek. 1:22-28, NIV, says this:

*"Spread out above the heads of the living creatures was what looked something like a vault, sparkling like crystal, and awesome. Under the vault their wings were stretched out one toward the other, and each had two wings covering its body. **When the creatures moved, I heard the sound of their wings, like the roar of rushing waters, like the voice of the Almighty, like the tumult of an army.** When they stood still, they lowered their wings. Then there came a voice from above the vault over their heads as they stood with lowered wings. Above the vault over their heads was what looked like a throne of lapis lazuli, and high above on the throne was a figure like that of a man. I saw that from what appeared to be his waist up he looked like glowing metal, as if full of fire, and that from there down he looked like fire; and brilliant light surrounded him. Like the appearance of a rainbow in the clouds on a rainy day, so was the radiance around him. This was the appearance of*

the likeness of the glory of the Lord. When I saw it, I fell face down, and I heard the voice of one speaking." (emphasis added)

Later, in Ezek. 10:1-5 (NIV), the prophet has a nearly identical vision:

*"I looked, and I saw the likeness of a throne of lapis lazuli above the vault that was over the heads of the cherubim. The Lord said to the man clothed in linen, "Go in among the wheels beneath the cherubim. Fill your hands with burning coals from among the cherubim and scatter them over the city." And as I watched, he went in. Now the cherubim were standing on the south side of the temple when the man went in, and a cloud filled the inner court. Then the glory of the Lord rose from above the cherubim and moved to the threshold of the temple. The cloud filled the temple, and the court was full of the radiance of the glory of the Lord. **The sound of the wings of the cherubim could be heard as far away as the outer court, like the voice of God Almighty when he speaks.**" (emphasis added)*

Similarly, the prophet Isaiah also had a vision of the Lord God upon a throne in Isa. 6:1-5 (NIV):

*"In the year that King Uzziah died, I saw the Lord, high and exalted, seated on a throne; and the train of his robe filled the temple. Above him were seraphim, each with six wings: With two wings they covered their faces, with two they covered their feet, and with two they were flying. **And they were calling to one another: "Holy, holy, holy is the Lord Almighty; the whole earth is full of his glory." At the sound of their voices the doorposts and thresholds shook and the temple was filled with smoke.** "Woe to me!" I cried. "I am ruined!*

13

For I am a man of unclean lips, and I live among a people of unclean lips, and my eyes have seen the King, the Lord Almighty."

In Revelation there are not just throne sounds but songs and chants being sung around the throne in heaven by a variety of beings. The first instance of this is found in Rev. 4:1-8 (NIV):

*"At once I was in the Spirit, and there before me was a throne in heaven with, someone sitting on it. And the one who sat there had the appearance of jasper and carnelian. A rainbow, resembling an emerald, encircled the throne. Surrounding the throne were twenty-four other thrones, and seated on them were twenty-four elders. They were dressed in white and had crowns of gold on their heads. **From the throne came flashes of lightning, rumbling and peals of thunder.** Before the throne, seven lamps were blazing. These are the seven spirits of God. Also before the throne there was what looked like a sea of glass, clear as crystal.*

*"In the center, around the throne, were four living creatures, and they were covered with eyes, in front and in back. The first living creature was like a lion, the second was like an ox, the third had a face like a man, the fourth was like a flying eagle. Each of the four living creatures had six wings and was covered with eyes all around, even under his wings. **Day and night they never stopped saying: 'Holy, holy, holy is the Lord God Almighty, who was, and is, and is to come.'"** (emphasis added)*

The 24 elders then speak another song in verse 11, and then in Chapter 5, verses 9-10, they sing a new song. They are then joined by more than 10 million angels in verse 11 who sing a new song in verse 12. Finally, Rev. 5:13 says, *"Then I heard every creature in heaven and on earth and under the earth and on the sea, and all that is in them, singing: 'To him who sits on the throne and to the Lamb be praise and honor and glory and power, for ever and ever!'"*

Now that's quite a choir – the largest one ever created, assembled or recorded in history – and apparently they don't even need a conductor! Rev. 14:1-3 even describes Jesus and a smaller choir of 144,000 singing to him on Mount Zion, again with many of the same details as in the other visions above! I believe the Spirit is saying through these examples in Scripture that just as there is worship around the thrones in heaven, each one of us as sons or daughters of God needs to create our own **"throne song"** and sing in the Spirit and/or sing a new song unto the Lord. (See Ps. 33:3, 47:6, 59:16, 68:4, 68:32, 96:1, 98:1, 98:4, 104:33, 105:2, 108:1, 144:9, 149:1; Isa. 42:10; 1 Cor. 14:26; and especially **Eph. 5:18-20,** NIV, *"Do not get drunk on wine, which leads to debauchery. Instead, be filled with the Spirit, speaking to one another with psalms, hymns, and songs from the Spirit. Sing and make music from your heart to the Lord, always giving thanks to God the Father for everything, in the name of our Lord Jesus Christ."*).

Our praise and worship is a weapon and a testimony of our faith, love and devotion to our King. It announces and signals to friend and foe alike our complete confidence, commitment and consecration to the One who died for us and rose again: Jesus of Nazareth. It is a sign of our authority and oneness in the Spirit. It also attracts the angelic host and releases fear and confusion in the enemy's camp.

THE THRONE OF LAW/GOVERNMENT

Some iterations of the Seven Mountains of Culture identify this particular mountain as either the mountain of "law" or the mountain of "government," so we'll identify with both in this chapter. For the remainder of this book it will simply be listed as the mountain of government. Webster's New Explorer Dictionary and Thesaurus defines **"Law"** as: A rule of conduct or action established by custom or laid down and enforced by a governing authority; also: the whole body of such rules; the control brought about by enforcing such rules; a science that deals with laws and their interpretation and application. It also defines **"Government"** as: Authoritative direction or control; rule; the making of policy; the organization or agency through which a political unit exercises authority. It is the complex of institutions, laws, and customs through which a political unit is governed. In the kingdom of God, law/government are the authoritative foundations of divine laws, principles and order that support the mandates, missions and merits of God's eternal purposes.

> *"The scepter shall not depart from Judah, nor a LAWGIVER from between his feet, until Shiloh comes; and to Him shall be the obedience of the people."*

> *(Gen. 49:10, GNB, emphasis added)*

> *"For unto us a child is born, unto us a son is given: and the GOVERNMENT shall be upon his shoulder ..."*

> *(Isa. 9:6, KJV, emphasis added)*

Lawgivers or kings governed, using the scepter as a display of official authority. Tradition holds that a king would hold his scepter out to a person who was permitted to approach the throne. To whom the king did not raise the scepter, that person was possibly put to death (Est. 4:11). The term **"Scepter"** comes from the Hebrew word: **"Shebet,"** meaning: To branch off, a stick for punishing, writing, fighting, ruling or walking. Scepters and thrones are directly related as symbols of law and government. Certainly we are not so harsh as to use physical contact in our dominion as kings today, but we do carry the authority to accept or reject matters of illicit or illegal approaches to the throne of righteousness

16

and to do so without compromise. However, armies of nations who are rightfully defending their territory against enemy attacks will use force to do so. When we discover diabolical plans of the adversary, we are charged with responsibility to reject, and not accept, detrimental terms. The scepter represents the righteousness of God which rules superior over all contrary issues.

"Thy THRONE, O God, is for ever and ever; the SCEPTER of thy kingdom is a right scepter. Thou lovest righteousness, and hateth wickedness: therefore God, thy God, hath anointed thee with the oil of gladness above thy fellows." (Ps. 45:6, KJV, emphasis added)

The Government or **"Misrah"** (Hebrew) of Christ, as found in Isa. 9:6-7, is the foundation for all government in the earth today. As we establish thrones in each of the Seven Mountains, we begin with the source of power where all authority and the ability to sit upon all other thrones is derived.

"Then God said, 'Let Us make man in Our image, according to Our likeness; and let them rule over the fish of the sea and over the birds of the sky and over the cattle and over all the earth, and over every creeping thing that creeps on the earth. God created man in His own image, in the image of God He created him, male and female He created them. God blessed them; and God said to them, 'Be fruitful and multiply, and fill the earth, and subdue it; and rule over the fish of the sea and over the birds of the sky and over every living thing that moves on the earth.'"

(Gen. 1:26-28, NAS)

"Government" on Earth actually began in the Garden of Eden when God gave a mandate to Adam to steward the Garden. When God

17

gives someone a "seed" and allows them to be responsible for its growth, safety, upbringing, and posterity, they are serving as "governors."

> **"Then the Lord God took man and put him into the Garden of Eden to cultivate it and keep it." (Gen. 2:15, NAS)**

Most people regard government in a more formal manner in terms of how it relates to the passing of laws and ordinances. All of this is government in a basic sense, but the government of God involves much more. Government is about the establishment of God's order and the provision of sustainability and resourcefulness for the well-being of humanity. We see "government" in law enforcement; the court systems; law practices; security agencies; local, state and national legislative offices; the monarchy; diplomatic agencies; cabinets of foreign ministries; public policy forums; ambassadorial offices and functions, and other organizations and environments that are charged with developing and maintaining law, order, consistency and accountability. There is a certain amount of "government" necessary in all of the Seven Mountains of Culture. This is why the government of Christ (Misrah) is the starting point for all throne-room culture.

Governments evolved in history by the establishment of nations, kings, councils and kingdoms. Different people groups and cultures began to develop over time. They all needed some form of laws, governance and oversight. History recorded the interactions between people, places and things and gives us accounts of how the issues of governance affected the nations of the world in both positive and negative ways. Wars have been fought and countless lives lost over issues of governance, with despotic leaders, coup d'états, genocide, civil unrest, divided nations and the establishment of territorial lines as the results. Human rights were violated in many instances when governments ruled without the fear of accountability or retribution. For this reason, righteous government must be restored with judgment and justice. The zeal of the Lord of Hosts will perform this (Isa. 9:7).

THE THRONE OF MEDIA

"The Lord gave the word: great was the company of those that published it."

(Ps. 68:11, KJV)

"Listen closely to the thunder of His voice, And the rumbling that goes out from His mouth. Under the whole heaven He lets it loose, And His lightning to the ends of the earth. After it, a voice roars; He thunders with His majestic voice, And He does not restrain the lightnings when His voice is heard. God thunders with His voice wondrously, Doing great things which we cannot comprehend...."

(Job 37:2-5, NAS)

Media is defined as: The means of communication, as radio and television, newspapers, and magazines that reach or influence people widely. (Dictionary.com) The Mountain associated with media is responsible for the collection, dissemination and articulation of information. People who work in this industry may be employed as reporters, broadcast journalists, radio reporters and announcers, television reporters and announcers, editors, technical support teams, meteorologists, traffic reporters, camera operators, producers, directors, writers, authors, and publishers.

Public perception of many of the events that happen in the world are based on how well or how poorly the media presents the information. It is said that the media is able to put a "spin" on just about anything, implying that craftiness and ulterior motives can shape how a story is released to the public, swaying their opinions, in perhaps the wrong way. Advanced technology and satellite systems allow information to span the entire globe in just minutes. This includes information that is not well prepared or presented, or even completely validated, making this industry a liability to the safety of our societies. With the advent of social media such as Facebook, Twitter, Instagram, and LinkedIn and the development of highly-sophisticated devices such as telephones, cameras, computers, electronic writing tablets and other devices, the media industry has a seemingly endless supply of information that is fed to distribution sources.

Photos, videos, voice recordings and text messages can go "viral," reaching millions of viewers or listeners in a short period of time. It is easy to see the positive or negative impact that information can have in today's world. If information is negative and if unhealthy programming is circulated worldwide, it will not take long for prejudice, misinformation and violence to contaminate the cultures and identities of people, places and things. Positives can become negatives in a matter of moments and the collateral damage can be phenomenal. The amount of damage control that must be conducted to repair major media missteps is enormous and the related fallout often seems surreal.

When "kings" take their place in the media industry, we are bound to see more sensitivity, wisdom, better communications, and the accurate distribution of information come to the forefront. Stories won't be presented just to start a "frenzy" and sell newspapers and advertising or spark interest at the expense of someone's privacy or moments of distress. More care will go into verifying the accuracy of details before a rush to "scoop" other agencies. With the promotion of kingdom citizens as the "kings" of this industry, policies can be changed and the structure of operations can be affected in positive ways. New cultures of civility and personal interaction can mold new attitudes in an agency environment that is used to doing things the "same old way." Human respect can rise to new heights. Although there is the risk of losing the competitive edge, the media industry has a chance of remaining viable and strong when the wisdom and the will of God are the driving forces behind its operations.

THE THRONE OF ARTS AND ENTERTAINMENT

"My heart is stirred by a noble theme as I recite my verses for the king; my tongue is the pen of a skillful writer."

(Ps. 45:1, NIV)

"See, I have called by name Bezalel, the son of Uri, the son of Hur, of the tribe of Judah. "I have filled him with the Spirit of God in wisdom, in understanding, in knowledge, and in all kinds of craftsmanship, to make artistic designs for work in gold, in silver, and in bronze,..."

(Ex. 31:3-4, NAS)

The Mountain of Arts and Entertainment is important to human survival. After a hard day at work nothing is more relaxing than listening to good music, watching a great TV program or movie or seeing an exciting game being played between your favorite teams. It's a way of life. People want and need the outlet and relaxation. Imagine this industry being influenced by believers who sit as "kings" in their areas of assignment at the tops of their mountains. Imagine the opportunities to help influence positive thoughts and actions in a huge way. This mountain covers the occupations that give us singers, musicians, songwriters, dancers, producers, performers, artists, agents and their products; the movie and theater world with its actors, agents, producers, directors, stage staff and equipment operators; the sports realm with players, coaches, stadium and arena staff, sponsors and spectators. And, there are countless behind-the-scenes participants in these industries that no one ever sees publicly.

This is a huge arena that handles astounding amounts of money, power and influence. The perception of life itself is often shaped by what is seen on "the big screen," or even the "small screen" for that matter. A day hardly passes without someone overhearing a conversation about the successes or failures of sports figures or teams. Player drafts, selections, team trades, terminations, brushes with the law and salaries are big talk at sports bars and coffee houses. Music is heard just about anywhere and we see people with headphones, telephones, radios, computers and the like, listening to music or watching movies. There is virtually nowhere you can travel where the Mountain of Arts and Entertainment is not having an influence.

There is a vast opportunity to experience the negative impact of something that enters our culture through arts and entertainment. Demonically influenced and socially inappropriate material slips into the mainstream activities of life, often un-noticed. Children are influenced by music and movies that they're watching on their phones and computers while clueless parents are only a few feet away. What is repeatedly seen and heard somehow becomes "endorsed" as a common way of life, and usually without any protest. Some people have just given up, believing that there is no way to turn this situation around. I disagree.

I have seen more Christian and biblically-based (even if very loosely) movies in the last 10 years than ever before. Authors are writing books and videos are being released that portray the kingdom of God and His people in a very positive light. Christian writers, producers, directors and actors are funding many of these movies themselves, without any large capital support from other sources. Wholesome journalism does indeed exist and there will be kings arising to cultivate this industry and support its growth. Certain professional sports figures are very open about their love for God and will pray on the field before games, unashamed of their relationships with God. Their faith and desire to see God glorified is their primary motive. As more of these very important believers rise to their places on their mountain and as they become established on thrones of influence, we will see and hear even more positive things happening.

THE THRONE OF BUSINESS

"It is the glory of God to conceal a matter, but the glory of kings is to search out a matter."

(Prov. 25:2, NAS)

"...money is the answer for everything."

(Eccl. 10:19, NIV)

"But remember the LORD your God, for it is he who gives you the ability to produce wealth, and so confirms his covenant, which he swore to your ancestors, as it is today."

(Deut. 8:18, NIV)

A business, also known as an enterprise or firm, is an organization involved in the trade of goods, services or both, to consumers. Businesses are prevalent in capitalist economies, where most of them are privately owned and provide goods and services to customers in exchange for other goods, services, or money (Wikipedia). Business, in some shape, form or fashion, takes place in every area of the Earth that's inhabited by mankind. It too, affects every other mountain of culture in terms of how the goods and services that are associated with each mountain are made available to the public. It is essential for the survival and upward mobility of cultures and societies on this planet. Higher Education systems have been established to teach the trade of business, with schools such as Harvard University, Stanford University, the London School of Economics, Yale University, Cambridge University, the University of Chicago, University of Pennsylvania, Dartmouth College, the Kellogg School of Business and numerous others, leading the way. Business is so important to the health of this planet that many nations form governmental regulatory groups to oversee transactions to ensure fairness and adherence to laws of trade and commerce.

Bankers, presidents and CEOs of corporations, investors, venture capitalists, hedge fund investors, corporate counsellors, auditors, certified public accountants, computer programmers and analysts, executive board members, business support teams such as office staff, home-based business owners, small business owners, consultants, administrators, and even the neighborhood paper carrier are involved in the Mountain of Business. This mountain serves every community in the world; therefore, it has a huge influence on the way of life in its respective areas. This mountain is also a favorite of the spirit of Babylon, which seeks to bring everyone and everything under its control.

"For the love of money is the source of all kinds of evil. Some have been so eager to have it that they have wandered away from the faith and have broken their hearts with many sorrows. But you, man of God, avoid all these things."

(I Tim. 6:10-11, GNB)

All of the other mountains have dealings with the business mountain, making it a very pivotal part of their culture as well. How people do business is either the cause for corrupt behavior or the cure for it.

"Wealth that you get by dishonesty will do you no good, but honesty can save your life. The Lord will not let good people go hungry, but he will keep the wicked from getting what they want. Being lazy will make you

poor, but hard work will make you rich. A sensible person gathers the crops when they are ready; it is a disgrace to sleep through the time of harvest. Good people will receive blessings. The words of the wicked hide a violent nature. Good people will be remembered as a blessing, but the wicked will soon be forgotten. Sensible people will accept good advice. People who talk foolishly will come to ruin. Honest people are safe and secure, but the dishonest will be caught."

(Prov. 10:2-9, GNB)

As the "kings" arise to their mountain and take their seats on their thrones, the business world will get a fresh revelation of righteous order, integrity and kingdom perspective and will help usher in the transfer of wealth to fund and further kingdom projects and programs.

THE THRONE OF FAMILY

"Sing to God, sing in praise to his name, extol him who rides on the clouds; rejoice before him – his name is the Lord. A father to the fatherless, a defender of the widows, is God in his holy dwelling. God sets the lonely in families, he leads out the prisoners with singing; but the rebellious live in a sun-scorched land."

(Ps. 68:4-6, NIV)

Family is defined as: A group of individuals living under one roof and under one head: Household. It is also a group of persons of common ancestry; a group of things having common characteristics; a social unit usually consisting of one or two parents and their children (Webster's New Explorer Dictionary and Thesaurus). The Mountain of Family is an important element in the production of healthy relationships, socially balanced people and as a "pool" from which the other mountains draw the people who make up their populations. It is an understatement

25

to say that many people have not enjoyed the experience of having loving and complete family units to draw strength from. Broken homes, homelessness, mental illness, poverty, spousal abuse, fatherlessness, drug and alcohol abuse, domestic violence, troubled neighborhoods, street violence, social injustice, racial profiling, discrimination and lack of strong educational support all factor into the types of families/homes that people emerge from.

"Kings" in the form of spiritual fathers and mothers can have a major impact on people who need to be embraced, encouraged and empowered. There are many people who will serve on their "thrones" to offer programs and financial assistance and to develop infrastructure and support systems for making families strong and self-sufficient. Even "parenting" can take on another level of identity with strong programs and support groups, headed by sensitive and anointed individuals who have the heart of the greatest parent ever – God the Father.

Professionally-trained believers who specialize in counseling, and who are able to offer emotional support, will have plenty of work to do in terms of providing healing and deliverance for those who need it. Members from other streams of the Seven Mountains can offer their respective skill-sets for mentoring and development, supporting those who did not have opportunities to rise up and take their rightful places in the Earth. Leaders who know how to galvanize others and create teams and networking groups can serve as the catalyst for developing the families/groups that some people never had the opportunity to experience.

God is about people; He always has been and always will be. It is for people that God gave His Son, Jesus Christ. The Holy Spirit came on the Day of Pentecost to fill "people" and bring them into the "family" of God. God is continuing to release wisdom about relationships and how to develop strong families, whether they are the nuclear family or extended ones.

THE THRONE OF EDUCATION

"Teach us to number our days carefully so that we may develop wisdom in our hearts."

(Ps. 90:12, HCS)

"The Lord GOD has given Me the tongue of those who are instructed to know how to sustain the weary with a word. He awakens Me each morning; He awakens My ear to listen like those being instructed."

(Isa. 50:4, HCS)

"He will be the sure foundation for your times, a rich store of salvation and wisdom and knowledge; the fear of the LORD is the key to this treasure."

(Isa. 33:6, NIV)

"Then the king ordered Ashpenaz, the chief of his officials, to bring in some of the sons of Israel, including some of the royal family and of the nobles, youths in whom was no defect, who were good-looking, **showing intelligence in every branch of wisdom, endowed with understanding and discerning knowledge,** *and who had ability for serving in the king's court; and he ordered him to teach them the literature and language of the Chaldeans."*

(Dan. 1:3-4, NAS, emphasis added)

*"**God gave these four young men an unusual aptitude for understanding every aspect of literature and wisdom.** And God gave Daniel the special ability to interpret the meanings of visions and dreams. When the training period ordered by the king was completed, the chief of staff brought all the young men to King*

27

Nebuchadnezzar. The king talked with them, and no one impressed him as much as Daniel, Hananiah, Mishael, and Azariah. So they entered the royal service. ***Whenever the king consulted them in any matter requiring wisdom and balanced judgment, he found them ten times more capable than any of the magicians and enchanters in his entire kingdom.***

(Dan. 1:17-20, NLT, emphasis added)

Education is defined as: The action or process of educating or being educated; a field of study dealing with methods of teaching and learning (Webster's New Explorer Dictionary and Thesaurus). The **Education Mountain** relates to the professionally-structured system of gathering and disseminating information to create an environment for learning, processing and acting upon what we've learned. What we learn as a human race is very important because it reflects upon how we conduct ourselves as citizens and how we contribute to the preservation of life, how we treat our resources and each other, and how we become productive, always seeking self-improvement. But, "how" we learn is important as well.

God is raising "kings" in this mountain who know how to stimulate the learning experience and how to pass on more information than we've ever known before. These are people who have new and creative ways of helping others become all that they can be through diversified teaching methods. Each one of the mountains of culture has an education process that empowers the people who function in the mountains, making a quality education of the highest importance. The advancement of best practices in any field or industry relies a great deal on how well its participants are educated.

"Behold, I will do something new, now it will spring forth; will you not be aware of it? I will even make a roadway in the wilderness and rivers in the desert."

(Isa. 14:19, NAS)

These influential educators will know how to effectively reach people of different races, creeds, colors and cultures, and even the sub-groups of "Baby Boomers," "Generation X-ers," "Generation Y-ers," "Millennials and others. The Education Mountain contributes to the development of technologies and the advancement of each of the other Seven Mountain spheres by providing the fundamental vehicle by which information that is specific to each mountain is ascertained and articulated and dispensed. Miseducation, non-education and under-education of citizens is criminal in the sense that it deprives human beings of the most fundamental of rights – the right to an education that gives them an opportunity to arise in life and have a fighting chance for survival in the world.

Since God gives us **"knowledge of witty inventions"** (Prov. 8:12, KJV), we have yet to enter the sphere of the full knowledge that God has for His people. Scientists, physicists, medical doctors, psychologists, psychiatrists, and other medical and scientific practitioners will arise with brilliance and intelligence that will astound the public. They will be able to teach, train and empower others to pass on information, technology, life lessons and discoveries that change the course of history and improve life. Mentors in the technological fields will help stimulate the inquisitive and curious minds of the people who love to "discover" things. Genocide, homicide, fratricide, suicide and other violent and destructive forces can be reduced through proper education. Racism and social unrest can be curbed through education. Through proper education, the world's best and brightest stars will shine and become the lights that help make this world what it should be. The best is yet to come!

THE THRONE OF RELIGION

"Then say to him, Thus says the Lord of Hosts, 'Behold a man whose name is Branch, FOR HE WILL BRANCH OUT from where He is; and He will build the temple of the Lord. Yes, it is He who will build the temple of the Lord, AND HE WILL BEAR THE HONOR AND SIT AND RULE ON HIS THRONE. Thus, He will be a priest on His throne, AND THE COUNSEL OF PEACE WILL BE BETWEEN THE TWO OFFICES.'"

(Zech. 6:12-13, NAS, emphasis added)

Religion is defined as: The service and worship of God or the supernatural; devotion to a religious faith; a personal set or institutionalized system of religious beliefs, attitudes, and practices; a cause, principle, or belief held to with faith and ardor (Webster's New Explorer Dictionary and Thesaurus).

The Mountain of Religion actually encompasses every religion in the world and not just the Christian faith. However, we'll remain focused on the context of thrones and how God is empowering "kings" to make this mountain more suitable for the purposes of the kingdom of God. The **Throne of Religion** embraces the *"two offices"* of **king** and **priest** after **the Order of Melchizedek** (Ps. 110:1, 4 and Heb. 5:10) as indicated in the text above. The singular ecclesiastical and traditional role of church leadership is now blended into a more diverse and effective role as Melchizedek and Jesus demonstrated in the Bible. This diversity heightens awareness of the "kingdom" message and not just the Gospel of salvation. Church leaders can now fulfill 2 Pet. 1:3 (KJV): *"According as his divine power hath given unto us all things that pertain unto life and godliness, through the knowledge of him that hath called us to glory and virtue."*

As "priests" who are also "kings," our spiritual leaders can develop a more diverse and prepared group of people who don't focus their entire existence within the four walls of the church building. They are now able to address issues that broaden the influence and effectiveness of local churches and their members. This increases the local members' ability to go into all the world and preach the Gospel and have the ability to do it through powerful lifestyles that reflect the miracles and virtue of Christ outside of the four walls of the church. Members are taught how to communicate in non-religious terms and how to show the love of God to a dying world. Believers won't suffer from "rapture fever" and will see the value of remaining in the earth to execute the mandates of the kingdom. Spiritual leaders can embrace "Seven Mountain" teaching and truly prepare their people to affect global environments.

In order to fully influence the Mountain of Religion, the "priest" must **"branch out"** and relate to the other "kings" and "mountaineers" in the remaining six Mountains of Culture. God is increasing the anointing, and adjusting the principles, perspectives and processes of how His spiritual leaders address world issues. Now, a more diversified and relational view is being embraced. In the past, some believers who were not involved in "full time" ministry didn't necessarily have value in the eyes of certain ecclesiastical leaders and there was a distinct line drawn between the "secular" and the "sacred" as it related to purpose and responsibility. The church is maturing and learning how to really represent the kingdom of God and respect the diversity that's in the Body of Christ. Whatever your secular occupation is, it has sacred underpinnings because you are part of the kingdom of God.

WE ARE "PROFESS"-IONALS!

"Let us, then, HOLD FIRMLY TO THE FAITH WE PROFESS. For we have a great High Priest who has gone into the very presence of God – Jesus, the Son of God. Our High Priest is not one who cannot feel sympathy for our weaknesses. On the contrary, we have a High Priest who was tempted in every way that we are, but did not sin. Let us have confidence, then, AND APPROACH GOD'S THRONE, WHERE THERE IS GRACE. There we will receive mercy and find grace to help us just when we need it."

(Heb. 4:14-16, GNB, emphasis added)

Because we can boldly and directly approach the throne of God in heaven, we can receive every measure of grace that we need to sit on thrones in the earth. Heaven's throne is the "master file" for thrones everywhere. Jesus is our High Priest who has been tested in every way possible and already has a plan mapped out for anything we'll face as we sit upon our thrones. Since Jesus has already been tested for us and took our sins upon Himself, provision has been made for our victory. We are now **"profess"-ional** kings who have taken lessons directly from the King of kings and Lord of lords! *"And Jesus increased in wisdom and stature and in favor with God and men."* (Luke 2:52, NKJV)

- **Wisdom** – The quality of having experience, knowledge and good judgment

- **Stature** – Reputation, position, prestige, distinction, importance, influence

- **Favor** – Approval, support and preference

32

Wisdom and stature and favor are some of a king's greatest assets. We'll have divine opportunities to go before other kings, the ability to stand in their palaces (have an audience with them) as Daniel and his colleagues did, and receive the type of favor that causes them to become our allies. Powerful partnerships will develop and mountains will move!

MY DECREE

I am called to be a "king" on the thrones of the Seven Mountains of Culture. I will listen diligently for God's voice of instruction about my assignment. I will follow the Word of the Lord and the leading of the Spirit of God so that I can be an instrument of kingdom conversion in the Earth. The power of my throne and my domain is found in the power of Christ on His throne. Without Him, I have no power or authority. But, He has equipped me for this assignment and I am confident in that. My place of assignment is either waiting for me or has already found me. I will ascend to my throne. God decided this before I was born. I will grow in grace and in the knowledge and favor of God. Like King Jesus, I will increase in wisdom and stature, and in favor with God and men.

I SEE *Thrones*!

I am called to be a "king"
on the thrones of the Seven
Mountains of Culture.

THE TECHNOLOGY
OF THRONES

"Let everyone be subject to the governing authorities, for there is no authority except that which God has established. The authorities that exist have been established by God."

(Rom. 13:1-2, NIV)

"**I Saw Thrones**" is a statement in the Book of Revelation that bridges the vision that John saw centuries ago with the exciting supernatural assignments that we have today. It's a revelation of the present and coming moves of supernatural governance and influence by the sons and daughters of God as we take our rightful places as the kings of the Earth above the Seven Mountains of Culture or Influence which are the pillars of influence of any society. By now, believers have been exposed to tremendous levels of teaching on the Seven Mountains of Culture by some of today's leading kingdom strategists and tacticians. We've come a long way since the initial introduction of the teaching on the subject back in the middle 1970's. The mountains or spheres of influence, which include Religion, Government, Business, Education, Family, Media, and Arts & Entertainment are extremely embedded in the transformational methods of God as He brings *Rev. 11:15* into reality. *"...The kingdoms of this world are become the kingdoms of our Lord and of his Christ; and he shall reign for ever and ever."*

In order to see this powerful transition take place, we'll have to undertake the process of mastering life from an elevated state of awareness upon **Mount Zion**, which is the **8th Mountain of Culture.** The number "8" represents *"new beginnings,"* an indication that we're going to see and experience new "heights" of supernatural awareness and expression as we sit upon our newly-appointed thrones. You'll see more on this subject in the Chapter entitled, **"Mount" Up with Wings like Eagles!**

"In the days to come the mountain where the Temple stands will be the highest one of all, towering above all the hills. Many nations will come streaming to it, and their people will say, Let us go up to the hill of the Lord, to the Temple of Israel's God. He will teach us what he wants us to do; we will walk in the paths he has chosen. For the Lord's teaching comes from Jerusalem; from Zion he speaks to his people."

(Mic. 4:1-2, GNB)

The grace and glory of God is being released to His people, giving the planet an answer to the cry of its heart... *"The whole creation waits breathlessly with anticipation for the revelation of God's sons and daughters. ...We know that the whole creation is groaning together and suffering labor pains up until **now.**" (Rom. 8:19, 22, KJV, emphasis added)*

The word **NOW** is an important indication of a brand new time of discovery and in the plan of God, "discovery" leads to "recovery!" It enlightens us to positive things that we might have overlooked in the past or it brings us into a sovereign season of special releases and manifestations

THE TECHNOLOGY OF THRONES

that overturn some of the ineffective or defective strategies and tactics of the past, giving us fresh new outlooks and new thought paradigms for today and tomorrow. With each new revelation comes new application.

This will directly relate to how we function on our thrones of assignment in the Seven Mountains of Culture or Influence. This governance and authority won't simply be "head" knowledge. It will be a manifested reality that transforms the kingdoms of this world into the kingdoms of the Lord and of His Christ where God's sons and daughters sit as "kings." As you continue reading, you'll see "kings" used throughout this book but I want to assure you that it's used only as a historical and technical reference to those who sat upon the thrones of the earth and not to divisively or dishonorably eliminate women from the culture of authority. In Christ there is neither male nor female (Gal. 3:29).

Historically, kings ruled and reigned from prominent and highlighted places of authority. It was necessary for them to rule from platforms that made their positions clear and it needed to be evident that they were in authority over their respective domains or territories. Thrones were usually elevated above ground level and ornately designed to render a sense of authority, power and splendor. The throne that we derive our power and authority and assignments from, as redeemed sons and daughters of God, is no different. It is a glorious throne and it's the model that all other thrones derive their most basic qualities and characteristics from. It is movable and exalted above all others. We as believers share in the royalty and honor of our Lord Jesus Christ who is elevated in the heavenly dimension *"Far above all principality and power, and might, and dominion, and every name that is named, not only in this world, but also in that which is to come" (Eph. 1:21, KJV).* He is the **"King of kings and the Lord of lords."** (1 Tim. 6:15)

> **Jesus Christ has *"...Made us kings and priests unto God and his Father; to him be glory and dominion forever. Amen."* (Rev. 1:6, KJV)**

A ROOM OF THRONES

One night, I had a vision of a *"room of thrones"* located in heaven. There were countless thrones in the room as far as the eye could see. There were various sizes and configurations and colors of thrones, with some being more ornate than others. I had a great sense of awe when I saw this magnificent sight. It was overwhelming. Even more curious was the fact that none of them were occupied by a person. I asked God what the vacancies meant. Why wasn't anyone on these thrones? He said, *"These are the thrones of assignment that I have for my sons and daughters on the earth."*

I asked again why none of the thrones were filled. He replied, *"They* ***ARE*** *filled, but they're presently occupied by people who are not assigned to sit there by me. So, I already see them as empty and ready for reassignment, waiting on those who have the right to come and sit upon them. Each throne has a person whom I have assigned to sit there. Many of my people believe that they are waiting on their success to come and they believe they're waiting on their 'thrones.'* [Places of success] *But actually, their success and their thrones are waiting on them."* I was astonished at this, because I realized that with all of the "wrong" people presently on thrones, it didn't supersede or disqualify or eliminate the proper, preordained and prepared kingdom citizens of God from taking their rightful places! In spite of who may be in power now, God sees us rising to our rightful places and He's kept our seats warm for us!

THE THEORY OF THRONES

I See Thrones! Igniting and Increasing Your Influence in the Seven Mountains of Culture is about empowerment. Thrones are about empowerment. The Bible lists the word **"throne" 173 times** and **"thrones" nine times.** The first Biblical mention of thrones is found in Gen. 41:40, GNB, where Pharaoh spoke to Joseph saying, *"You shall have charge over my house, and all my people shall be governed according to your word [with reverence, submission, and obedience]. Only in matters of the **throne** will I be greater than you are."* The final Biblical reference to thrones is found in Rev. 22:3, GNB which says, *"There shall no longer exist there anything that is accursed (detestable, foul, offensive, impure, hateful, or horrible). But the **throne** of God and of the Lamb shall be in it, and His servants shall worship Him [pay divine honors to Him and do Him holy service]."* The remaining Biblical verses about thrones show us a powerful and diverse overview of thrones, the types of people who ruled and the circumstances surrounding their reign.

According to Webster's New Explorer Dictionary and Thesaurus a "Throne" is defined as: **The chair of state of a sovereign or high dignitary; royal power: sovereignty.** Thrones are very important in secular and biblical history as they represent the seat of power in nations and kingdoms. Today, many nations of the world establish their systems of governance, power, influence and authority through various means, among them being: succession within a monarchy, the democratic process of elections, political succession, military or police authority and action, war, subjugation, coup d'états, anarchy, genocide, manipulation of social systems, and other forms of illegal or dark influence. Many of these methods are not lawful or even humane. However those in power obtained it, the essence of their authority is based on having leadership and influence of some type that affects people, places and things. They may not have established a central location to function from but their actions force others to recognize their power. Therefore, thrones can be **literal** or **implied.**

"And I saw thrones, and they that sat upon them, and judgment was given unto them..."

(Rev. 20:4, KJV)

The word **"Judgment"** is from the Greek term **"Krima,"** meaning: A decision (the function or the effect, for or against ["crime"]): avenge, and go to law. The type of judgment described by Strong's Concordance indicates a type of judicious but not necessarily judicial or professional representation of law. Being judicious simply means to do something with a good sensibility, intelligence, prudence and wisdom. The term "judicial" suggests a career in the application of the principles of law such as a judge or magistrate.

> **As believers who sit on thrones, we are called to reinstate the balanced, civil, righteous, and wise influence that Jesus would, if He were in our place.**

Thrones, though not always identified as such, represent kingdoms, authority, governance, supervision, accountability, resourcefulness and in the case of godly authority: love, kindness, forgiveness, mercy, peace, humanitarianism, and good stewardship. Nearly every culture, climate and community on earth understands the presence of thrones as the seat of rulership and a source which regulates, delegates, supervises, supports, protects and manages people, places and things. Even insect and animal kingdoms are fashioned after a type of monarchy, structural hierarchy, or other influential pattern of leadership that gives guidance and provides structure and order to promote the survival of the species.

Thrones are a necessary part of government, governance and influence, including democratic governmental structures headed by elected officials or appointed leaders and in other forms of corporate or administrative organizations. Military organizations and para-military organizations such as police, fire and emergency medical services conform to some type of organizational hierarchy or structure. Even the family unit and the neighborhood block club celebrate authority in some form or another. Thrones exist within the scope of each of the Seven Mountains of Culture and are not necessarily accompanied by public recognition, ceremonialism or large supporting infrastructures.

> "Thrones" are everywhere, whether they are recognized and acknowledged or not!

God is the first and foremost example of governance and authority that mankind has to guide us in our application of authority in our own lives. The eternally powerful Father, with His loving and kind authority, is certainly no pushover or weakling in His application of divine order. His order is designed to first, redeem, then reform the disorder of planet Earth and its citizens brought about by the fall of mankind in the garden. The fall brought about systemic issues of disorder, displacement and defeat that became embedded in the nature and culture of the human race. This resulted in erratic behavior patterns in humanity and led to the disruption of how the human race managed the planet and its resources, often resulting in self destructive policies, platforms and programs that eroded societies and systems, along with the physical structure of the planet.

GIVE ME THIS MOUNTAIN!

"Now therefore give me this mountain, whereof the Lord spake in that day; for thou heardest in that day how the An'akim were there, and that the cities were great and fenced: if so be the Lord will be with me, then I shall be able to drive them out, as the Lord said."

(Josh. 14:12, KJVA)

Thrones and mountains are embedded in the culture of governance in both natural and spiritual arenas. Whoever possesses the "mountain" has the greatest vantage point and can launch attacks from high places against enemies. One can see great distances in a 360-degree angle from a mountaintop. Mountains are a valuable commodity in times of **war** and **exploration**. Mountains also represent any force or influence that looms over us as a deterrent to progress. In the technology of thrones and kingdom influence, the possession of mountains is equally as important as the possession of crowns. In the Seven Mountain Culture, we'll encounter forces who want to maintain and increase their influence in the mountains. Many of them are driven by the engines of Babylonian influence which desires to elevate itself above other cultures for the purpose of exalting its identity and dominating others.

When Joshua said, *"Give me this mountain,"* he was saying something very strategic. The word **"Give,"** in Hebrew means: Add, appoint, assign, commit, grant, restore and occupy.

    ⃠ **Add** – New assignments are being revealed according to our destinies and purposes

🔊 **Appoint –** We receive official authorization for these to be our mountains of influence

🔊 **Assign –** We have an endorsement from God to navigate the territory of these mountains

🔊 **Commit –** God gives His sovereign support to our activities

🔊 **Grant –** Special favor is given to us so that we can leverage our influence

🔊 **Restore –** We are empowered to reverse the negative influence and return the mountains to their original purposes

🔊 **Occupy –** Kingdom forces begin to dwell in and overtake the sphere of influence and bring positive results

Here are seven strategic and tactical points that lead to getting a **"Mountaintop Mentality."** When a point of vantage is achieved on a mountain, a "king" can set up camp and establish a throne. Even if the apex, or highest point hasn't been achieved yet, there is still a strategic and tactical advantage of being higher than you were before.

"And Saul and the men of Israel were gathered together, and pitched by the valley of Elah, and set the battle in array against the Philistines. And the Philistines stood on a mountain on the one side, and Israel stood on a mountain on the other side: and there was a valley between them."

(I Sam. 17:2-3, KJVA)

Often, two opposing forces watch each other from elevated positions on mountains, meaning that each group has achieved a certain level of prominence or victory. In life we encounter many opposing forces like this. As they look directly toward us it can be intimidating, but we have to know the purpose of God in the conflict. In this case, the opposing army was the Philistines or **"Pelesheth,"** (Heb.) a people whose name means: **To roll in dust.** This is also a reference to the nature of the serpent in the garden who was cursed by God to *"Crawl on your belly and eat dust as long as you live" (Gen. 3:14, GNB).* The Philistines represent the enemy of Israel and the kingdom of God.

As the story later unfolds, it is not the army of Israel that defeats the Philistine giant, Goliath, but an up and coming kingdom figure named David. He was not yet the sitting king but he possessed a "Mountaintop Mentality." In fact, King Saul and his army were intimidated by Goliath and his boasting. God used a very unlikely figure to circumvent the power of Goliath and his army and to take the victory for Israel. This act of courage by David at an early age helped contribute to his stature when it was time for him to become the actual king. He had a reputation for being anointed by God to come against greater odds and achieve victory for the kingdom. We are no different. We'll have great victories along the way as we ascend in influence and advance to our full assignment on the throne and we must remember, it was God who anointed and appointed David, and it's God who anoints and appoints us.

"How you've fallen from, heaven, morning star, son of dawn! [Lucifer] You are cut down to earth, helpless on your back! You said to yourself, I will climb up to heaven; above God's stars, I WILL RAISE MY THRONE. I'LL SIT ON THE MOUNT OF THE ASSEMBLY, on the heights of Zaphon. I'll go up to the cloud tops; I'll be like the Most High! But down to the underworld you are brought, to the depths of the pit."

(Isa. 14:12-15, CEB, emphasis added)

Satan, with his technology of Babylonian influence, always looks to assert a "parallel position" in the affairs of the kingdom of God, hoping to look "eye to eye" with you on the mountain as the Philistines did with

King Saul and the army of Israel. He hopes to reduce our confidence. Knowing that the Seven Mountain Culture exists among mankind, and that Mount Sinai, Mount Zion and other mountain figures in the Bible represent kingdom authority, he sets out to duplicate the position that godly forces possess. In the previous text, he boasts of *"raising his throne,"* and going to *"sit on the mount of the assembly"* in an attempt to make himself equal with kingdom forces.

> *"Next, we turned around and headed back toward the wilderness along the Red Sea road, exactly as the Lord instructed me. We traveled all around Mount Seir for a long time. Eventually the Lord said: You've been traveling around this mountain long enough. Head north."*

> (Deut. 2:1-2, CEB)

THE LAW OF SOVEREIGN ATTRACTION

The text of Deut. 2:1-2 is a typology of believers wandering around perplexing situations without progressing. It's no coincidence that the very mountain that stalled God's people on their journey is named **"Seir,"** which means: **"Devil"** in the Hebrew language! But nothing abolishes the power of a "devilish" mountain like a renewed mind and fresh instructions from God. When God told the people to **"Head north,"** He was sending them directly into alignment with **"The Law of Sovereign Attraction,"** a powerful kingdom principle that helps believers on their thrones to achieve their goals with supernatural support, resources, anointing, grace, angelic forces, wartime alliances, good relationships and other much needed supplies. Here's how it works…

"Beautiful for situation, the joy of the whole earth is mount Zion, on the sides of the north, the city of the great king. God is known in her palaces for a refuge."

(Ps. 48:2, KJV)

Mount Zion, which is the **8ᵗʰ Mountain** for believers, represents the seat of power for us. It puts us in position above the Seven Mountains and serves as a type of "Holy Headquarters," where we get strategic input from God in our quest to engage the other seven mountains. Turning *"north"* gives us new beginnings and new strategies and tactics for gaining ground for the kingdom. It's a safe place to dwell. You'll see more about it in the section of this chapter entitled, *"A Beautiful Situation"* and in the chapter entitled *"Mount" up With Wings Like Eagles!*

When we get distracted or discouraged and end up circling *"Mount Seir,"* we waste precious time, energy and resources. God will providentially tell us what He told Israel, *"You're going in circles! Head north, toward my kingdom!"* This meant that Israel was to begin following the flow of a pre-positioned supernatural force called **the sovereignty of God.** Just as the Earth has a natural force or magnetic field that runs from the North Polar Region to the South Polar Region, and that force makes compass needles point north. Likewise, when something is magnetic, it attracts objects that contain iron. We too have a supernatural, attractive force that works on our behalf.

A simple grammar school experiment demonstrates the power of magnetic attraction. Take a metal pole and place it near pieces of metal like paper clips. The clips are not attracted to the pole because it is not magnetic. Then take the metal pole and balance it across a block of wood or some other object so that it runs lengthwise in a north-south direction. Strike the pole on the north end with a metal hammer. Now place the end of the pole near the paper clips and watch them connect to the pole. You made the pole become magnetic by striking it sharply and temporarily "disconnecting" the molecules so they could reform, a split second later, under the "authority" of the preexisting magnetic field!

The power of attraction was already there, but the pole had to be struck to temporarily disconnect its molecules from their old "non-attractive nature" and reform them under a pre-existing physical law. The pole had to face in the direction where the law of attraction was already in effect. The Law of Sovereign Attraction works the same way. *"My message is like a fire, and like a hammer that breaks rocks in pieces." (Jer. 23:29, GNB)* When we allow the Word of God to "hit" those "rocky" areas of our lives and rearrange our "non-attractive" nature, we "reform" in a new kingdom nature that attracts the assets of the kingdom. When we face the kingdom of God and its principles (north), we become supernaturally attractive and **"all these things will be added to us!"**

"But seek ye first the kingdom of God, and his righteousness; and all these things shall be added unto you."

(Matt. 6:33, KJV)

SOVEREIGN ATTRACTION - CASE STUDY

I know of a case involving a believer who always felt impressed to help the city that he lived in and worked in for many years. He contributed a great deal to the city during his career there and soon retired and moved to another state, still wondering if his desire to do something positive in that city would ever be fulfilled. The city was facing mounting hardships, dwindling resources and a decreasing population. He had received numerous prophetic words over the years – words about doing positive things and having success there. This man went on with his assignment in the new location but always kept thinking about his old hometown. One night many years later, the man had a dream where an angel took him into the sky above his old city. The place appeared dark and lifeless. He asked the angel the meaning of the darkness and the angel simply said, "Watch this." As the man watched, the lights began to come on, first in one area, then another, until the entire area over the city was illuminated.

The man was inspired by the vision and kept hope in his heart that it would eventually come to pass. Again, years passed and the man was shopping in a store that he frequently visits. He had no real purpose for being there on that particular day. He just "felt" that he should go. To his surprise, he ran into an old former co-worker, whom he had not seen in nearly 18 years and who still worked in the city that the man retired from. They talked, exchanged business cards and said they'd like to meet again soon. The friend turned out to be a believer too and as it turns out, the friend was in an influential position and invited the man to participate in events that involved the community. The reconnection grew. They were both influential in spearheading promotions and events that benefitted each of them greatly. They formed a powerful alliance between their two organizations and amazingly the meeting location was in the area directly below where the angel had shown the believer those many years ago!

Their partnership evolved and resulted in a widely-recognized program that enjoyed international exposure and put their old city back into a positive limelight. Other resourceful people saw their program, and on their own, many began to come and support. This included business groups, social agencies, major corporations, schools, churches, community groups, youth groups, and governmental agencies. The news media and others began to join in to support their efforts. God was faithful over what he had put in the believer's heart so many years earlier. *The Law of Sovereign Attraction* kicked in for both of them because each one had remained faithful to seeking the kingdom of God. The believer that moved away now travels back to the old city frequently to participate in positive and successful ventures; all after being gone from that city for over 20 years! Everything that was needed to make the prophetic word and the purpose of God successful began to connect to the process supernaturally.

MOUNTAINTOP LEADERSHIP MODELS

Throughout the Bible we find numerous examples of good and bad leadership, righteous and unrighteous kings and queens, and successful and unsuccessful leadership models. We have examples of people whose allegiance to their leaders had both positive and negative results as well as those who were totally disloyal and fostered treason, rebellion and betrayal among their peers. We see those who disrupted otherwise peaceful conditions for their own selfish gains and quite a few examples of despotic leaders who practiced atrocities against their own people. We also see influential people who were not recognized as "kings" or "queens" nor did they sit on literal thrones according to their titles. But, they contributed to the recovery of people, places and things and restored safety and prosperity to many. These leaders located their respective *"mountains of influence,"* found their particular places of assignment and brought victory in many different ways. There were people such as:

ꝏ **Noah** - The builder of the Ark and preserver of the human race

ꝏ **Abraham** - The "Father of Faith" and patriarch of nations

ꝏ **Sarah** – Wife of Abraham and woman of great faith who believed God against all odds

ꝏ **Jacob** - The son of promise and progenitor of Israel

ꝏ **Joseph** - The "Dreamer" who sovereignly restored Egypt and other nations from famine

ꝏ **Joshua** - A General in the army of God and an expeditionary leader

∞ **Ruth** - A woman with a loving heart and who accepted God against her traditions

∞ **Gideon** - A mighty warrior who fought against insurmountable odds, became victorious and was offered a crown but refused it

∞ **Deborah** - A prophet of God and a judge of Israel

∞ **Mary** - A young woman found worthy to birth Christ into the Earth

∞ **Elizabeth** – The" Miracle Mother" who gave birth to the Prophet John in her old age

∞ **Peter** - The apostle and witness to the power of Christ to the first century church

∞ **Paul** - The apostle and the revelator of New Testament/kingdom truth

∞ **John** – The revelator, apostle and survivor of the Patmos exile

These people are proof that it doesn't take a literal throne to be influential and to respond to the purpose of God. They still made an incredible difference in the outcome of their conflicts. We can learn from them and give ourselves to God for His righteous and supernatural influence to make us successful in our assignments as well.

A few years ago, when I read the statement *"I saw thrones"* in Rev. 20:4, I immediately felt a spark of interest and knew something supernatural was about to happen. I began to read about thrones and how judgment was given to those who sat on them. I started to sense how powerful it would be if the "judges" of the earth would arise and take their rightful places in society. When I refer to judges, I am not talking about those who've chosen a secular judicial career, but those who God has anointed to disrupt the systemic disorder that we see on the earth. As the historical "judges" of the Old Testament made great changes for the good of the people according to God's order, I believe that righteous authority and judgment is being restored today and believers will do even greater works.

Through history, and today, we see a wide range of methods regarding how people obtain thrones or positions of authority and influence. They do so by inheritance, or by succession, or by the transfer of duty, assignment and honor; as a reward for dedication and service, and by the display of virtue and proper character. We see others who rise to power by usury, warfare, brutality, trickery, or deceit. The ungodly hearts of men have been very creative throughout history showing just how desperate, crafty, greedy and driven they were to possess the power to rule over people, places and things. Even today in some nations torn with civil war, strife, unrest and the lust for power, there seems to be virtually no limit to how far some will go to exercise rule over others. It has been said that if you want to see what is in the heart of a person, give him an opportunity to rule or rise to power.

The expression *"Absolute power corrupts absolutely"* comes to mind. Power hungry people have caused the loss of many lives and the destruction of entire nations in their quests. Humanity has suffered for countless centuries because of this. Nonetheless, we cannot deny nor refute the need for authority or governance in the earth simply because something has gone wrong in the past with systems and methods of governance. We cannot deny the fact that we serve in a kingdom and it is the nature of kingdoms to rule and reign and to challenge opposing kingdoms. The thrones of God's kingdom, while being strong, inherently confident and influential, also contain the love, mercy and kindness of God. We must be diligent in understanding and applying the dual nature of our thrones just as David, the worshipping warrior did. He knew how to exercise a tender heart and the boldness of a warrior as situations dictated.

> "And from the days of John the Baptist until the present time, the kingdom of heaven has endured violent assault, and violent men seize it by force [as a precious prize - a share in the heavenly kingdom is sought with the most ardent zeal and intense exertion]." (Matt. 11:12, AMP)

A BEAUTIFUL SITUATION

"Great is the Lord, and greatly to be praised in the city of our God, in the mountain of his holiness. Beautiful for situation, the joy of the whole earth is Mount Zion, on the sides of the north, the city of the great King. God is known in her palaces for a refuge. For, lo, the kings assembled, they passed by together. They saw it, and so they marveled..."

(Ps. 48:1-5, KJV)

The heavenly dimension or the realm of God's throne-room is the place where creation has its design and beginning. It is where, for the most part, we identify the location of the throne of God and the dwelling place of heavenly hosts. It is the domain of the kingdom of heaven and all of the prime directives of life itself are issued from the heavenly throne-room of God and His Son Jesus Christ. It is the **"situation room"** of the kingdom. The U.S. Government has a place known as **The White House Situation Room.** It is a 5,525 square-foot conference room and intelligence management center in the basement of the West Wing of the White House.

The National Security Council staff runs this place as a strategic and tactical meeting place for the President of the United States and his advisors; the National Security Advisor, Homeland Security Advisor and White House Chief of Staff. In this location they monitor issues of crisis in American and abroad and have the capacity to maintain secure communications channels through advanced technology so that the Commander in Chief can maintain effective governance over the United States and its interests. Likewise, we are poised and ready to enter the "situation room" of God which is dispensing intelligence, wisdom, strategies, tactics, resources and other valuable assets toward the fulfillment of destiny and purpose.

"To those who win the victory I will give the right to sit beside me on my throne, just as I have been victorious and now sit by my Father on his throne."

(Rev. 3:21, GNB)

It is likely assumed that the technology of thrones applies to kings, queens, monarchs and other sovereign dignitaries. This also includes presidents, prime ministers, secretaries of state, governors, congressmen, senators, mayors, judges, magistrates, college president, principals, CEOs, administrators, executives, military officers and other types of leadership, encompassing many other specific roles of authority that may not be listed here. It applies to men and women of God who have worthwhile assignments and positions of influence that are relevant to the enlargement of God's kingdom no matter which of the mountains of influence they serve in. The list is actually much larger because the context of restored and revitalized kingdom authority is expanded to include believers involved in many other leadership or stewardship roles and positions of influence that may not appear as strong positions of governance or have any apparent or direct relationship to the destiny of nations or the kingdom of God.

Working for God is no longer expressed primarily through the ecclesiastical offices or through those who have their primary mission in the mountain of religion. But, every person on earth has a call and destiny given to them by God. Everyone has a place of authority, and a span of governance or influence that may not be readily apparent to themselves or to others. As small as the scope of their influence may appear to be, it can be no less influential than the famous "mustard seed" of Matt. 17:20, AMP.

"...For truly I say to you, if you have faith [that is living] like a grain of mustard seed, you can say to this mountain, Move from here to yonder place, and it will move; and nothing will be impossible unto you."

While the mustard seed appeared small and insignificant, it forever holds a place in history as a part of one of Jesus' greatest teachings on how little becomes much when faith is at work! As a matter of fact, every seed is an example of the "**GENIUS**" of God. The seed or "**GENE**" of God's glorious throne-room assignment is placed inside of the believer through destiny. He or she then confesses, "**I**" am the "king" that God assigned to sit upon my throne. The "**GENE**" contains supernatural blueprints that transform the "**I**"-dentity of the believer. Knowing that he is powerless alone, the believer becomes one with Christ, who sits on the throne. Now, the believer can confess that it's no longer just Christ on the throne, now it is the two of "**US**" on the throne! This is the "**GENE-I-US**" of God at work!

WISDOM TO DO THE WORK

God is the supreme and sovereign authority over all creation. How could we be made in His image and likeness and not receive the nature of leadership or stewardship that God Himself possesses. God's commission to Adam in the Garden of Eden makes it clear that He delegated authority and stewardship to His most perfect creation... mankind. *"So God created human beings, making them like himself. He created them male and female, blessed them, and said, Have many children, so that your descendants will live all over the earth and bring it under their control..." (Gen. 1:27-28, GNB)* The supernatural intelligence of God is manifesting in believers to accommodate their new positions on the throne. This is what the wisdom of God does for us. It enables us to serve in influential positions without always making a complete mess of things!

"We honour God for what he conceals; we honour kings for what they explain. You never know what a king is thinking; his thoughts are beyond us, like the heights of the sky or the depths of the ocean. Take the impurities out of silver and the artist can produce a thing of beauty. Keep evil advisors away from the king and his government will be known for its justice."

(Prov. 25:2-5, GNB)

The book of Proverbs is an essential place of study for believers who have places of influence and authority in the Seven Mountains of Culture. The importance of wisdom can never be emphasized enough, because it serves to prevent many mistakes that can have far-reaching implications and disastrous results.

"The proverbs of Solomon, son of David and king of Israel. Here are proverbs that will help you to recognize wisdom and sound advice, and understand sayings with deep meaning. They can teach you how to live intelligently and how to be honest, just and fair. They can make an inexperienced person clever and teach young people how to be resourceful. These proverbs can even add to the knowledge of the wise

and give guidance to the educated, so they can understand the hidden meanings of proverbs and the problems that the wise raise."

(Prov. 1:1-6, GNB)

When "kings" sat upon thrones in Biblical history, they were expected to govern with wisdom, compassion and strength. However, there are many examples of both godly and ungodly or irresponsible leadership in the Bible, with the majority of the kings in Israel's history being unwise and ungodly. According to the Thompson Chain Reference Bible - 5th Improved Edition (1988), the kings of the United Kingdom in Israel's history included **Saul**, an unwise king who was deposed; **David**, a sometimes unwise but spiritually sensitive king; and **Solomon**, a man of great wisdom but one who was blind-sided in many areas.

During the period of the kings of Israel known as the divided kingdom, there were rulers in both Israel and Judah, with the kings of Israel **all** being considered evil. They were: Jeroboam I, Nadab, Baasha, Elah, Zimri, Omri, Ahab, Ahaziah, Jehoram, Jehu, Jehoahaz, Jeroboam II, Zachariah, Shallum, Menahem, Pekahiah, Pekah and Hoshea. This shows how unstable their hearts were and of the deplorable conditions that the people must have endured under their reign.

> **"Righteousness makes a nation great; sin is a disgrace to any nation." (Prov. 14:34, GNB)**

In Judah, 14 out of 20 of their kings were considered evil. The evil kings were: Rehoboam, Abijam, Jehoram, Ahaziah, Athalia (a queen), Amaziah, Uzziah, Ahaz, Manasseh, Amon, Jehoaz, Jehoiakim, Jehoiachin, and

Zedekiah. Those considered to be good kings were: Asa, Jehoshaphat, Joash, Jotham, Hezekiah, and Josiah.

"The plans of the mind and orderly thinking belong to man, but from the Lord comes the [wise] answer of the tongue. All the ways of a man are pure in his own eyes, but the Lord weighs the spirits (the thoughts and intents of the heart). Roll your works upon the Lord [commit and trust them wholly to him; he will cause your thoughts to become agreeable to His will, and] so shall your plans be established and succeed. The Lord has made everything [to accommodate itself and contribute] to its own end and His own purpose—even the wicked [are fitted for their role] for the day of calamity and evil. Everyone proud and arrogant in heart is disgusting, hateful, and exceedingly offensive to the Lord; be assured [I pledge it] they will not go unpunished. By mercy and love, truth and fidelity [to God and man—not by sacrificial offerings], iniquity is purged out of the heart, and by reverent, worshipful fear of the Lord men depart from and avoid evil. When a man's ways please the Lord, He makes even his enemies to be at peace with him."

(Prov. 16:1-7, AMP)

After reading this powerful truth from the Word of the Lord, it is my hope that all of us in positions of authority, governance or influence will seek the wisdom of God, and thereby avoid the calamitous results of some of our predecessors. There are countless examples of failed or undesirable leadership models in our more recent history. In the 20th century alone, we have: Adolph Hitler – responsible for the uprising of a group of superiorists who were involved in the deaths of between 30 and 50 million people in raging acts of genocide; Josef Stalin – A Soviet leader, who himself was responsible for over 20 million deaths through famine and so-called purging and other atrocities; Mao Zedong – A Chinese revolutionary and Head of State of the People's Republic of

China. Many of his acts led to famine and the deaths of over 50 million people. Other atrocious, despotic, infamous leaders include: Pol Pot, Idi Amin, The House of Saud, Robert Mugabe, Isaias Afewerki, Sadam Hussein, Osama Bin Laden, and others.

In fact, Adolph Hitler had an exact replica made of the "Seat of Satan" mentioned in Rev. 2:12-13 in Pergamos (Pergamom) and discovered and excavated by German archaeologist Carl Humann, who began excavating the ancient Red Temple site there on Sept. 9, 1878 – and to his amazement located a giant chair and altar – a literal "throne". "The throne and altar was then fully excavated, and eventually shipped to Germany and there reconstructed. Kaiser Wilhelm II celebrated its completion in Berlin in 1902. Soon after, Germany became embroiled in the "The Great War" (WW I). Then, in 1933 Adolph Hitler was elected Chancellor of Germany. In 1934 he became "Der Furher" and ordered construction of the Tribune at Zeppelin Field in Nuremberg for his Nazi rallies."

"Hitler's architect, Albert Speer, used the Pergamon Altar with Satan's Throne as the model for the Zeppelintribüne. The Führer's pulpit and the Pergamon Throne was in the center of the tribune, which was built from 1930 – 1937. **Hitler would actually sit on this throne as he reviewed the troops at Zeppelin Field. Adolph Hitler, from this ancient throne, then precipitated World War II in 1939.** At the conclusion of World War II, the Soviets took the Pergamon Altar and Throne to Leningrad in 1948 (Same year as Israel was formed) as spoils. Satan's Throne was later returned to Germany in 1958. It seemed Kruschev was spooked by some strange paranormal anomalies around the "Throne". Today, the Pergamon Altar – the literal Throne of Satan, is in a Berlin museum." (Source: Dr. A. True Ott, The Literal Throne of Satan – The Book of Revelation Evidences Examined, Jan. 14, 2013, emphasis added) https://atrueott.wordpress.com/2013/01/14/the-literal-throne-of-satan-the-book-of-revelation-evidences-examined/

Even the mountain of religion is not exempt from having destructive and selfish leaders who are bent on domination and oppression. Many remember the Jonestown massacre of 1978 in which Reverend Jim Jones led a church membership of over 900 persons to their death in a mass suicide. Surely this is an atrocity and abomination on a mass scale. Earlier historical periods or eras have produced and witnessed what could be described as "dueling thrones," or centers of power, vying for control and political supremacy. One such instance was the fight which began in 1205 between King John of England and Pope Innocent III over who the successor appointee would be for the Archbishop of Canterbury position. They were not able to agree on a candidate and in 1208 Pope Innocent placed England under interdiction and in 1209 he excommunicated King John. This bitter, hostile dispute was settled in 1213 when King John capitulated, and rebellious nobles forced John to sign the Magna Carta peace treaty in 1215. King John died the following year, largely a broken man. (Wikipedia)

Time and space will not permit an exhaustive review of the negative leadership that the world has seen, neither is it particularly valuable in encouraging present-day believers to greater heights of good character and godliness. Rather, we will accentuate the positive message of this book and hope that readers will focus on it.

TOOLS OF THE TRADE

"And it shall come to pass in that day, that I will call my servant Eliakim the son of Hilkiah: And I will cloth him with thy robe, and strengthen him with thy girdle, and I will commit thy government into his hand: and he shall be a father to the inhabitants of Jerusalem, and to the house of Judah. And the key of the house of David will I lay

upon his shoulder; so he shall open, and none shall shut; and he shall shut, and none shall open. "

(Isa. 22:20-22, KJV)

There is a distinctive spirit of honor that comes to people who sit on thrones and reign with good character, honor, justice and integrity. The text above gives an example of how a newly installed palace administrator is being symbolically empowered by God with certain garments and "tools of the trade." Although the kings in today's assignments may or may not have distinctive garb that separates them for their office, there is still significance in the fact that being enthroned gives one a "change of garments," thereby "suiting" and preparing them for their official capacity to govern. There are three specific terms that are important in the text above. As Eccl. 4:12, GNB states: *"Two people can resist an attack that would defeat one person alone. A rope made of three cords is hard to break."* Looking at the Hebrew translations we can see a powerful revelation forming.

- ◦ **Robe – "KeThoneth"** – To clothe; the shoulder as being the place where the garments hang. This has special significance as the place where the Mantle of Misrah is laid upon us. *"And the government shall be upon his shoulder."* (Isa. 9:6, KJV)

- ◦ **Girdle – "Abnet"** – A girdle. *"Stand therefore [hold your ground], having tightened the belt of truth around your loins…"* (Ephesians 6:14, AMP)

- ◦ **Key – "Maphteach"** – An opener. Also taken from the word: **"Pethach,"** meaning: To open wide, begin, plow, carve, let go free, and to unstop.

When we are assigned as kings to a throne, we are equipped by having the Mantle of Misrah or government of Christ upon us. Our ability to govern is not based on our own ambitions or strength but on Christ, who created all things and defeated our enemies through the foreknowledge of God. When God **"commits the government"** to us, we need more than a desire to be successful. We need the tools of the trade. We also wear "truth" firmly held in place so that we are not easily dissuaded from the assignment and purposes of God. Finally, we have supernatural empowerment with keys to open doors and remove obstacles and hindrances that have been in place.

"Keys" also suggests that one has special knowledge and endowments that enable them to have favor in royal places, where others cannot enter, such as the young Hebrew men in the Book of Daniel. (Luke 11:52 supports the fact that "knowledge" is a key. The young men possessed skills that gave them access to the king's palace. They were, *"Youths without blemish, well-favored in appearance and skillful in all wisdom, discernment, and understanding, apt in learning knowledge, competent to stand and serve in the king's palace-and to teach them the literature and language of the Chaldeans." (Dan. 1:4, AMP)*

> **We are equipped with supernatural tools to stand in our official assignments.**

And I will fasten him like a peg or nail in a firm place; and he will become a throne of honor and glory to his father's house."

(Isa. 22:23, KJ21)

As we accept our assignments and become equipped with the tools of the trade we take on yet another level of competence and stability. Today we are called, not only to sit upon thrones, but to become as **"living thrones"** in our assignments. In the original Hebrew text, the word **"become"** is from the term **"Hayah,"** which means: To exist, be, become, to pass, be a beacon, happen, or require. We virtually become the assignment and what we do is no longer "second nature" – now, its first nature! This suggests that we are able to reign, not only when we are in our dedicated places of assignment, but we can maintain a victorious mindset and be ready to "leap into action" whenever we are needed in an impromptu setting.

"Preach the word. Be ready to do it whether it is convenient or inconvenient. Correct, confront, and encourage with patience and instruction."

(2 Tim. 4:2, CEB)

Although the text is referring primarily to preaching, I believe that it also represents the fact that we should be ready to do the work of the Lord at any time. The fact that God will fasten one like a peg or nail suggests the stability, firmness and assurance that comes with being assigned to a throne by God. It is the sovereign foreknowledge of God that puts us there in the first place and we'll need to be assured of this as we face challenges to our positions. Becoming **"a throne in our father's house"** is significant not only because we are of the House of God but we can become brightspots in our respective companies, teams, groups, governments, teams, and even neighborhoods and families.

Thrones are not designed to bring failure, they're designed to bring victory. As we sit upon thrones let's be conscious of the fact that the glory of the Lord is there and there is a countenance that reflects His glory. The glory of God also contains the wisdom of God. Wisdom is a vital resource that we as kings cannot afford to do without. Rulership and authority without temperance and good judgment are a dangerous combination.

"I am Wisdom, and I have insight; I have knowledge and sound judgment. To honour the Lord is to hate evil; I hate pride and arrogance, evil ways and false words. I make plans and carry them out. I have

understanding, and I am strong. I help kings to govern and rulers to make good laws. Every ruler on earth governs with my help, officials and nobles alike. I love those who love me; whoever looks for me can find me. I have riches and honour to give, prosperity and success. What you get from me is better than the finest gold, better than the purest silver. I walk the way of righteousness; I follow paths of justice, giving wealth to those who love me, filling their houses with treasures. The Lord created me first of all, the first of his works, long ago. I was made in the very beginning, at first, before the world began."

(Prov. 8:11-23, GNB)

CASE STUDY – ENTHRALLED BY A THRONE

There is great responsibility in being enthroned by God. *"For unto whomsoever much is given, of him shall much be required; and to whom men have committed much of him they will ask the more." (Luke 12:48, KJ21 A)*

A great example of irresponsibility with authority is found in the life of King Nebuchadnezzar of Babylon. The power and favor that God gives to kings is exactly that... a favor. At no point can we allow our own ambitions, selfish motives, delusions of grandeur or even the misplaced motives and influences of friends or peers divert us from our focus. Our lives must be centered on God and His purposes and we must frequent the company of men and women with whom we can be open and honest about ourselves and from whom we can receive instructions, counsel and correction if need be. We must be accountable for the authority that we carry at all times. King Nebuchadnezzar was a person who violated these principles and faced the correction of God.

"At the end of twelve months he was walking in the royal palace of Babylon. The king said, Is not this the great Babylon that I have built as the royal residence and seat of government by the might of my power and for the honor and glory of my majesty? While the words were still in the king's mouth, there fell a voice from heaven, saying, O King Nebuchadnezzar, to you it is spoken: The kingdom has departed from you, And you shall be driven from among men and your dwelling will be with the living creatures of the field. You will be made to eat grass like the oxen, and seven times [or years] shall pass over you until you have learned and know that the Most High [God] rules in the kingdom of men and gives it to whomever he will."

(Dan. 4:29-32, AMP)

Now, for the recovery process…

"At the same time my reason and understanding returned to me; and for the glory of my kingdom, my majesty and splendor returned to me, and my counselors and my lords sought me out: I was reestablished in my kingdom, and still more greatness [than before] was added to me. Now I, Nebuchadnezzar, praise and extol and honor the King of heaven, Whose works are faithful and right and Whose ways are just. And those who walk in pride He is able to abase and humble."

(Dan. 4: 36-37, AMP)

King Nebuchadnezzar is a good example of an individual who became lifted up in pride, challenging even the authority of God Himself. We should fare much better in our reign as kings since we have more spiritual resources and greater systems of accountability and relationships around us. But let us never forget that God will not share His glory with "another," which means a person of a different kind. If you are not "another" but of the same substance and fellowship as those He calls His own, then you are blessed indeed.

MY DECREE

I believe that I am the righteousness of God in Christ. I am created in the image and likeness of God and I possess the presence of God in my life. I have been created as a special and unique instrument in the hands of God. I am the only one who God has made to be "ME!" Therefore, I will not overlook my destiny or purpose and I will not fade into obscurity. I will not allow myself to forget what God says about me. I will invest in my identity, my throne and in the purpose for which I have been created. There are people who need me to be "ME." I will not strive with others for my own identity, destiny and purpose to be revealed or confirmed. I will be confident in God's ability as a craftsman. I will trust Him to build me as I should be. I will not interfere with the process. I have been called to fulfill a purpose in the Seven Mountains of Culture. I will trust God and His purpose in me as I face my adversary on the mountain.

I SEE *Thrones*!

I SEE *Thrones!*

THE MANTLE
OF MISRAH!

B elievers not only have the wonderful gift of redemption and the forgiveness of sins, but a life filled with the presence of a wonderful, eternal God who restored us to a state of fullness intended for Adam before the fall of mankind. But, the salvation of our souls is not the only concern that God has. He created planet Earth, placed mankind over it as stewards and custodians of its rich resources and when man lost his authority to the power of sin, not only was his soul in jeopardy, the planet itself was at stake. Everything within the systematic order of the planet was shifted off course.

It is acknowledged by most people that Christ came to save souls and redeem us from the curse of sin, but He also came to fully restore mankind to the level of authority that Adam once had. Mankind must be restored to fellowship with God and to the full authority to reign on earth as its lawfully-appointed guardian. This includes the management of **souls, systems and societies**, the three lost elements in Earth's culture.

"For the Son of man is come to seek and to save that which was lost."

(Luke 19:10, KJV)

The work of Christ redeemed the souls of mankind and the systems of the earth that man uses to sustain the planet and provide for continual resources that coming generations need. He restored the societies of mankind and provides for the social balance that promotes healthy living and productivity. As we occupy thrones on the Seven Mountains of Culture, we help provide:

- ๕ **Substance** – Pertinent skill-sets, thoughtfulness, reliability, good character

- ๕ **Balance** – Proper perspectives, fairness, civility, wisdom and right thinking

- ๕ **Oversight** – Responsibility, diligence, care, management

- ๕ **Creativity** – Artfulness, ingenuity, flexibility

- ๕ **Stewardship** – Understanding the value of time, resources and relationships

- ๕ **Governance** – Righteous authority, understanding of purpose, proper motives

- ๕ **Peace** – The mind of Christ, kindness, humility

- ๕ **Other vital elements** that keep mankind on a path of upward mobility and generational sustainability

One of the most powerful works of supernatural grace is summed up in what God accomplished through Christ when He restored the

THE MANTLE OF MISRAH!

Government of God to the Earth. God planted the seed that inclusively solves major systemic issues and imbalances in the educational, business, religious, governmental, media, arts & entertainment, and family spheres in the earth. When disorder and chaos emerge, only righteous order will circumvent the problems and bring repair and restoration. The only cure for darkness is light. The only cure for failure is success. The only cure for hatred is love. The only cure for war is peace. The supernatural solution that God has given us is the Governmental Mantle of Jesus Christ. It's called **Misrah**, which is a Hebrew word that means: **Empire, government and ruling power.** It also relates to the Hebrew name **"Sarah"** [Abraham's wife] which means: **One who prevails.**

"For to us a Child is born, to us a Son is given; and the government shall be upon His shoulder, and His name shall be called Wonderful, Counselor, Mighty God, Everlasting Father [of Eternity], Prince of Peace. Of the increase of His government and peace there shall be no end, upon the throne of David and over his kingdom, to establish it and to uphold it with justice and with righteousness from the [latter] time forth, even forevermore. The zeal of the Lord of hosts will perform this."

(Isa. 9:6-7, AMP)

"The government shall be upon his shoulder" is a supernatural description of God's government resting upon Christ. He wears the mantle of government as the sovereign and supreme creator of all things. Because we are in Christ as His Body, we have the privilege of wearing the governmental mantle as well. (For more on the Mantle of Misrah, read my book *Authority for Assignment: Releasing the Mantle of God's Government in the Marketplace* – Kingdom House Publishing, 2011). Because of the Mantle of Misrah, the Government of God is transferred to us to enable us to sit upon thrones of responsibility and influence in the earth and to reign supernaturally.

With this mantle, the power of government gives way to an increase of peace that is endless. It empowered David, who wore the mantle in a type of prophetic relationship with the pre-incarnate Christ, and it empowers us who came after Christ. The *throne of David* is a type created after *the Order of Melchizedek*, wherein we are both king and priest, worshipper and warrior. It is the best of both worlds, enabling us to resume our rightful governance in the earth, following the order of Christ, the Last Adam, who Himself, is a priest after the Order of Melchizedek (Heb. 5:6).

The Mantle of Misrah holistically contains the creative DNA, which is the original descriptive and structural code of everything that exists. When God assigns us to thrones, they are always predetermined and programmed to give us a place of purpose according to divine assignment. Christ made everything; therefore, the original blueprints are in His Words, His Ways and His Will! When we wear His Mantle, we have access to all of that information!

"In the beginning the Word already existed; the Word was with God, and the Word was God. From the very beginning the Word was with God. Through him God made all things; not one thing in all creation was made without him. The Word was the source of life, and this life brought light to humanity. The light shines in the darkness and the darkness has never put it out."

(John 1:1-5, GNB)

Wearing the Mantle of Misrah provides us with the ability to sit on thrones in every area of our God-given assignments. We govern with the authority of Christ Himself!

THE MANTLE OF MISRAH!

THE POWER TO PREVAIL

The "government" or Misrah of God is a powerful force that defends the constitution of the Kingdom of heaven and defends believers against the onslaught of the spirit of Babylon – the demonic force that exalts itself against the knowledge of God (2 Cor. 10:4-5). The term Misrah is also related to the name Sarah, who was the wife of Abraham. Her name means: *One who prevails.* As we carry the nature of the Mantle of Misrah, we carry prevailing power. This type of enduring spiritual energy is needed to confront the opposing powers of darkness which do as Nimrod and the original Babylonians did. They exalted themselves to the highest level possible and sought to build themselves a name and a tower that would reach the heavens. This served as a challenge to God Himself. Although Babylon doesn't exist as a geographical location any longer (except for Babylon, NY), the spirit is still threatening to dislodge believers from their places of purpose in the kingdom. Babylon is about exalting anything and everything other than God and His kingdom.

Sarah is a good role model for prevailing power in the fact that she faced tremendous setbacks concerning child-bearing. She witnessed her younger counterpart Hagar, give birth to a child by her husband. This was a difficult thing for any woman to endure. But, she had a promise from God who knew she was an aging woman and was past the child-bearing years. The promise of God was strong and so was her faith.

"Because of faith also Sarah herself received physical power to conceive a child, even when she was long past the age for it, because she considered [God] Who had given her the promise to be reliable and trustworthy and true to His word."

(Heb. 11:11, AMP)

71

The power of God brought a renewal to Sarah's womb and gave her strength to conceive seed! Without the strength to *accept* the seed of God, she would never have been able to produce Isaac, the son of the promise for Abraham. She received "strength" or **"Dunamis,"** in the Greek language. It means: force, miraculous power, a miracle itself, mighty deed and wonderful work. It translates into the word **"dynamite"** in English! Like Sarah, we need the power to prevail against all of our lost hopes, forgotten dreams, and feelings of failure that try to darken our futures. With the power to prevail through Misrah, like Sarah, we prevail against time constraints, aging, discouragement, fear, anxiety and every other force of darkness. There are many Sarahs who are waiting in the wings for their "seed" to come alive, even if it's been a long time coming.

We are called to be the **"Sarahs of the Seven Mountains,"** prevailing against our enemies. Imagine the intensity that can arise in the hearts of believers who find out that God has a place of victory for them after all. Imagine the entrepreneurs, inventors, scientists, investors, media moguls, consultants, students, teachers, musicians, entertainers, parents, governmental leaders, corporate leaders and others who take on the spirit of Sarah and prevail against circumstances even when they feel left behind! They will no longer be stopped because of memories of past failures. They'll forge ahead to see the purposes of God fulfilled before their eyes. They will exercise their mantles, and their creativity and ingenuity will begin to flow again. A day of accomplishment will come again!

THE SHIELDS OF MISRAH!

"Sing praises to God, sing praises! Sing praises to our King, sing praises! For God is the King of all the earth; sing praises in a skillful psalm and with understanding. God reigns over nations; GOD SITS UPON HIS HOLY THRONE. The princes and nobles of the peoples

*are gathered together, a [united] people for the God of Abraham,
FOR THE SHIELDS OF THE EARTH BELONG TO GOD; He
is highly exalted."*

(Ps. 47:6-9, AMP, emphasis added)

The government of Jesus Christ is upon our shoulders, and it's steadily increasing along with our peace! We sit on the throne of David, we have kingdom order, and everything we do is established with proper judgment and with justice; it will last forever, and best of all... we don't have to do it on our own! **The zeal of the Lord of Hosts will do it for us.** My interests are protected by God. I am shielded from having to stress and struggle about how to fulfill my assignment. I am covered by the purposes of God and the final results are under supernatural protection! Isa. 9:7 says that *"The zeal of the Lord of Hosts"* will perform for us. The word **"Zeal"** is from the Hebrew term, **"Qanna,"** which means: **Jealous.** Jealousy is a very possessive and protective emotion.

"So the angel who talked with me said to me, Cry out, Thus says the Lord of hosts: I AM JEALOUS FOR JERUSALEM AND FOR ZION WITH GREAT JEALOUSY."

(Zech. 1:14-15, AMP, emphasis added)

God is very protective of His investments in believers who govern and influence culture from the 8th Mountain – Mount Zion. This supernatural protection of "God's jealousy" is called **"The Shields of Misrah."** Have you looked at the emblems or crests of certain organizations that exercise authority? It's very likely that you will see a "shield" as part of their emblem. This suggests that there's protection of the **ideology, nature, assets, culture** and **purpose** of the organization. Spiritual government is no different. God protects what He projects. In order for the government of God to steadily increase and never wane in strength it must have an eternal security system built in to give it sustainability against the decay

73

of the natural, negatively influenced environments we are exposed to. The Shields of Misrah protect our:

- ❧ **Patterns** – The divine design of our identity and character

- ❧ **Pathways** – The course of our journey through life

- ❧ **Purpose** – The desired results of God's influence on our lives

- ❧ **Assets** – The resources that God provides for the assignment

- ❧ **Abilities** – Skill-sets and special endowments

- ❧ **Assignments** – The application of divinely-appointed mission, mandate and motives of God

PRONOUNCING PEACE

"He that is slow to anger is better than the mighty; And he that ruleth his spirit, than he that taketh a city."

(Prov. 16:32, ASV)

Since this book is about thrones and the increase of the government of Christ, it's only reasonable that there's a great deal of discussion on authority, governance and influence. But, there is also another very important element that we can't afford to overlook. *"Of the increase of His government and PEACE there will be no end."* (Emphasis added). Peace is a very important byproduct of the government of God. When people think of government, they are prone to think of masterful strategies of warfare, conflict and the power to "outgun" an enemy. The government or Misrah of God is very flexible, because God will always approach the issues by looking back at His own creative purposes embedded within the situation and moving forward from that perspective. He won't always have to "go to war" to make things correct. He looks back to "why" he created something, then extracts and emphasizes the original purpose for doing it.

Many times God has only to "remind" things that they were created by His Word. He does this through us, who live on the earth as custodians of this world. We make decrees and prophesy using the Word of God, speaking to the planet to realign it with God's original purposes. The Word retains "rights of ownership" and commands things to yield to His government.

"And there arose a great storm of wind, and the waves beat into the ship, so that it was now full. And he was in the hinder part of the ship, asleep on a pillow: and they awake him, and say unto him, Master, carest thou not that we perish? And he arose, and rebuked the wind, and said, Peace, be still. And the wind ceased, and there was a great calm."

(Mark 4:37-39, KJV)

Jesus spoke **"peace"** to the unruly, contrary waves of the sea. The elements "remembered" who the Almighty Creator was and they yielded to His authority and influence.

"The peace that Christ gives is to guide you in the decisions you make; for it is to this peace that God has called you together in the one body. And be thankful. Christ's message in all its richness must live in your hearts. Teach and instruct each other with all wisdom..."

(Col. 3:15-16, GNB)

"For the full content of divine nature lives in Christ, in his humanity, and you have been given full life in union with him. He is supreme over every spiritual ruler and authority."

(Col. 2:9-10, GNB)

CASE STUDY – MISRAH MOVES MOUNTAINS

A local authority figure in municipal government was assigned to lead a bankrupt city department with a long list of ills. The supervisor was a believer and a kingdom citizen but he had accepted the job not realizing the dire state that the organization was in. Employees were disgruntled and working without a contract for about five years beyond the expiration date of the old one. Their workplace was drafty because doors wouldn't seal properly, the roof leaked and there was little money for repairs. To make matters worse, they had vehicles that were over 20 years old, leaked fluids and would occasionally stall or not start at all. Every attempt to get help from the town's mayor or council members was met with a stern "NO!"

This went on for about a year when the supervisor felt an unction to change the strategy of the "battle" and began to make decrees over the workplace, the equipment, the budget and the issues that plagued the organization. He claimed his authority for the assignment knowing that God had placed him there to make a difference. He had received prophetic words about going to that job many years before he even got there so he knew that God was "paying attention" to the issues. He began to "speak to the mountain" that loomed over his situation and believed God for positive, supernatural results.

A short time later, he received a call from a bank group about 500 miles away whom he had never heard of. They said they had "heard" that

76

he was in need of a low interest loan to secure an equipment purchase and they'd like to help. They contacted the city treasurer and the loan was approved for over $1.4 million dollars without "jumping through any hoops or hanging from a wire!" Previously, the community had also applied for federal grants for tools and equipment and had always been turned down. Not this time! The grant for $100,000.00 was awarded!

Surprisingly, money was found, and repairs were made to the facilities. Suddenly, it was like the dam had broken. Since things were "on a roll" the supervisor felt inspired to develop a new uniform code, giving the workers a new look and employee morale skyrocketed. The union contract dispute with the municipality had been terribly stalled but suddenly the supervisor received a fresh idea on how to negotiate the deal and both sides left the table satisfied. The contract was ratified shortly afterward. People asked the supervisor how he had "pulled it off," and he said, "Well, now that you ask, I didn't do it simply as a supervisor, but I did it with the power of God! I made decrees that shifted the climate and released resources."

This was Misrah in action! The supervisor leveraged the power of authority for the assignment and called in angels and resources to accomplish the purposes of God for a local community. The results were phenomenal.

CASE STUDY – REPELLING THE POWERS OF DARKNESS

"Jesus knew everything that was going to happen to him, so he stepped forward and asked them, 'Who is it you are looking for?' Jesus of Nazareth,' they answered. 'I am he,' he said. Judas, the traitor was standing there with them. When Jesus said to them, 'I am he,' they moved back and fell to the ground."

(John 18:4-6, GNB)

This is no simple case of someone tripping over a rock; this is the governmental power of Christ in action. Jesus' declaration, **"I am he,"** was powerful because He was declaring His identity, as if to even say, "I am Alpha and Omega, the beginning and the ending, the first and the last." It was the same as if He had said, "I AM THAT I AM!" It was the declaration of the eternal identity of Jesus Christ that caused the soldiers to fall. It was an "involuntary" act of submission that came when they heard His voice. As simplistic as this seems, the sound of a supernaturally-inspired word releases the government of God and things are shaken as a result.

"See that you do not refuse Him who speaks. For if they refused Him who spoke on earth, much more shall we not escape if we turn away from Him who speaks from heaven, WHOSE VOICE THEN SHOOK THE EARTH; but now He has promised, saying, 'YET ONCE MORE I SHAKE NOT ONLY THE EARTH, BUT ALSO THE HEAVEN. Now this, 'Yet once more,' indicates the removal of those things that are being shaken, as of things that are made, that the things which cannot be shaken may remain. Therefore, since we are receiving a kingdom which cannot be shaken, let us have grace, by which we may serve God acceptably with reverence and godly fear. For our God is a consuming fire."

(Heb. 12:25-28, NKJV, emphasis added)

The Word of God is like both a fire and a hammer, according to Jeremiah 23:29. It has the power to "burn down" or "break down" all opposition. We'll see the supernatural Shields of Misrah work for us when the Word is released from our mouths. It will shake the situation so that only what is in concert with the kingdom of God can remain intact!

MY DECREE

I am a Misrah (man or woman). I am built strong with the government of God upon my shoulders. I have been created as one who prevails. When my government increases, so will my peace. I am a worshipping warrior like King David, and a peacemaker. It is "supernaturally natural" for me to rule and reign in my assignments. I will walk in supernatural thinking, timing and truth. I will go through supernatural doors because it is my destiny. The "Shields of Misrah" will cover and protect my assets, abilities and assignments. I will succeed at the purposes of God. I am created to do good works in Jesus Christ. All that was lost will be restored to me so that I can fulfill my destiny. My mountain of assignment will be blessed when I arrive there! MISRAH!

I SEE *Thrones!*

I SEE *Thrones!*

"MOUNT" UP WITH WINGS LIKE EAGLES!

"But those who wait on the Lord shall renew their strength; They shall mount up with wings like eagles..."

(Isa. 40:31, NKJV)

"**M**ount" up with wings like eagles and go to the highest mountaintop level possible! It's a play on words but it works to get the idea across that there is plenty of supernatural energy in high places!

"In the days to come the mountain where the Temple stands will be the highest one of all, towering above all the hills. Many nations will come streaming to it, and their people will say, 'Let us go up the hill of the Lord, to the Temple of Israel's God. HE WILL TEACH US WHAT HE WANTS US TO DO; we will walk in the paths he has chosen. For the Lord's teaching comes from Jerusalem; from Zion he speaks to his people.' He will settle disputes among the nations, among the great

powers near and far. They will hammer their swords into ploughs and their spears into pruning knives. Nations will never again go to war, never prepare for battle again. Everyone will live in peace among his own vineyards and fig trees, and no one will make him afraid. The Lord Almighty has promised this."

(Mic. 4:1-4, GNB, emphasis added)

This is truly a tall order if we view the text only from a natural perspective. But, viewed in the context of how God's creative will and purpose are changing how we function in our assignments, it becomes a template, not only for what is possible, but what is already decided upon and sealed by the immutable and providential counsel of God. I realize that the text has prophetic and historical connotations regarding Israel, but we all know that God packs a tremendous amount of truth into a text, providing for things that are still in the future and are yet undisclosed. This text says more than we may realize about the season of thrones and the shifting of the power grid in the mountains of culture and influence. Like the Israelites in the text, we have a strategic and tactical advantage by being in the temple or as it is today, *being* the temple of God. As the temple of God, we are living vessels that house the glory that is described in the illustration of Zion.

"Surely you know that you are God's temple and that God's Spirit lives in you!"

(I Cor. 3:16, GNB)

Observe how **"the mountain where the Temple stands"** is positioned above the other mountains and hills (The Seven Mountains of Culture), being described as **"the highest of them all."** The superiority of God's **"8th Mountain,"** or the Mountain of the Kingdom of Heaven, with the number eight signifying **new beginnings**, shows us the opportunity for brand new things to happen. The "8 Mountain" gives us stature that is above the other mountains and by having a position higher than the opposition, the climate of conflict drastically changes. The government of God increases for us because the Mountain of God and the Temple outrank all other mountains and authorities.

> *"The Lord is great and is to be highly praised in the city of our God, on his sacred hill. Zion, the mountain of God, is high and beautiful; the city of the great king brings joy to all the world. God has shown that there is safety with him inside the fortresses of the city."*

> (Ps. 48:1-3, GNB)

Zion is "the city of the great king" and can now be called the **"city of kings"** because there are now many of us in Christ, and we are qualified to dwell there and sit upon thrones. We dwell upon new heights and receive knowledge and wisdom commensurate with our new assignments on the thrones of the Earth. *Because we are the temple of God on Mount Zion, new benefits emerge...*

- Believers become the "temple" or dwelling place of God's presence

- Nations will stream or flow to the source of God's fresh presence and demonstration of power in the newly-anointed kings

- People will acknowledge the superiority of the wisdom and presence of God in us, as we serve as "the Temple" of God

- They will sense that God is "teaching" us new things and will hunger and thirst for it

- They will sense His willingness to share His knowledge with us and sense His heart for planet Earth and humanity because they will see the tremendous solutions that are coming from us

    Walls of offense will be broken between mankind and God. People will begin to seek God as never before

    Forgiveness and amnesty will be offered to people and organizations and they will experience new beginnings

    The science and art of conflict resolution will take on a brand new identity

    Truth will be spoken to those in power and many will acknowledge it

    There will be an increase of "Government and Peace" according to Isa. 9:6-7

    We will operate on pre-determined paths of sovereignty and "wandering" will be greatly reduced or removed altogether

    People will serve out their assignments according to their God-given special destinies and designs and will reproduce others of their kind according to their destinies and spiritual DNA

> **We have official residency on Mount Zion, the headquarters of the Kingdom of "the Most High!" Mount Zion stands high above the Seven Mountains of Culture.**

Much of this will happen because God has empowered a new company of kings who navigate things differently than in the past. God empowers His "kings" to produce supernatural miracles in places where miracles didn't normally occur. Many people are well acquainted with the power and demonstration of miracles, signs and wonders on the altar of a Sunday morning church service where physical healings take place. But, miracles are about to become widespread in areas that are not accustomed to religious activity. It won't be because someone sets up a pulpit with a choir singing in the background. The Mountain of Religion won't be the predominant technology behind this new wave of miracles. These miracles are specially tailored to each "throne" that is located on the mountains. Thrones carry assignments, and there is power in each one to produce specific results.

ABOVE AND BEYOND

"But in the last days it shall come to pass, that the mountain of the house of the Lord shall be established in the top of the mountains, and it shall be exalted above the hills; and people shall flow unto it. And many nations shall come, and say, Come, let us go up to the mountain of the Lord, and to the house of the God of Jacob; and he will teach us of his ways, and we will walk in his paths: for the law shall go forth out of Zion, and the word of the Lord from Jerusalem."

(Mic. 4:1-2, KJV)

I find it interesting that the mountain of the Lord, being above all other mountains, is called **"the house of the God of Jacob."** The name **"Jacob"** is from the Hebrew word *"Ya'aqob,"* meaning: **Supplanter.** Vocabulary.com states: A *supplanter* is one who takes over or takes the place of someone else, usually on purpose. *Supplanter* often refers to governments and rulers of countries, and it comes from the verb *supplant*, which evolved from the Latin *supplantare*, meaning "to trip up or to overthrow."

Being empowered by the God of Jacob carries a propensity or inclination to sense the intentions of God and at some point, to also sense the shift of assignment and the possibility of being moved into greater positions of authority and influence. But, there are already people at the tops of each of the seven mountains with seniority in places of influence. They are not necessarily kingdom citizens in the family of God. Many of them are so embedded in the cultures of those mountains that no one can even imagine their decline or fall from ultimate power at this point in time. Therefore, believers who "see thrones" are not being assigned from a parallel position adjacent to those already in power, but from the throne-room of God Himself, in Mount Zion, above the Seven Mountains.

I do believe that in some cases, partnerships and/or alliances may develop between those presently in power and those coming into power. All reassignments are not necessarily "hostile take-overs" and "take-downs" and many are done in completely peaceful ways. As a matter of fact, the 3M Project Global Initiative, which is our Global Effect Movers & Shakers Network (GEMS) platform for community transformation relies on partnerships and alliances to shift the balance of power. In a spiritual sense, "supplanting" can often be more about the eventual results of the shift and reassignments for God's purposes than it is about the public display of the shift. If God can perform a "subtle supplanting" process, quietly and unobtrusively, then He will.

"But the Lord says, 'Do not cling to the events of the past or dwell on what happened long ago. Watch for the new thing I am going to do. It is happening already - you can see it now! I will make a road through the wilderness and give you streams of water there. Even the wild animals will honour me: jackals and ostriches will praise me when I make rivers flow in the dessert to give water to my chosen people.'"

(Isa. 43:18-21, GNB)

Results follow the shift of authority that we experience when we actively begin leveraging our stature on the "8th Mountain." Our confessions put on muscle because we now believe for greater outcomes and we have a tangible spiritual technology to rely on. We train our hearts and mouths to speak like kings. As kings we will begin to **"declare roads"** to be built and release **"streams of water"** in the wilderness. Even resistant **"wild"** forces can become tamed under that level of authority.

"For the word of a king is authority and power, and who can say to him, What are you doing? Whoever observes the [king's] command will experience no harm, and a wise man's mind will know both when and what to do. For every purpose and matter has its [right] time and judgment, although the misery and wickedness of the man lies heavily upon him [who rebels against the king]."

(Eccl. 8:4-6, AMP)

INTERCHANGEABLE IDENTITIES

"And [He] hath made us kings and priests unto God and his Father; to him be glory and dominion for ever and ever. Amen."

(Rev. 1:6, KJV, emphasis added)

We are truly blessed to be called kings and priests today. The Order of Melchizedek gives us the restored offices of king/priest so we can fulfill the entire purpose and counsel of God for our lives and for planet Earth. Since the "priest" speaks to God for mankind, we now have an unrestricted communication link to God through the sacrificial blood offered by the High Priest, Christ Jesus. We can boldly approach the throne of grace for every need and every situation (Heb. 4:16). The spiritual side of us wants to always be in touch with our priesthood. It feels like such a safe place; it feels like we can always talk with our

Father, and because we can, there is great comfort in that. But, the king cannot be neglected.

"Yes, [you are building a temple of the Lord, but] it is he Who shall build the [true] temple of the Lord, and He shall bear the honor and glory [as of the only begotten of the Father] and shall sit and rule upon His throne, and the counsel of peace shall be between the two [offices – Priest and King]."

(Zech. 6:13, AMP)

We also sense confidence and strength when we are faced with challenges and the spirit of the "king" becomes activated. *"Where the word of a king is, there is power, and who can say unto him, What doest thou?"* Knowing that we carry this word of power gives us a charge like no other. We know that the adversary responds to our governmental authority and we see great victory with it. But, what happens when we have a tendency to gravitate to our priesthood more than our king-ship. Do we have to pick up one and put the other down? Or, can we be spiritually sensitive, balanced and well trained enough to recognize which office we should project, based on our current assignment? Sometimes it may not be so clear.

> **We have dual citizenship in heaven and on Earth and we have a dual commissioning as kings and priests.**

We may suffer from *"Manifestation Mood-swings."* At times we're undecided as to whether we are in the king mode or the priest mode. It's easy to have a predisposition toward the office we have functioned in the most often. But, since God has given us both offices and they are equally important, there may be difficulty there. It would be a mistake to assume that being a king is all about a display of power, authority or forcefulness. David, the worshipping warrior, often displayed sensitive moments as he sought God. After all, he is known as the sweet psalmist of Israel. So, you're not a "king" when you feel "tough" and a "priest" when you feel "mild" and soft tempered; you still are both. David understood the Order of Melchizedek, and knew the value of warfare and worship. How did he decide which office to function in at a given moment? How do we know which one to emphasize at a given moment?

"Grace and peace be multiplied unto you through the knowledge of God, and of Jesus our Lord, According as his divine power hath given unto us all things that pertain unto life and godliness, through the knowledge of him that hath called us to glory and virtue."

(2 Pet. 1:3, KJV)

Everything in existence operates from a type of technology. **"Life"** and **"godliness"** are the two technologies that are emphasized in this text. Traditionally, priests minister to God for the people and excel in matters of "godliness" and the things that pertain to faith, righteousness and relationships with God. The technology of kings involves the exercise of authority which is used to influence quality of life issues and deals with resourcefulness and the administration of the substance of the world. When we find ourselves dealing directly with communicating with God and administering the presence and power of God to people, places and things, we are operating primarily as "priests." When we deal with aspects of how life is lived in a physical sense, we are operating primarily as "kings."

In a basic sense the identity of the "priest" is where we get the ability to:

- **Pray** – Communicate intimately with God

- **Pardon** – Forgive others of their transgressions, sins or debts against us

- **Petition** – Make requests for God to move in the Earth realm on behalf of the people

- **Prophesy** – Speak the mind, will and purposes of God

- **Preach** – Declare the message of the Gospel of Christ and of the kingdom

- **Pronounce** – Speak forth the mandates and edicts of God

The "king" releases the power to:

- **Command** – The written or verbal release of orders, rules, policies and procedures

- **Control** – Exercise dominion and restraint over contrary forces

- **Commandeer** – Seize or repossess resources taken by an enemy

- **Confront** – Speak truth to power or address issues of disorder

- **Contain** – Develop parameters for the safekeeping of assets, abilities and assignments

- **Create** – Birth, conceive, give life to, originate

- **Capitalize** – Adequately resource

- **Communicate** – Cast vision, set course and direction, proclaim

- **Collaborate** – Find ways and identify mutually-beneficial common causes to strategically partner, cooperate or ally with other kings.

In many cases the lines are not always so clearly drawn, and we function in a state of constant "interchangeability" like Melchizedek, David or Jesus. Let's just get comfortable in whatever the present situation dictates because grace and peace are multiplied to us for the accomplishment of everything that pertains to life and godliness. We are well equipped for both roles, so let us have peace in the exercise of both.

"Even he shall build the temple of the Lord; and he shall bear the glory, and shall sit and rule upon his throne; and he shall be a priest upon his throne: and the counsel of peace shall be between them both."

(Zech. 6:13, KJVA)

SETTING THE TONE TO RULE ON THE THRONE

Just because we have thrones and crowns, it doesn't mean that we will be good leaders or have a positive influence on those around us. Thrones are everywhere and it becomes evident that everyone who has one doesn't necessarily do well with it. Two of the areas of inconsistency and incompetence deal with the kinds of influence that people use and the type of character they express while in power. I want to point out the need for righteousness or at least a sense of nobility, fairness, good character and values such as honesty and integrity. Virtually anyplace that you see authority, power, governance, the control of currency, the oversight of land or political territories, the ability to establish policy and to legislate laws, influence cultures, oversee organizations, control resources, experience social activities, deliver goods and services, influence people or groups, there will be thrones. God's perspective of "assignment" on thrones is about influence and affecting the outcome of the kingdom mandate found in *Rev. 11:15*, *"…The kingdoms of this world are become the kingdoms of our Lord and of his Christ, and he shall reign forever and ever."*

The Seven Mountains of Culture include: **Business, Government, Education, Family, Media, Arts & Entertainment,** and **Religion.** In essence, thrones are located wherever **"power"** or **"resources"** are distributed. Thrones may be found wherever there are established structures of governance, authority and influence that may be accompanied by a system or form of allegiance toward a **person, and plans, programs and/or policies** associated with the person. These are called **"Issues of Influence."**

    ℽ **Person** – The individual who is in a position of authority or influence

    ℽ **Plans** – The ideology or vision of the one in authority or a position of influence

    ℽ **Programs** – The means by which the person, policies and plans are administered

    ℽ **Policies** – The culture and power of enforcement behind the person, plans and programs

All thrones are not physically visible but may be found in less grand or conspicuous settings. They don't necessarily promote a public presence, but are still effective in leveraging power/resources. The less conspicuous thrones may still display a culture and a system of allegiance with people who believe in and support the vision and those who wield influence in their areas. Regardless of the **"level of leverage"** assigned to a throne, its purpose is to wield **influence.** The more organized systems of governance are more likely to present influence in an orderly and planned fashion. Leaders can influence people either positively or negatively, and either intentionally or unintentionally. Sometimes the results are mixed. Whether the person in authority has planned to do so or not, influence appears in some form or another by way of personal interaction, methodology or technology. The less prominent thrones have their place according to the purpose of God and serve to bring about His desires. There may be a less formal display of governance but in the eternal plans of God, everything is important in its own way.

When God gives an assignment or commissions a believer to sit on a throne, He doesn't do it on a "whim." God is very methodical in His planning. After all, everything He does comes from an eternal perspective. God *"establishes"* those He has called to sit on thrones. In some shape, form or fashion, God uses formalized training, mentoring, life experience, success, failure, weakness, strength, friendships, betrayals, the person's desires, familial DNA and culture, His Word and the power of His Spirit to influence the preparation process for each person chosen to sit on a particular throne. God is very conscious of the **"details"** and makes sure that every little thing counts toward the finished product. He exercises *"sovereignty"* in establishing His purpose in us.

> **"I know that whatever God does, It shall be forever. Nothing can be added to it, And nothing taken from it." (Eccl. 3:14, NKJV)**

We have to go into this journey knowing some very important foundational facts of our case. The adversary will attempt to **"add chapters"** to your destiny and life story, or he'll try to **"omit"** a few of them. It would be like reading a novel with a few pages missing from each chapter. When you get to the end of the story, you see what it is, but you're left a little puzzled by how all of the issues relate to one another. You may end up reading about characters or situations that weren't properly *"introduced"* into the story line. Something seems to be missing! If the adversary *"adds"* material to the story line, it influences how you process the end results and it may cause you to focus on certain points that aren't really essential to the results that God wants.

That's a big distraction! Knowing the *"life story"* the way God has planned it for us is essential to our survival and success. God uses every single part of our experiences, both the highs and the lows, because that's where we gain the *character, fortitude, experience, temperament* and **ability** to leverage our experience, and to positively influence someone or something God's way. The development of Godly character is built in us during those trying times.

"Behold, I have refined thee, but not with silver; I have chosen thee in the furnace of thy affliction."

(Isa. 48:10, KJV)

Take courage, believer... God has reserved your throne according to His eternal purpose! But, even in the furnace of affliction, remember to keep an open heart and mind about doing things to please the Father, and never allow yourself to be driven by ambition, ego, performance, your own personal agenda or pressure from others. Jesus remained focused on His Father's agenda and stayed humble throughout the process of His journey on the way to His ultimate throne; the one from which He proclaimed... *"All power is given unto me in heaven and in earth!"*

"Let this mind be in you, which was also in Christ Jesus: Who being in the form of God, thought it not robbery to be equal with God: But made himself of no reputation, and took on the form of a servant, and was made in the likeness of men: And being found in fashion as a man, he humbled himself, and became obedient unto death, even the death of the cross. WHEREFORE GOD ALSO HATH HIGHLY EXALTED

*HIM, AND GIVEN HIM A NAME WHICH IS ABOVE EVERY
NAME: THAT AT THE NAME OF JESUS EVERY KNEE
SHOULD BOW, OF THINGS IN HEAVEN, AND THINGS IN
THE EARTH, AND THINGS UNDER THE EARTH."*

(Phil. 2:5-10, KJV, emphasis added)

By contrast, King Nebuchadnezzar in the Old Testament is a good example of a person who became quite "full of himself" during his reign on the throne of Babylon. He attributed too much of his success to himself, virtually excluding God from the process altogether. This spells trouble! Fortunately, after a "wake up call" from an angel of God, and a season of "self-realization," Nebuchadnezzar recovered his senses and gave God the glory, after which his kingdom was returned to him.

ESTABLISHING MAJESTY

The text below shows two very important aspects of kingdom success – **Establishment** and **Majesty**. These are qualities that are added to one's *"throne-room experience"* by God as a result of humility and attributing the position to God and not one's self.

"And at the end of the days I Nebuchadnezzar lifted up mine eyes unto heaven, and mine understanding returned unto me, AND I BLESSED THE MOST HIGH, AND I PRAISED AND HONORED HIM THAT LIVETH FOREVER, WHOSE DOMINION IS AN EVERLASTING DOMINION, AND HIS KINGDOM IS FROM GENERATION TO GENERATION: And all the inhabitants of the earth are reputed as nothing: and he doeth according to his will in the army of heaven, and among the inhabitants of the earth: and none can stay his hand, or say unto him, What doest thou? At the same time my reason returned unto me; and for the glory of my kingdom, mine honor

and brightness; and my counsellors and my lords sought unto me; AND
I WAS ESTABLISHED IN MY KINGDOM, AND EXCELLENT
MAJESTY WAS ADDED UNTO ME."

(Dan. 4:34-36, KJV, emphasis added)

The word **"Established"** is from the Hebrew term **"Te'qan,"** **meaning:**
To straighten up, and confirm. The word **"Majesty"** is from the Hebrew
term **"Rebuw,"** meaning: Increase of dignity. It also derives meaning
from the Hebrew term **"Rabah,"** meaning: Increase, continue, enlarge,
excel, to be in authority, yield, gather, multiply and be plenteous. In other
words, when a person has proper character and attributes the power of
the throne to God, He will add the confirming grace of Majesty and
Establishment.

OPPORTUNITY OR ASSIGNMENT?

I'd like to point out something very important related to having success
on a throne. We all realize that there are a number of ways to end up
on a throne and not all of them are proper, safe or righteous. History
teaches us that kings rise to power and are often overthrown not long
afterward. Some buy their way into power through manipulation and
the use of money, politics, social disorder and an appeal to bring change,
often in a disruptive way. Some create their own "crisis situation" in
order to conveniently be on the scene to offer solutions and relief. Often
this is accomplished through forcefulness and conflict. Some rise to
power through rights of succession as in a monarchy or are handed the
scepter through allegiance to the former leader or through a democratic
political process.

Others create or develop their own platforms or business models and
form a corporate structure through which they rise to greater levels of
power and influence. Some are even given special opportunities to which

they may or may not have a right to by people called "Kingmakers." *Wikipedia* defines a **Kingmaker** as: "A person or group that has great influence in a royal or political succession, without being a viable candidate. Kingmakers may use political, monetary, religious, and military means to influence the succession. Originally, the term applied to the activities of Richard Neville, the 16th Earl of Warwick – "Warwick the Kingmaker" – during the Wars of the Roses of England.

In any case, for kingdom citizens, a very important issue must be taken into account, and the following queation answered. **IS THIS JUST AN OPPORTUNITY OR AM I ON ASSIGNMENT?** It's easy to look at a simple opportunity and mistake it for an assignment if it looks like a chance to finally be successful or financially stable. It may take you to great places in the world, introduce you to the movers and shakers of the day or to a position in an exciting new organization. When considering a position in life, we must remember that it's God's life and we are "bought with a price." This means that our lives as kingdom citizens are not our own and we owe allegiance to God before anything else. There is a great difference between an opportunity and an assignment. **"Opportunity Knocks!"** We've all heard that one. But, when the door opens there's no guarantee that destiny will be staring you in the face!

CASE STUDY - LOOK BEFORE YOU LEAP!

I learned an important lesson during my 30 years in the fire service. After fires were extinguished, we'd walk through the building to check for hidden fires or to locate victims. We'd often come to a door that was closed. I would tell the firefighter not to open the door and briskly walk through because the floor may be missing on the other side. Often *"there was no floor beyond the door!"* I believe this is good advice for kings today.

"Opportunity may knock" and invite you to come running through the door because it's a chance you just can't afford to pass up. Be careful and remember, that when God knocks, there is always a "foundation" to stand on – on the other side! It will always relate to the unique purpose that God has for your life, a purpose imagined by God long before you were born. Not only that, but Jesus always walks **TOWARD** you when you open a door that He was knocking on. Then after you "eat together" or come to realize the purposes of God, you will follow Jesus back through that door to the place of fulfillment! "Look before you Leap!

"Listen! I stand at the door and knock; if anyone hears my voice and opens the door, I will come in and eat with them, and they will eat with me."

(Rev. 3:20, GNB)

> **True assignments will be of a "destiny-driven design" and will bring certain foundations that will produce a "destiny-based response."**

AUTHORITY FOR ASSIGNMENT

"Then the word of the Lord came unto me, saying, Before I formed thee in the belly I knew thee; and before thou camest forth out of the womb I sanctified thee, and I ordained thee a prophet to the nations. Then said I, Ah, Lord God! Behold, I cannot speak: for I am a child. But the Lord said unto me, Say not, I am a child: for thou shalt go to all that I shall send thee, and whatsoever I command thee thou shalt speak. Be not afraid of their faces: for I am with thee to deliver thee, saith the Lord. Then the Lord put forth his hand, and touched my mouth. And

the Lord said unto me, Behold, I have put my words in thy mouth.
See, I have this day set thee over the nations and over the kingdoms,
to root out, and to pull down, and to destroy, and to throw down, to
build and to plant."

(Jer. 1:4-10, KJV)

When you are given an assignment, you'll also receive "authority" for
the assignment. Believers often fail in an undertaking because they
had a "desire" for the assignment rather than an "authorization" from
God Himself.

God gives authority through…

- **The Word of the Lord** – God's endorsement through scripture,
rhema or prophetic words, or authorized authority figures

- **God's "Pre-Approval"** – His foreknowledge of your destiny
which predates time itself

- **God's Purpose** – The intentions of the assignment

- **God's Touch** – His hand is on you as the instrument of the
assignment

- **God's Words** – The ability to communicate the assignment
(Either you will speak or another will speak for you or your
works will speak)

- **The Description of the Assignment** – More specific applications
of your assignment with projected results based on God's
sovereign plans

- **Anointing** – The gift or baptism of the Holy Spirit is available to
all believers today. In the Old Testament, 1 Samuel 16:13 NLT,
"So as David stood there among his brothers, Samuel took the flask

of olive oil he had brought and anointed David with the oil. And the Spirit of the LORD came powerfully upon David from that day on." Or 1 Samuel 16:13 NAS, *"Then Samuel took the horn of oil and anointed him in the midst of his brothers; and the Spirit of the LORD came mightily upon David from that day forward."*

౿ **Commissioning** – Appointing or conferring rank or position, setting into office. See for example Jesus' commissioning of the Twelve in Matt. 10:1-3, Mark 3:14-19, Luke 6:13-16. For a fuller description, read *Aligning with the Apostolic, Volume 1* – Kingdom House Publishing, 2013.

Let's take this authority and mount up with wings like eagles!

MY DECREE

I am a Melchizedek King/Priest and I make my home on Mount Zion. The kingdom call is on my life and I am empowered to rule and reign in high places. Wisdom and truth abide in me because I am called to make a difference in my assigned mountain. God has given me great and precious promises that provide everything I need for life and godliness. I reject every "bootleg chapter" that the enemy tries to add to my destiny. I reclaim the "lost chapters" of my life today! I will discern the difference between an opportunity and an assignment. When doors open for me, Jesus is there to feed me and lead me back through. I will exercise the power of my "8th Mountain Mentality" and I will have complete victory!

I SEE *Thrones!*

A REVERSAL OF
MISFORTUNE

"This is the decision of the alert and watchful angels. So then, let all people everywhere know that THE SUPREME GOD HAS POWER OVER HUMAN KINGDOMS AND THAT HE CAN GIVE THEM TO ANYONE HE CHOOSES – EVEN TO THOSE WHO ARE THE LEAST IMPORTANT."

(Dan. 4:17, GNB, emphasis added)

One of the most profound *"rags to riches"* accounts in the Bible is the one of Joseph, the dreamer, an imprisoned "para-prophet" who faced degrading opposition from his brothers only to rise to the level of Egypt's royal court. The same spirit of sovereign purpose, process and positioning is on us today, as God prophetically reveals, early on, the persons we are yet to become. When we receive prophetic words, we often see little or nothing to indicate how effective or influential we are going to become. In fact, things often get much worse before they get better. However, the negative circumstances do not define the final outcome as far as God is concerned. It was His plan all along to raise Joseph to royalty, even as it is to make each of us effective and influential in some shape, form or fashion, according to the destiny He has chosen for us.

> *"The king and his officials approved this plan, and said to them, 'We will never find a better man than Joseph, a man who has God's Spirit in him.' The king said to Joseph, 'God has shown you all this, so it is obvious that you have greater wisdom and insight than anyone else. I will put you in charge of my country, and all my people will obey your orders. Your authority will be second only to mine. I now appoint you governor over all Egypt.' The king removed from his finger the ring engraved with the royal seal and put it on Joseph's finger. He put a fine linen robe on him, and placed a gold chain round his neck. He gave him the second chariot to ride in, and his guard of honor went ahead of him and cried out, 'Make way! Make way!' And so Joseph was appointed governor over all Egypt."*

> (Gen. 41:37-43, GNB)

A very significant thing happened with Joseph and the king of Egypt. The king removed a signet ring from his own finger and placed it on Joseph's finger. In ancient Egypt it was customary for a king to wear a ring that had a seal for certifying documents or authenticating his signature. The design on the ring was the king's own and was not allowed to be duplicated in any form. Hot wax was the agent used for sealing envelopes or packages and the ring left an impression indicating authenticity. In the kingdom of God, we are "sealed" with the Holy Spirit as an indication of our legal inheritance and authority in Christ (Eph. 1:13-14). As kings in the Seven Mountains of Culture, we have the ability and authority to **"seal"** or make decrees over projects, programs, principles, processes, plans, people, places, provisions, pulpits and platforms to release the authority of God's purpose. We literally become God's seal of approval and have the grace to bring a transfer of God's favor to our places of assignment and to surrounding territories.

"In that day, saith the Lord of hosts, will I take thee, O Zerubbabel, my servant, the son of Shealtiel, saith the Lord, and will MAKE THEE AS A SIGNET: FOR I HAVE CHOSEN THEE, saith the Lord of hosts."

(Hag. 2:23, KJVA, emphasis added)

Natural authority figures have tremendous influence in the formation of laws, edicts, rules, regulations and operating systems that form trends and infrastructure for how things will operate in their spheres. When we arrive on the scene as kings, God will place that type of authority on many of us, to change culture in positive and influential ways. We can literally go from being people who appear to have little or no effect, to people who become the "movers and shakers" of our industries.

REASSESSMENT, REASSIGNMENT AND REALIGNMENT

"And thou, profane wicked prince of Israel, whose day is come, when iniquity shall have an end, Thus saith the Lord God; REMOVE THE DIADEM, AND TAKE OFF THE CROWN: this shall not be the same: exalt him that is low, and abase him that is high. I will overturn, overturn, overturn, it: and it shall be no more, until he come whose right it is; and I will give it him."

(Ezek. 21:25-27, KJV, emphasis added)

This text is a good template for *authority reassessment, reassignment and realignment* even for today's leadership structure and models. Some of the details are different but the process is very much the same. Israel was going through a difficult time when they were straying in their dedication to God. Iniquity and transgression were rampant. God's solution to this disruptive attitude was to focus on the leader or "Prince" of the nation. This **"Nasi,"** or king and ruler (Hebrew) had lost sensitivity toward God. (This term is also from the Hebrew word **"Nacah,"** meaning: **To lift, furnish, further, exalt,** [wear] **armor, and obtain.**)

This leader should have been able, by virtue of his anointing and assignment— to lift, furnish, exalt, protect and acquire substance for his nation! Instead, he did not do this. The Lord God was literally saying, *"If you can't rule properly, or be the resourceful leader that the people need, I'll find someone who can!"* Today, the transition and transfer process is still moving throughout the earth. As the kingdom of God progressively advances, we see more and more improvements in areas that were formerly much more difficult.

Using the text above, please observe the key points of the transition and transfer process.

    ℴ *The Word of God comes to initiate the process of transfer and transition – "Thus saith the Lord"*

    ℴ *An announcement of termination comes against "the present time" and its conditions – "Iniquity shall have an end"*

    ℴ *Previous authority symbols are "defrocked" or visibly removed from power – "Remove the diadem, and take off the crown"*

    ℴ *A reversal, shift or exchange of authority occurs – "Overturn, overturn, overturn"*

∞ *New rulership is positioned on the throne – "Exalt him that is low, and abase him that is high"*

∞ *New authority figures accept and assert their assignments – "He comes whose right it is"*

∞ *New authority becomes godly, established authority – "I will give it to him"*

The account of Zerubbabel, the Governor of Judah, is another example of a divinely appointed "overturning" and a "takeover" of a throne. It shows how God leverages His resources to support His chosen replacements for dissident rulers. A believer who is chosen by God has the forces of heaven and Earth at his or her disposal.

"On that same day, the 24th of the month, the Lord gave Haggai a second message for Zerubbabel, the governor of Judah: 'I am about to shake heaven and earth and overthrow kingdoms and end their power. I will overturn chariots and their drivers; the horses will die, and their riders will kill one another. On that day I will take Zerubbabel my servant and I will appoint you to rule in my name. You are the one I have chosen.' The Lord Almighty has spoken."

(Hag. 2:20-23, GNB)

With sin in the world, everything is exposed to its demonically-engineered influences, but the power of our sovereign God and the shed blood of Jesus Christ recovers us from its effects. We are delivered from the power of darkness and have been translated into the kingdom of God's Son. God is a God of order and structure, as His entire creation demonstrates and is bringing everything into kingdom order. Creation itself is held together in an orderly fashion only because a God of order is governing through the Word of His power. We, as kings, now have the privilege and power to govern with **"the word of a king."**

"For the word of a king is authority and power, and who can say to him, What are you doing?"

(Eccl. 8:4, AMP)

Finally, the example of Shebna and Eliakim is enlightening and a study in contrast of stewardship styles, fiduciary faithfulness or the lack thereof, and profiles in power. Shebna's abuse of position, power and privilege as palace administrator in Jerusalem for self-benefit drew God's attention and judgment and Isaiah was told to prophesy to Shebna a change in leadership and location and legacy, and the name of God's chosen replacement Eliakim. In contrast, Eliakim would inherit royal robes, royal title, royal authority and the key to the house of David, while bringing honor to his family name and being a father to the people of Judah and Jerusalem. God's intervention in this matter was decisive and conclusive.

"This is what the Lord, the LORD of Heaven's Armies, said to me: "Confront Shebna, the palace administrator, and give him this message: "Who do you think you are, and what are you doing here, building a beautiful tomb for yourself—a monument high up in the rock? For the LORD is about to hurl you away, mighty man. He is going to grab you, crumple you into a ball, and toss you away into a distant, barren land. There you will die, and your glorious chariots will be broken and useless. You are a disgrace to your master! "Yes, I will drive you out of office," says the LORD. "I will pull you down from your high position. And then I will call my servant Eliakim son of Hilkiah to replace you. I will dress him in your royal robes and will give him your title and your authority. And he will be a father to the people of Jerusalem and Judah. I will give him the key to the house of David—the highest position in the royal court. When he opens doors, no one will be able to close them; when he closes doors, no one will be able to open them. He will bring

honor to his family name, for I will drive him firmly in place like a
nail in the wall. They will give him great responsibility, and he will
bring honor to even the lowliest members of his family."

(Isa. 22:15-24, NLT)

A DECISION FOR REVISION

A very important purpose of the Kingdom of God in us and the reason
for our placement upon thrones is to bring about the reformation of
life on this planet as we currently know it and to cause the kingdoms
of this world to become the kingdoms of our Lord and of His Christ
(see Rev. 11:15). This is an often repeated text in this book because the
entire premise of "I See Thrones!" is based on the kingdom conversion
principle and process. It's about restoring the orderly format of all
creation as God originally intended, and in doing so we must create
cultures of interest, learning and on-going relationships with people,
places and things that support upward mobility and improvement.
The throne of the earth's greatest King, Jesus Christ, becomes the
template for all governance and authority and how we are to derive
and demonstrate power.

"Thus says the Lord God: Remove the [high priest's] miter or headband
and take off the [king's] crown; things shall not remain as they have
been; the low is to be exalted and the high is to be brought low. I will
overthrow, overthrow, overthrow it; this also shall be no more until
He comes Whose right it is [to reign in judgment and in righteousness],
and I will give it to Him."

(Ezek. 21:27, AMP)

Here is a prophetic preview of the coming Christ who will rule over
His creation, replacing the reign of unrighteous kings. It's about the

restoration of the kingdom of God under the Order of Melchizedek, where we are restored to the righteous king/priest positions that God intended. God is virtually turning thrones **"upside down"** or as the King James Version of the Bible says, God is working to **"overturn"** them to make way for His people to take their rightful places! Since we are found "in Christ," He will rule and reign through His Body, the Church.

Most of the spiritual technology that we'll witness in this season of transformation is not primarily used to rid the world of the unjust rulers as much as it is to properly prepare and project the believers who are to rise to their rightful positions. Turning a throne **"upside down"** shakes it free of anyone who may have been sitting there unrightfully. But the process isn't complete **"Until he comes whose right it is!"** The primary impetus of this book is to ignite the fires of faith and destiny and propel forward the believers who know that it's time to advance the kingdom of God. It would be an easy task for God to simply remove the unqualified or unrighteous leadership found on Earth today. After all, who can sit on a throne that's been "overturned?" The task of throne conversions isn't simply about removing the wrong person and putting in the right person. It's more about preparing believers to step up to their positions of purpose that God ordained. The challenge is to bring believers to the place where we all know beyond a shadow of doubt that we are the ones "Whose right it is," and "whose God-given assignment it is."

SITTING IN SOVEREIGNTY

We now sit in that same place with Christ, as His Body, not only in the heavenly realm but also on the earth, because here, on earth, our rulership and influence will have the greatest effect. God the Father has a throne, His Son Jesus has a throne and we, the Body of Christ in the earth, each have a place in the throne with Christ and an additional place of assignment which can literally be interpreted as "our own throne." It's a **transformational authority** and it's not simply given for us to flex our muscles against the forces of darkness. Neither do we become *"blessed bullies"* who go around wreaking havoc on weaker individuals. There is accountability and fiduciary responsibility with this.

"And the seventy returned again with joy, saying, Lord, even the devils are subject unto us through thy name."

(Luke 10:17, KJV)

"Notwithstanding in this rejoice not, that the spirits are subject unto you; but rather rejoice, because your names are written in heaven."

(Luke 10:20, KJV)

Transformational authority is given to bring about the purposes of God. All righteous authority derives its power from the throne of God in heaven but we need thrones in the earth to execute the plans, pursuits, purposes, perspectives and powers of God. This is the only way that God's true reality can be seen on the earth. It has to be done through redeemed mankind, made in His image and likeness whose power and authority are legally derived from Him. The Body of Christ has tremendous revelations about the times of reformation and restoration that are to come. However, we also need strong confidence in our ability to govern the respective territories and systems of the earth that God hands over to us.

"The heaven, even the heavens, are the Lord's: but the earth hath he given to the children of men."

(Ps. 115:16, KJV)

God intends that we recover the state of dominion that Adam first enjoyed in the Garden of Eden. The Earth belongs to the children of men, so God is igniting our hearts once again to take our rightful places in the earth. Divine order and power have been restored and you are

109

about to see another "throne-room technology" that God is using to usher in this powerful transition. The word is **"Sovereignty!"** Kings exercise a right known as **"Sovereignty"** which is: Supremacy in rule or power; the power to govern without external control or the supreme political power in a state. [Sovereignty is the activity of a sovereign or one who is] **predominant, paramount or preponderant** (Webster's New World Dictionary). We are kings under the sovereign authority of the reator King Jesus Christ. As His Body we leverage the power of His decree found in **Matt. 28:18, KJV...** *"All power is given unto me in heaven and in earth."* We must believe this and act upon it.

> **Sovereignty affects our individual destinies as well as the destinies of nations and kingdoms.**

In the past, the subject of sovereignty was often sequestered into conversations and issues relating to the universal church and to its history and relation to world events. Sovereignty had more to do with the aspect of eschatology and the judgment of nations rather than with the individual people who live in them. But, how can sovereignty relate only to nations without including the individual people who live in them? Can sovereignty overlook the actual human beings, the souls who Christ shed His blood for and died to show the desire of God to reconcile all things to Himself?

Is sovereignty more about history than "His-Story" of the redemption of mankind and about man's restored authority on the earth and the recovery that will bring all things back into alignment with the purposes of God? Can sovereignty overlook each person's important role in the destiny of nations or the fact that God is a "Father" who wants an orderly family structure and that He wants His children living in a loving and personal relationship with Him? Indeed, the sovereign work of God through Christ is about what He accomplishes in the lives of each individual, making every personal link in the chain contribute to the strength of the entire chain – the chain of humanity.

Sovereignty is a power that overtakes the demonically-engineered systems of the earth that run rampant, not because they are superior to us, but because the governing skills of mankind are often not fully empowered, engaged or expressed. As mankind is restored to the divine government of Jesus Christ, we'll see the systems of earth sovereignly reformatted to the divine purposes they were originally created for. We are learning how to leverage the influence of our thrones, how to redeem earthly systems, how to rule and reign as the Body of Christ and how to unseat illegitimate rulership and regain lost destinies.

LED INTO LORDSHIP

The kingdom journey of the believer not only leads to our ascension to "thrones," but also to the assignment of **"lordship."** Lordship deals with the responsibility that we receive over **t**erritories, technologies, resources, relationships and reservoirs of supernatural provisions.

"...And the Lamb shall overcome them; for he is Lord of lords, and King of kings: and they that are with him are CALLED, and CHOSEN, and FAITHFUL."

(Rev. 17:14, KJV)

Webster's New World Dictionary and Thesaurus defines a **Lord** as: A person of great power in some field. Therefore, **"lordship"** is a term relative to special **"fields"** or assignments within Seven Mountain territory. As God gives us authority to rule and reign in our assignments, we are led into ever expanding and increasing responsibilities. The **"lord"** is the **"specialist"** in his or her field. He or she is **"called," "chosen,"** and **"faithful"** in respective areas of assignment, as Rev. 17:14 shows. We are about to see phenomenal advances in breakthrough technology and ideas that rattle and shake "status quo" environments and normalcy. The unusual and the uncommon are about to happen. So, take courage because your increase is closer than you think!

"Sing, O Barren, thou that didst not bear, break forth into singing, and cry aloud, thou that didst not travail with child: for more are the children of the desolate than the children of the married wife, saith the Lord. ENLARGE THE PLACE OF YOUR TENT, AND LET THEM STRETCH FORTH THE CURTAINS OF THINE HABITATIONS; SPARE NOT, LENGTHEN THY CORDS, AND STRENGTHEN THY STAKES; FOR THOU SHALT BREAK FORTH ON THE RIGHT HAND AND ON THE LEFT; AND THY SEED SHALL INHERIT THE GENTILES, AND MAKE THE DESOLATE CITIES TO BE INHABITED. Fear not; for thou shalt not be ashamed: neither be thou confounded; for thou shalt not be put to shame: for thou shalt forget the shame of thy youth, and shalt not remember the reproach of thy widowhood anymore."

(Isa. 54:1-4, KJV, emphasis added)

CATCHING UP WITH THE KINGDOM CALENDAR

"He raises up the poor out of the dust and lifts the needy from the ash heap, to make them sit with nobles and INHERIT THE THRONE OF GLORY. For the pillars of the earth are the Lord's, and he has set the world upon them."

(1 Sam. 2:8, AMP, emphasis added)

It is the Father's good pleasure to give us the kingdom, as Jesus told His disciples. And many of the people who are destined to rule and reign don't necessarily see it at the present time. They may feel *inadequate, insignificant, unqualified, unnecessary, unprepared, undesirable, unfulfilled and unloved.* Now it is time to "**UN – TIE**" the negativity! Every one of has experienced some of these feelings from time to time, but it's important to develop and keep a healthy kingdom mindset and look at God's plan for our elevation and fulfilled destinies. The text above shows us that we can start out insignificant, but through the grace of God, we rise to the top and inherit His throne of glory. If the poor person and the beggar can rise up, then anyone can! But, rather than just sitting around, waiting for this to happen, we need to take time to develop our "**throne-room thought-life.**" Part of that process is understanding how to handle "time" and the issue of "waiting on our time to come."

The Lord began to explain what He meant when He said that *"People believe they are waiting on their success and their thrones but their success and their thrones are actually waiting on them."* Look at the natural calendar and see how it reaches forward into the future by showing dates that haven't even arrived. Yet, the dates are posted in sequential order on a calendar with holidays and special events already listed on them. How's that for foresight?! Even the phases of the moon are shown months ahead of time with an expectation that the moon will actually look that way when those dates arrive! Astronomy magazines can project the positions of planets, stars, galaxies and constellations far into the future. They can plot the courses of comets and predict the dates for a comet's return on its flight past the earth decades ahead of time. This is great information and we thank God for the intelligence to do something like this. But, we are encouraged to do the same for spiritual matters and for the destinies and assignments that are "waiting" on us! We have the Word of God and the Holy Spirit to give us the "facts" about what is to come.

"However, when He, the Spirit of truth has come, He will guide you into all truth; for he will not speak on His own authority, but whatever he hears he will speak; and HE WILL TELL YOU THINGS TO COME."

(John 16:13, NKJV, emphasis added)

Nothing brings us up to date faster than hearing about future plans directly from the Holy Spirit! Paul the Apostle had a clear perspective on this...

"I do not claim that I have already succeeded or have already become perfect. I keep striving to win the prize for which Christ Jesus has already won me to himself. Of course, my brothers and sisters, I really do not think that I have already won it; the one thing I do, however, is to forget what is behind me and do my best to reach what is ahead. So I run straight towards the goal in order to win the prize, which is God's call through Christ Jesus to the life above. [High calling] All of us who are spiritually mature should have this same attitude. But if some of you have a different attitude, God will make this clear to you. However that may be, let us go forward according to the same rules we have followed until now."

(Phil. 3:12-16, GNB, emphasis added)

Paul was a revelator! The "rules" that he followed were rules of revelation knowledge that constantly shifted his thinking paradigms. Paul made it very clear, that in this instance, what is before us is more important than what is behind us. He pointed out the importance of "forgetting those things which are behind" or the things that seem like they are "following us!" This could be our personal mistakes, failures, unpleasant memories, failed business ventures, disappointments, loss of momentum, unhappiness, bewilderment, depression, church splits, divorce, job termination, family squabbles, and even those times when our personal dedication to God faded for a time and we didn't listen to God diligently. What's more important is what is in front of us!

The prize of God's high call upon our lives is now in front of us! Every day of our lives is highlighted with an inventory of benefits that were predetermined by God long before the actual day arrives. *Psalm 68:19* tells us *"Blessed be the Lord, who daily loadeth us with benefits."* This high calling is the ultimate assignment from God. It's a heavenly calling and a call of destiny and divine purpose. The King James Version of the text calls it the "high calling of God." The word **"High"** is from the Greek term **"Ano,"** meaning: Upward, on the top, or above. It refers to the fact that God's calling on our lives wasn't invented on the earth, but in a creative thought dimension far superior to that of mankind. It's actually heaven's version of our lives. The word **"Calling,"** is taken from the Greek term **"Klesis,"** meaning: **Invitation.** We have been officially invited to take on the image of our identities as we appear to God in heaven.

> **If earth's version of your life is a total failure, then it's a "bootleg" copy of your destiny! Go for the real deal!**

Believers often use the old "default" confession that they are "waiting" on God. They feel like there is nothing to do but watch time pass to "see" if anything changes. I do believe that God places things on a timeline and that timeline is divine. Some things should only happen if and when God decides and I want to make it clear that I believe this, but there are also things that we can do to join God in the process of walking into destiny through interlocking with strong prophetic words, studying the Word of God, interacting with strong believers in fellowship and giving God the dedicated life He wants from us.

"But they that wait upon the Lord shall renew their strength; they shall mount up with wings as eagles; they shall run, and not be weary; and they shall walk and not faint."

(Isa. 40:31, KJV)

In this text the term **"Wait"** doesn't primarily mean to pass time. It comes from the Hebrew word **"Qavah,"** meaning: To bind together by twisting, to expect, to gather together. For us, waiting is about interlocking ourselves in relational service to God and walking out the God-given secular assignments that we have. From that, we have healthy expectations of what God has put in place through His providence, foreknowledge and sovereignty. We gather together every resource, revelation and relationship that God gives us and we come forth in victory. We'll mount up with wings like eagles and our strength will be renewed!

You are being placed on thrones that are predetermined by God's will and counsel. You are "coming into your own" as the saying goes. Naturally, I had to ponder over what God said and I realized how powerful His statement was. He asked me *"How can you wait on something that is ahead of you?* If you are walking and someone is in front of you, are you waiting on them or are they waiting on YOU! You can only wait on someone or something that is BEHIND you! So, you are not waiting on the future, the future is waiting on YOU! Thrones are waiting on us to come "whose right it is!" according to Ezek. 21:27.

"PARDON ME... I BELIEVE THAT'S MY SEAT!"

All of us probably remember going to a concert, game or other event that was filled with a crowd. It was a task trying to find a seat if you didn't have reserved seating. It's even worse if you went with another person and needed two or more seats next to each other. There's probably not a very good solution available in this case but next time it would be better to purchase seats in advance and receive assigned seat numbers. If you arrive only to find someone else sitting in your assigned seat, you have a "legal recourse" to the situation. You may politely ask the individual to move, showing him the stub verifying your pre-assigned seat and hope that he's a person of good character.

On occasion you may run into a more rash and brazen individual who wants to argue and defend his "stolen goods" and imply that he has a right to them, even after seeing your ticket stub with the seat number on it! He may even claim the old "first come-first served" clause, but legally his claim doesn't apply because a legal matter of preassigned seating takes precedence. We may discover similar circumstances when we locate our assigned "thrones" only to find someone else in our "seat," and that "someone" doesn't intend to move!

"I beheld till the thrones were cast down, and the Ancient of days did sit, whose garment was as white as snow, and the hair of his head like pure wool: his throne was like the fiery flame, and his wheels as burning fire."

(Dan. 7:9, KJVA)

"Cast down" is a term from the Hebrew words **"ReMah,"** meaning: To throw, hurl or carry and **"MeAl,"** meaning: **The setting** and/or **"Alal,"** meaning: Thrusting oneself in, to enter, introduce, bring in. Collectively, I believe this means: To throw down or hurl away a throne

117

and its powers who have set themselves in a place of authority and attempt to rule as the true authority.

There are opposing forces occupying many thrones within the Seven Mountains of Culture. The supernatural displacement that God brings may not be a "clean sweep" in every situation. First off, don't expect demonic powers to be polite. Even though these dark forces know they are in violation of divine law and order, they attempt to maintain their stand hoping we that we're not aware of our rights or are afraid to confront the issue. In this spiritual battle we must be aware of our position and the privilege that we have to invoke the power of divine law and order, issued from the high court of heaven by the Chief Magistrate of creation. The strategies and tactics of this battle are decided in the high court long before we enter the fight. Most cases are tried in lower courts and the appeals process works its way up to the higher courts. In our case, this is just the opposite. Our cases are tried in the high court first! Eventually, with the correct application of **"situational sovereignty,"** these thrones will be **"cast down."**

What is **"situational sovereignty?"** It is: The application of God's immutable intentions (purpose and counsel) that are applied to specific cases of human involvement, so that even when the human will resists the invitation and mercies of God and the orderly framework of the Spirit of God, the Lord will override the matter for the greater good and preservation of His original plans. It is His exercise of creative privilege. *"Heaven belongs to the Lord alone, but he gave the earth to the human race." Psalm 115:16 (GNB)* normally applies, but He will intercept the issue and override it as He sees fit.

"...Blessed be the name of God forever and ever, for wisdom and might are His. And He changes the times and the seasons; HE REMOVES KINGS AND RAISES UP KINGS..."

(Dan. 2:20-21, NKJV, emphasis added)

118

> **"For exaltation comes neither from the west nor from the south, But God is the Judge: HE PUTS DOWN ONE, AND EXALTS ANOTHER."**
> **(Ps. 75:6-7, NKJV, emphasis added)**

Remember the revelation of **"The Room of Thrones?"** There were empty seats waiting on God's chosen ones to occupy them. These seats of authority or influence may not yet be empty on earth but they are empty as far as heaven is concerned. This is why we can expect a shift of power in the earth. The process of removal has already begun. Now we have a fresh revelation of life and a different way to do things! We won't "fight" our way to the top anymore. We'll assert our rights to inheritance through the spirit dimension where God Himself will "turn over" the seats of authority to His sons and daughters! In the meantime, we will do our diligence to be people of good character and operate in our skillsets with excellence and nobility.

"While I was looking, THRONES WERE PUT IN PLACE. One who had been living for ever sat down on one of the thrones. His clothes were white as snow, and his hair was like pure wool. His throne, mounted on fiery wheels was blazing with fire, and a stream of fire was pouring out from it."

(Dan. 7:9-10, GNB, emphasis added)

All thrones that oppose God's kingdom structure and order will eventually be cast down! The thrones of the king of Babylon, the spirit of Babylon and Satan are all the same when it comes to God's judgment!

119

"You will take up this taunt against the king of Babylon: How the oppressor has ceased! How the flood has receded! The Lord has broken the staff of the wicked, the rod of tyrants that struck peoples in rage with ceaseless blows, that ruled nations with anger, with relentless aggression. All the earth rests quietly, then it breaks into song. Even the cypresses rejoice over you, the cedars of Lebanon: 'Since you were laid low, no logger comes up against us!' The underworld beneath becomes restless to greet your arrival. It awakens the ghosts, all the leaders of earth; it makes the kings of the nations rise from their thrones. All of them speak and say to you: 'Even you've become weak like we are! You are the same as us!' Your majesty has been brought down to the underworld, along with the sound of your harps..."

(Isa. 14:4-11, AMP)

CASE STUDY – "KING SAUL... YOU'RE FIRED!"

One of the best examples of a leader being deposed from a throne and replaced by God's choice is that of King Saul. Saul was not God's first choice to be the King of Israel. As a matter of fact, God Himself wanted to be Israel's king but they rejected Him. God's next choice for Israel would be an unlikely candidate for rulership, a boy named David. David was later described as a man after God's own heart, a position that he must have had in God's eternal purposes all along. God knew David before he was formed in his mother's womb and God knew what his heart would be like and how he would worship God with a tender heart yet fight vehemently for the kingdom at the same time. God's sovereign foreknowledge already positioned David to become the King of Israel and to be the forerunner of Christ, who would be known as "the son of David."

> **Although King Saul was on the literal throne for quite some time, he was already removed as king in the spirit dimension. Saul's throne was "empty" even while he sat on it, waiting on David to rise to his assignment as king.**

Here's a good example of how the people of a group, company or organization, and even nations, can make decisions to select authority figures that don't carry out the purposes of God. *"The heaven, even the heavens, are the Lord's: but the earth hath he given to the children of men"* (Ps. 115:16). We realize that the results of mankind's decisions can be disastrous!

"Rebellion against him is as bad as witchcraft, and arrogance is as sinful as idolatry. Because you rejected the Lord's command, he has rejected you as king. 'Yes, I have sinned,' Saul replied. 'I have disobeyed the Lord's command and your instructions. I was afraid of my men and did what they wanted. But now I beg you, forgive my sin and go back with me, so that I can worship the Lord.' 'I will not go back with you,' Samuel answered. 'YOU REJECTED THE LORD'S COMMAND, AND HE HAS REJECTED YOU AS KING OF ISRAEL.' Then Samuel turned to leave, but Saul caught hold of his cloak, and tore it. Samuel said to him, 'The Lord has torn the kingdom of Israel away from you today and given it to someone who is a better man than you.'

(I Sam. 15:23-28, GNB, emphasis added)

Let's fast forward to a future account involving Saul's throne where he enlisted the help of a soothsayer to call up the spirit of the deceased Samuel to see if he could maintain his throne. He wanted to see if Samuel's original decree against him had changed.

> *"Samuel said to Saul, 'Why have you disturbed me? Why did you make me come back? Saul answered, 'I am in great trouble! The Philistines are at war with me, and God has abandoned me. He doesn't answer me anymore, either by prophets or by dreams. And so I have called you, for you to tell me what I must do.' Samuel said, 'Why do you call me when the Lord has abandoned you and become your enemy? THE LORD HAS DONE TO YOU WHAT HE TOLD YOU THROUGH ME: HE HAS TAKEN THE KINGDOM AWAY FROM YOU AND GIVEN IT TO DAVID INSTEAD. You disobeyed the Lord's command and did not completely destroy the Amalekites and all they had. This is why the Lord is doing this to you now. He will hand you over to the Philistines. Tomorrow you and your sons will join me, and the Lord will also hand the army of Israel over to the Philistines."*

> *(I Sam. 28:15-19, GNB, emphasis added)*

Many years had passed between the texts of 1 Sam. 15:23-28 and 1 Samuel 28:15-18. Some theologians estimate that the timespan is between 15 and 20 years before David came to reign in Israel after he was first anointed and crowned king in Hebron. Yet on Saul's second meeting with the prophet Samuel, he received the same rebuke that he was given many years before. The battle with Amalek and the cause of God's rebuke took place many years ago, yet God still considered Saul's disobedience as grounds for dismissal from office. Nothing had changed. In the mind of God it was as though no time had passed at all.

Amazingly, Saul continued on the throne but in the mind of God, his reign was terminated. This is proof that when God deposes someone, it doesn't matter whether the natural timeline reflects it or not. Although David had to wait for King Saul to be removed from the throne, he was growing in maturity and wisdom during that time and building his team so that when it was time to take the throne, he was ready. God makes use of every single moment in time and nothing is wasted!

"This is the decision of the alert and watchful angels. So then, let all people everywhere know that THE SUPREME GOD HAS POWER OVER HUMAN KINGDOMS AND THAT HE CAN GIVE THEM TO ANYONE HE CHOOSES – EVEN TO THOSE WHO ARE THE LEAST IMPORTANT."

(Dan. 4:17, GNB, emphasis added)

The eternal spiritual verdict is already in! You may say, what about the will of the people, who, in the case of Saul, made a bad decision that affected them all? We are now living in a special prophetic season where there are many more anointed and capable believers, intercessors and kingdom ambassadors on the scene who heavily influence the climate of the earth. They shift atmospheres, and the timeline of the expansion of God's kingdom is much more advanced than in the days of Saul.

There are more believers on the earth than ever before and if we are able to be enlightened with throne-room thinking, we can influence the culture of the Seven Mountains and life on earth in more positive ways than ever before. There are many despotic forces that occupy the physical dimension of authority and power and influence but in the mind of God they are already deposed, waiting for those to come who are "better" suited to fulfill the purposes of God than they are. In Isa. 9:6-7 God promised to "Overturn" the situation. I believe that He's doing that for us today.

CASE STUDY – DIAMONDS IN THE ROUGH

I was made aware of a case about a believer who had fallen into a situation where he had violated a law and was sentenced to prison. He was extremely remorseful and repentant but had to serve out his sentence, nonetheless. He was a community leader and was loved and respected by many. Ironically, about two years prior to the incident, a prophetic leader who was meeting this man for the first time said, "I see you going into a season where you enter a very dark place. It's a place that would frighten most people, but don't fear because the Lord will be with you in that place. You are going to go in and 'mine the diamonds' that you find there." Time passed and the man was tried, convicted and sent away. No doubt, this was a dark period in his life. But, after the man was in prison, he found great favor with the administration who recognized that he had a good spirit and was very personable and was a great leader.

He was placed in charge of a small group of men and was so influential that the officials gave him a larger group to work with. In fact, he ended up being in charge of men who were with other groups but left them and joined with him because of his abilities and demeanor. He was so successful that he was able to stop violence and unrest within the prison. Men came to him for counsel and to learn about how to move forward with their lives. He held classes, had worship services and taught the men about unity and strong character. He virtually became their "pastor" while in prison and was able to influence them to go straight when they emerged from the system. Even verified gang members looked to this man as their leader. He encouraged them to walk with respect and honor toward one another. He led over 200 men while in the "dark place."

After a few years, he was released, went back to his occupation and later discovered that some of the men that he had influenced while he was incarcerated had gotten out and become successful in their endeavors.

They attributed their successes to him. In spite of being in the dark place, this man had truly found his **"throne!"** Today, he is a highly regarded leader and has raised up other leaders in America and beyond. As is very common with "kings," he discovered *"diamonds in the rough"* and was able to help them find their thrones, too.

MY DECREE

I am a King (Queen)! A place has been prepared for me before I was formed in my mother's womb. The adversary of my destiny has already been defeated. I have a scheduled meeting with success, and fulfillment and victory. There is order, sovereignty and strength in my life because the Creator and Possessor of Heaven and Earth esteems my purpose. I will use my time wisely while awaiting my throne. I will invest in my calling, my destiny and my purpose. I will invest in right relationships and I will invest in my skill sets for the glory of God. I am continually improving in everything I do.

I SEE *Thrones*!

I SEE *Thrones!*

THE DAYS OF
HEAVEN ON EARTH

*"And thou shalt write them [The words of the Lord] upon the door
posts of thine house, and upon thy gates: That your days may be
multiplied, and the days of your children, in the land which the Lord
sware unto your fathers to give them, AS THE DAYS OF HEAVEN
ON EARTH."*

(Deut. 11:20-21, KJV, emphasis added)

"Heaven on earth**"** is probably the desire of every believer in the
world. Who wouldn't want to live in a trouble-free environment
filled with wonderful blessings and prosperity and freedom from every
challenge that threatens our peace and tranquility? Who wouldn't want
to have their every desire granted? But, does *"heaven on earth"* mean all of
that? Christ certainly came that we would have abundant life, and God
blesses us in tremendous ways, but we still face heavy trials, persecutions
and difficult challenges at times. Then, what does *"heaven on earth"*

mean? Let's unpack this revelation to see how it applies to our lives today and how our positions of assignment on our thrones are affected.

This will help to expand, yet balance our expectations about life on earth from heaven's perspective. God does a great deal to encourage His people in times of conflict and recovery from difficult times. But usually, He'll make recovery a "process." God considers the process of the journey to be a valuable experience. I often say *"The process is just as important as the product,"* in God's perspective. For many years I've maintained that idea and I believe it explains one of the reasons why God often appears to take long periods of time to bring a promise to fruition.

God is the greatest multi-tasker ever, and we can depend on Him to accomplish a myriad of sovereign issues during the "process" of recovery. He's developing us, and the circumstances including people, places and things that relate to His desired outcome. This is why the idea of *"Heaven on earth"* can't be construed as a means of escape from all responsibility and effort, hoping to bring about a glorious and victorious outcome. It takes effort to manifest the Kingdom of God on the earth because with any "birth" there are always birth pains.

SEIZING YOUR SOVEREIGNTY

"And from the days of John the Baptist until the present time, the kingdom of heaven has endured violent assault, and violent men seize it by force [as a precious prize-a share in the heavenly kingdom is sought with most ardent zeal and intense exertion].

(Matt. 11:12, AMP)

The Greek word for **"Force"** is **"Harpazo,"** meaning: **To seize.** The time has come to **"seize"** the kingdom of God. We are in seasons of sovereignty that empower us to accelerate the process of recovering the kingdoms of this world and reassigning them as the Kingdoms of our Lord and

Christ according to Rev. 11:15. This is a realistic focus and expectation of kingdom citizens. Our outlook is both realistic and holistic because it includes a healthy balance of challenges and victories, a blend of conflict and triumphs, and the opportunities to face challenges head-on with the power of God in our lives. This attitude and approach gives us more powerful "ground level" perspectives of kingdom life and how we are to leverage our influences in the Earth.

It is a blend of grace that gives us unmerited favor and ability in areas where we have no strength or courage and the application of obedience, faith and courage, in action. Believers have to "step out of the boat" at the command of Christ as Peter did. This is a viable and realistic explanation and expectation provided by biblical history and in researching the lives of God's most notable servants in biblical history, who can argue against it? In the lives of our favorite biblical champions, there was one thing common to all; they had to rely on the power of God against both human and demonic challenges. There were battles, and there was the exercise of faith, and there was victory. Nothing came then without a price, and the same thing holds true today.

One thing is certain; the Word of the Lord provides great expectations of an eventual, favorable outcome as we forge ahead applying the principles, strategies, faith and perseverance of champions – with the foreknowledge of God being one of our most strategic and tactical tools. It's our on-going application of kingdom principles that enables us to develop the fortitude and apply the leverage and influence that it takes to overcome adversity. We have to be active participants in the process and not just casual observers of those who apply the process and get powerful results. We are now both **Kings** and **Priests** according to the Order of Melchizedek, and we are able to exercise the rights and privileges of dual citizenship. For an in-depth revelation on the Order of Melchizedek, please read the powerful book by my covenant brother Dr. Francis Myles called *The Order of Melchizedek: Rediscovering the Eternal Priesthood of*

Jesus Christ and How it Affects Us Today. This book is a must read for those who want to see why being kings and priests in today's world is so vital and powerful.

As Kings we exercise **"sovereignty,"** which is: Supremacy in rule or power; the power to govern without external control or the supreme political power in a state. [Sovereignty is the activity of a sovereign or one who is] **predominant, paramount or preponderant** (Webster's New World Dictionary). Because Christ is the King of kings, the sovereign nature of His heavenly rulership is passed down to us. We are kings under the authority of the Creator King Jesus Christ.

"From John to the seven churches in the province of Asia: Grace and peace be yours from God, who is, who was, and who is to come, and from the seven spirits in front of his throne, and from Jesus Christ, the faithful witness, the first to be raised from death and WHO IS ALSO THE RULER OF THE KINGS OF THE WORLD. He loves us, and by his sacrificial death he has freed us from our sins and made us a kingdom of priests to serve his God and Father. To Jesus Christ be the glory and power for ever and ever. Amen."

(Rev. 1:1-6, GNB, emphasis added)

Realistically, the promise in the text above is not just about blessings and bliss but also about the **recovery** and **reinforcement** and **replication** of divine patterns that have sovereign and sustainable qualities built-in – qualities that are needed on planet Earth.

   ↄ **Recovery** – The redemption of man, the reconciliation of all things back to God and the re-formation of original creative DNA

   ↄ **Reinforcement** – The establishment of kingdom order that holds everything in place with constant reminders of originality of purpose

ℵ **Replication** – The ability to reproduce godly patterns, systems, activities and generations thereafter

Heaven is a sovereign dimension in which everything is within the purview of the eternal creative wisdom of God. Heaven is a realm that represents the "throne" of God – the place where divine foreknowledge has its seat of origin. God uses the idea of a throne and a seat in heaven to give a recognizable point of reference to all things that are created so they can sustain their existence by Him. We look to His sovereignty as our King, provider and source of life. Humanity and creation both need to recognize and realize that it's God who upholds all things by the word of His power (Heb. 1:3). Creation needs to be able to look up to its Creator to continually draw from His original plan and foreknowledge for survival.

Creation derives its nature and form from God Himself and is powerless and without purpose aside from Him. The splendor and glory of God aren't limited to heaven, although God chose to manifest from heaven to establish it as the capitol of His recognized sovereignty and authority. He can manifest glory wherever he chooses and He has chosen to do it through us. Truthfully, God is sovereign, no matter where He is, as His omnipotence dictates and we are His instruments on earth, following heaven as a type and shadow of what earthly life should be like. This isn't a fantasy or euphoric hallucination. This is kingdom-level transformation in action and a mandate of our assignments and missions on earth.

AMBASSADORS ON ASSIGNMENT

In order to introduce the kingdom of heaven to earth and to convert the kingdoms of this world into the kingdoms of God, there must be the full institution of kingdom-level ambassadorship through believers. Among theologians there has risen a debate about the terms *"kingdom of heaven"* and *"kingdom of God"* and whether they can be used interchangeably. What you are about to read is not designed to settle that argument but to unveil a perspective that directly reflects upon our missions and assignments as "kings" on thrones of the Seven Mountains of Culture. I believe that the kingdom of heaven is the realm surrounding the domain and territory of God upon His throne. It encompasses the structure of sovereign order, the ranks of angels and other heavenly beings and the atmosphere of eternity itself.

God is seated on His throne with Christ seated next to Him (Rev. 22:3). All power comes from God upon His throne. The term *"kingdom of God"* is an expression of a more focused and direct application of God's ruling *power and presence* when experienced inside of a believer. When the Pharisees enquired of Jesus about how the kingdom of God would be revealed, He gave them a profound answer, and one which they didn't expect. It answers the question, "Where is the kingdom of God?"

"Some Pharisees asked when the kingdom of God would come. His answer was, 'The Kingdom of God does not come in such a way as to be seen. No one will say, 'Look, here it is! Or, 'There it is!'; because the KINGDOM OF GOD IS WITHIN YOU."

(Luke 17:20-21, GNB, emphasis added)

This suggests that the kingdom of God is more identifiable inwardly, in the spirit of the believer, than outwardly in a physical location. First, God imparts *the kingdom of God* to believers to transfer His *"authorization code"* to us so that we can function as His official representatives. And since *the kingdom of heaven* belongs to God and not vice versa, it is reasonable to believe that heaven can only become authorized to "move to Earth" by God Himself, or by an authorized representative (ambassador) who has already received *the kingdom of God.*

> **We need the kingdom of God inside of us before we can bring the kingdom of heaven to Earth.**

"Instead, be concerned above everything else with the Kingdom of God and with what he requires of you, and he will provide you with all these other things."

(Matt. 6:33, GNB)

"But seek (aim at and strive after) first of all His kingdom and His righteousness (His way of being right), and then all these things taken together will be given to you besides. Do not worry or be anxious about tomorrow, for tomorrow will have worries and anxieties of its own. Sufficient for each day is its own trouble."

(Matt. 6:33-34, AMP)

The **kingdom of heaven** is God's **"real estate"** or the **"real"** location of His kingdom **"estate."** And in order to bring visitors to the property to "see it," the owner (God) must authorize the **"real estate agent"** (sons and daughters) to do so. Remember, the kingdom of heaven is the domain, territory and atmosphere of heaven. The **kingdom of God** is His personal presence and His authorization to present the **kingdom of heaven** to Earth. This enables/entitles the ambassadors (sons or daughters) to request that "heaven comes to Earth." Heaven can legally and lawfully be "summoned" to earth by an authorized ambassador. If the kingdom of God enters you first, then we are empowered with the **"Law of Sovereign Attraction"** and causes **"all these things,"** or the rest of God's estate in the kingdom of Heaven to be **"added unto you!"**

133

"I assure you that whoever believes in me will do the works that I do. They will do even greater works than these because I am going to the Father. I will do whatever you ask for in my name, so that the Father can be glorified in the Son. When you ask anything in my name, I will do it."

(John 14:12-14, CEB)

> **The resources of heaven are at our disposal and as "kings" we are authorized to "command" the resources of heaven to come to Earth so we may experience "the days of heaven on Earth!"**

THE STATE OF THE "UNION"

"...The kingdoms of this world are become the kingdoms of our Lord and of his Christ, and he shall reign forever and ever."

(Rev. 11:15, KJV)

Clearly, we have an invitation from heaven to join with it and become one unified kingdom as our Lord prayed according to **Luke 11:2** (KJV, emphasis added), *"...Thy kingdom come. THY WILL BE DONE. AS IN HEAVEN, SO IN EARTH."* Experiencing the days of heaven on earth and the mandate to make all earthly kingdoms become the kingdoms of our Lord and His Christ is exciting! Increase is coming because Heaven and Earth are one realm! There is a **"union."**

"And thou shalt write them [The words of the Lord] upon the door posts of thine house, and upon thy gates: That your days may be multiplied, and the days of your children, in the land which the Lord sware unto your fathers to give them, AS THE DAYS OF HEAVEN ON EARTH."

(Deut. 11:20-21, KJV, emphasis added)

The text of Deut. 11:20-21 says that our **days** would be **"multiplied"** or increased. We're not living life on earth as a singular and separate dimension of creation, isolated from God, but we are being included in what happens in heaven! Heaven's best is being attached to us, multiplying our value and resourcefulness. Every assignment that we have on Earth originated in the mind of God, and reflects His original plans and intentions. The word **"Multiplied"** comes from the Hebrew term **"Rabah,"** meaning: To increase, continue, enlarge, be multiplied, bring in abundance, and to yield through the process of time. The multiplication process is about receiving results as heaven dictates.

When we encounter the difficult issues of life, one of the first things we should do as believers is to consult the Word of God to see what God says about our situation. We get "heaven's" perspective, then we develop the faith and courage to forge ahead. As *"faith comes by hearing and hearing by the word of God,"* (Rom. 10:17), so our beliefs are formed. We become determined and forceful in possessing the will of God for ourselves. *"...The kingdom of heaven suffers violence and **the violent take it by force!"*** (Matt. 11:12, emphasis added). When we get a "taste" of heaven we become more aggressive and adamant about claiming our inheritance to possess the same plans and purposes of God on Earth. He is the Most High God, the possessor of heaven and earth and His will is to be done in both places! (See Gen. 14:22)

> ## Life on Earth is not a singular and separate event from what goes on in heaven.

What would life be like if we aggressively proclaimed *"the days of heaven on earth?"* We would begin to see new patterns of victory and accomplishments that we've never experienced before. You may even ask, "Why didn't this happen before?" We are growing in the grace and knowledge of God and there is a continually-unfolding revelation of power and victory that belongs to us in Christ! We can have better lives and experience greater victories, but there is a process that God wants everyone to understand. Part of this process is the unpacking and unfolding of fresh revelation knowledge!

There is a divine **"union"** between heaven and Earth that we haven't fully realized, but are coming into now. Heaven and Earth were really meant to share some of the same experiences, the way God sees it. We are beginning to understand **the state of the "Union!"** Yes, that's a play on words for us who live in the United States. Each year we listen to our president reveal the "state" or condition of the U.S. economy, social and political status, climate change and other issues of concern. Now, we have to ask ourselves, "What is **'the state of the union'** in our own lives?" How does this revelation apply to the global community? How do we leverage the power of our assignments and thrones around the world to bring positive changes to life as we know it?

It begins with fresh knowledge and perspectives on our identities in Christ. **Are we taking advantage of the benefits of heaven or are we just trying to get there really fast?** We don't want to develop an escapist's mentality, focusing only on the afterlife and avoiding all responsibility for what takes place on Earth. We are the custodians of this planet and always have been according to God's eternal plan.

The season when sin entered and the devil took over was just a temporary "glitch" in Earth's history! It's time to restore the state of the union between heaven and Earth and take our rightful places on our planet!

"Having made known unto us the mystery of his will, according to his good pleasure which he hath purposed in himself: THAT IN THE FULNESS OF TIMES HE MIGHT GATHER TOGETHER IN ONE ALL THINGS IN CHRIST, BOTH WHICH ARE IN HEAVEN AND WHICH ARE ON EARTH; EVEN IN HIM."

(Eph. 1:9-10, KJV, emphasis added)

God is taking His mind's view of your heavenly life and superimposing or overlaying it as a template or pattern onto your life on the Earth. Christ is the Word of the Lord, who, according to John 1:3 took part in the creation of everything that exists. Everything in its original state in God, is full of the Word of the Lord and full of divine purpose. Things in the Earth are not necessarily so pure but need to be reconciled back to their original purposes. In the "fullness of times," or the "sovereign season" of a person's life, God is gathering together "in one" all things so that the Earthly version mirrors the heavenly version. God is gathering things together so there is only "one version" of things concerning us. Interestingly, the words "gather together" come from the Greek term **"Anakephalaiomai,"** meaning: **To sum up or comprehend.** As believers we must be able to "sum up and comprehend" the fact that heaven and Earth are longing to join together as the one eternal kingdom platform of God.

Let's look back for a moment to one of our foundational texts for this revelation, *Deut. 11:12*, *"…The eyes of the Lord thy God are always upon it, [the land, field or assignment] from the beginning of the year even unto the end of the year"* (emphasis added). It helps to reflect again on the fact that **"Year,"** or **"Shanah,"** is the Hebrew word for **Duplication and Repetition.** In other words, what God does in heaven, He does on Earth. He'll keep overlaying and superimposing the heavenly template onto the earthly pattern until Earth looks like heaven!

> **A multi-dimensional convergence is**
> **taking place each time we declare**
> **"The days of Heaven on Earth!"**

This is a powerful tool in the hands of kingdom citizens! Imagine knowing what your heavenly destiny looks like and being able to virtually "call it down" to Earth just as God did in Rev. 21:10 when He caused New Jerusalem to descend to Earth covered with the glory of God! It's exciting to know that we don't have to reinvent the wheel! His plans are already in place in the **"Dominion Dimension!"**

THE DOMINION DIMENSION

"...Thy kingdom come. Thy will be done, AS IN HEAVEN, SO IN EARTH."

(Luke 11:2, KJV, emphasis added)

I intentionally used the King James Version of the text in Luke because it mentions heaven before earth. In the other Gospels it is written *"On earth, as it is in heaven."* I want to share more powerful revelations about the days of heaven appearing on Earth and about a decree that we can make to accelerate the shift. Heaven is mentioned first because heaven, where God dwells and where His will originates within Him, and where everything He created has its origins, is the original pattern and template for Earth. The kingdom "comes" to Earth from heaven, or it's overlaid or superimposed onto Earth.

In the text shown below, I intentionally chose the Jubilee Translation of the Bible because it uses the phrase, *"The days of heaven on earth."* Again, heaven is mentioned first. This is what I call... the **Dominion Dimension** – the place where the authority of Heaven is realized and released on planet Earth. It's a realm that recognizes our dual citizenship and doesn't treat us as *"visitors or violators."* heaven doesn't turn its nose up at us but treats us as residents with authorization to operate from the throne of Jesus Christ; neither does the Earth reject our authority because it realizes that we were born here and have a right to steward the planet.

"THE EYES OF THE LORD ARE ALWAYS UPON IT, [the land] FROM THE BEGINNING OF THE YEAR EVEN UNTO THE END OF THE YEAR."

(Deut. 11: 12 (b), JUB, emphasis added)

> **We exercise authority in heaven and in Earth because we are residents of "The Dominion Dimension!"**

The Lord made a promise to keep His eyes on the land of His people, from the beginning of the year to the end of it. God will never take His eyes off of us or the things He has promised us. He preserves both to the fulfillment of His purposes. The word **"Year"** comes from the Hebrew term **"Shanah,"** meaning: Duplicate or transmute. **Transmute** means: To change in form, alter, adapt, metamorph or translate. It's the period of time when God is taking His heavenly ideas and translocating them onto the Earth realm so it begins to look like heaven in terms of the fulfillment of purpose in His people. It doesn't mean that the streets will turn to gold or that we'll have wings, harps and halos. It simply means that God's original design for us, which He originated in His heart, will now have the opportunity to manifest in us, with **NO loss of transmission, translation, transition, transformation,** and eventually – **transmutation.**

§ **Transmission** – God generates His Word to mankind

§ **Translation** – The plans are received by mankind with no misinterpretation or variation

§ **Transition** – The process of shifting to "dual citizenship" is realized

§ **Transformation** – The end results will be according to God's original design

§ **Transmutation** – The will of God is done "As in heaven, so in Earth."

The "days of heaven on earth" are part of the focused and watchful attention that God is giving them for the entire year or "Shanah," or duplication period. He is watching from the beginning of "Shanah" (year) until the end of "Shanah" (year) or the beginning of the duplication period to the end of it. This is a parallel concept to *"alpha and omega, the beginning and the ending, the first and the last."* And, consequently, He won't stop until "His kingdom comes, and His will is done, as in heaven, so in earth!" We are to become, on earth, who we are in heaven! (Rev. 22:13)

THE "SHANAH SHIFT" – WHEN KINGS AND KINGDOMS COME!

"...Thy kingdom come. Thy will be done, as in heaven, so in earth."

(Luke 11:2, KJV)

The **"Shanah Shift"** has already begun! The transition process is underway for you even as you read this book. Your mentality is changing and when that happens, your mentality becomes your reality! This is not simply an opportunity... it's an assignment from the Lord Jesus Himself. It is impossible for the "kingdom" to come without also releasing corresponding kings to rule and reign in their respective spheres, territories or places of assignment. The coming of kings and kingdoms is exactly how the will of God will be done on the Earth. It's a divinely sequential process of events.

"And I appoint unto you a kingdom, as my Father hath appointed unto me."

(Luke 22:29, KJV)

The word **Appoint: "Diatithemai"** (Greek) is composed of the words – **Dia**: A channel, through, or by occasion; and **"Tithemi" (also Theo)**, meaning: To place in a passive or horizontal position. When you are first "appointed" by God you may appear to be asleep and not very noticeable! You may feel "undiscovered and unnecessary or feel that your dreams and visions are not finding fulfillment. But, when the appointed time comes, God gives a "resurrection" or rise to your assignment. He'll call the "rivers of living water," the power of the Holy Spirit, to begin rising and rushing forth out of your being.

"He that believeth on me, as the scripture hath said, out of his belly shall flow rivers of living water. (But this spake he of the Spirit, which

they that believe on him should receive: for the Holy Ghost was not yet given; because that Jesus was not yet glorified.)

(John 7:38-39, KJV)

The mighty waters of the kingdom of God are being called up and out of us by the Word of the Lord. The text below is a type and shadow of supernatural kingdom waters rising up in the believer. It should be noted once again that the "north" represents the kingdom of God (Ps. 48:2). Just as a compass aligns its needle with the magnetic "north" within the Earth's atmosphere, we align with the power of the kingdom to bring supernatural shifts within the spheres of influence on the Earth.

"The word of the Lord that came to Jeremiah the prophet against the Philistines, before that Pharaoh smote Gaza. Thus saith the Lord; Behold, waters rise up out of the north, and shall be an overflowing flood, and shall overflow the land, and all that is therein; the city, and them that dwell therein..."

(Jer. 47:1-2, KJV)

"And the waters returned, and covered the chariots, and the horsemen, and all the host of Pharaoh that came into the sea after them; there remained not so much as one of them."

(Ex. 14:28, KJV)

"The voice of the Lord is upon the waters: the God of glory thundereth: the Lord is upon many waters."

(Ps. 29:3, KJV)

It is the strategic plan of God to shift the posture and influence of despotic, demonic, unequipped, unrighteous or inflexible kings and begin to call forth the realignment of proper governing and ruling forces on this planet. God changes the times and seasons and reveals them to us so that we can stand in agreement with corresponding actions. We'll see the physical manifestation of these changes as the Body of Christ understands whose "right it is" (Ezek. 21:27) to sit on thrones. The release of "living waters" will supernaturally shift the "player roster" of influential people.

"Daniel answered and said, Blessed be the name of God for ever and ever: for wisdom and might are his: And he changeth the times and the seasons: he removeth kings, and setteth up kings: he giveth wisdom to the wise, and knowledge to them that know understanding. He revealeth the deep and secret things: he knoweth what is in the darkness, and the light dwelleth with him."

(Dan. 2:20-22, KJV)

WHEN HEAVEN SPEAKS...

A supernatural phenomenon took place in the upper room on the day of Pentecost. The people were gathered there at the command of Jesus who told them to wait there for the promise of the Father to be manifested.

"When the Day of Pentecost had fully come, they were all with one accord in one place. And suddenly there came a SOUND FROM HEAVEN, as of a rushing mighty wind, and it filled the house where they were sitting. Then there appeared to them divided tongues, as of fire, and one sat upon each of them. And they were all filled with the Holy Spirit and began to speak with other tongues, as the Spirit gave them utterance."

(Acts 2:1-4, NKJV, emphasis added)

143

The word **"Sound"** comes from the Greek term **"Echos,"** from which we get our word **"Echo,"** which means: A repetition of a sound caused by a reflection of sound waves. The supernaturally inspired language of "kings" on the Earth "reflects" the sovereign design of God's purposes. "The days of Heaven on Earth" represents that fact that we speak from the original design and architecture of God for this planet. We don't have to "reinvent the wheel," neither do we "make up the script along the way."

"Therefore settle it in your hearts not to meditate beforehand on what you will answer; for I WILL GIVE YOU A MOUTH AND WISDOM WHICH ALL YOUR ADVERSARIES WILL NOT BE ABLE TO CONTRADICT OR RESIST."

(Luke 21:14-15, NKJV, emphasis added)

MIRACLE MATHEMATICS

God instructed His people to keep His laws visible before their eyes so they could learn His ways. He promised that if they kept His laws, He would **multiply their days as the days of heaven on earth.** Today, we are not under the laws of that time, but we are subject to "spiritual laws" that affect atmospheres and produce kingdom-level results. If we stay conscious of them we can shift spiritual climates! The word **"Multiply"** is from the Hebrew term **"Rabah,"** which means: To increase, make abundant, BRING UP, and yield. This means that God **"brings up"** the earth to heaven's level, which is the same as bringing heaven down to earth's level and the results are multiplied and increased. We need to be conscious of seeking for wisdom in how to effectively execute the plans of heaven on earth. Some people tend to get "religious" or overly spiritual in things and have no practical process for walking out a spiritual plan. There's an old expression about people who are *"so heavenly minded that they are no earthly good!"*

Jesus set this pattern in motion with the disciples in **Luke 11:2 KJV** when he said, *"And when ye pray, say, Our father which art in heaven, Hallowed be thy name. Thy kingdom come. Thy will be done, AS IN HEAVEN, SO IN EARTH"* (emphasis Added). The kingdom of God has come to Earth from heaven and it brings the will of God with it. The kingdom of God is sovereign, as most earthly kingdoms are in their own rights, but the kingdom of God is the first true sovereign kingdom in existence. **The will of the king manifests wherever his sovereignty exists.** It's a natural order for the will of the king to be revealed after his kingdom shows up!

"Divine Duplication" is a powerful principle of sovereignty. This powerful truth is available to us as a practice and not just a promise and a principle! Part of the new glory on ground level experience will come through a change in perspective. God is the Father of glory and He's removing the *"Ichabod Issues"* from us. The word "Ichabod" means that the glory of God has departed from God's people. This is the sad state of affairs that the Prophet Ezekiel spoke of in his writings. When Ichabod is removed, new glory comes in. Fresh vision and revelation come through a renewal of glory in our minds.

"And ask the God of our Lord Jesus Christ, the glorious Father, to give you the Spirit, who will make you wise and reveal God to you, so that you will know him. I ask that your minds may be opened to see his light, so that you will know what is the hope to which he has called you, how rich are the wonderful blessings he promises his people, and how very great is his power at work in us who believe. This power working in us is the same as the mighty strength he used when he raised Christ from death and seated him at his right side in the heavenly world. Christ rules there above all heavenly rulers, authorities, powers and

lords; he has a title superior to all titles of authority in this world and in the next. "

(Eph. 1:17-21, GNB)

"Glory" appears to be one of the transforming agents in this text. The glory of God gives us illumination and revelation and the glory of our inheritance reveals the richness of His resources and power toward us. The word **"Glory"** is from the Greek term **"Doxa,"** meaning: Light or something very apparent. If something becomes very apparent, it is easier to understand and apply. God wants us aware of what our assignments are and of the rights and privileges that we, as kingdom citizens and sons and daughters of God, possess. Here is a list of "Glorified Gifts" that come from the light...

- The spirit of wisdom and revelation in the knowledge of Him
- Enlightened understanding
- Enhanced hope of success in the assignment
- Increased awareness of the inheritance
- Awareness of increased power
- Awareness of the posture and position of Christ and His church

The presence of light not only increases our awareness of our privileges but there's an "Image Enhancement" program built into it! Everyone uses mirrors. Mirrors are important to everyday life in some way or another. Even if you aren't very vain and spend half of your day in front of a mirror, they are still essential to life. You can't safely operate a motor vehicle without them. They are important for maneuvering and positioning your vehicle and for discovering that someone may be approaching your car too closely! But, as wonderful as mirrors are, they are virtually useless without one important thing... **light!** No mirror can work without light. In our kingdom life we need **"light and mirrors"** to completely see what God wants us to become. This is the only way to experience the kingdom-level image enhancement that God desires for us.

"But we all, with open face, [eyes] beholding as in a glass [mirror] the glory of the Lord, ARE CHANGED INTO THE SAME IMAGE FROM GLORY TO GLORY, even as by the Spirit of the Lord."

(2 Cor. 3:18, KJV, emphasis added)

Glory is the "DNA" of God. It contains all that He is and all that He knows.

This is why we have to be exposed to His glory. When we face the glory and spend quality time in it, we are transformed into the same image as Christ. With each level of exposure we experience, another facet of God and the Christ nature is superimposed over us. The Spirit of the Lord brings this miraculous event into play. Being changed into "the same image" means quite a bit. We are not masquerading as "little gods" in the earth or spiritual "wannabes." As human beings we are already made in His image and likeness, making us the most advanced life form on this planet.

In fact, one of Jesus' prime missions was to reconcile us back to God so we can resume our place as the custodians of planet Earth, just as Adam had been assigned in the Garden of Eden. We have been restored to prominence as kingdom citizens and we carry a royal heritage as "sons of God." It is the image of the "Son of God" Jesus Christ, and our transformation into His body that makes us eligible to **"manifest His majesty on the Seven Mountains of Culture."** When Jesus walked the

147

Earth He was an example of *"glory on ground level."* The template that Jesus followed is found below.

"Believe me when I say that I am in the Father and the Father is in me. If not, believe because of the things I do. I am telling you the truth: those who believe in me will do what I do – yes, they will do even greater things, because I am going to the Father. And I will do whatever you ask in my name, so that the Father's glory will be shown through the Son. If you ask for anything in my name, I will do it."

(John 14:11-14, GNB)

WORKING THE "DAY" SHIFT

"I must work the works of him that sent me, while it is day: the night cometh, when no man can work. As long as I am in the world, I am the light of the world."

(John 9:4-5, KJV)

It's a new **"Day!"** As kingdom citizens, we have a lot of work to do, and we have to clearly discern the times and seasons of *"assignment."* We can't afford to mistake an *"opportunity"* for an *"assignment."* When opportunity knocks, it may not be God at the door! We can't let our desperation to succeed in life summon us into a tangled web of ambition and desire only to "outrun" the sovereignty and foreknowledge of God in the process. We must keep pace with the plans of God and remain in the *"light."* This powerful season of the restoration of thrones is highly dependent on how well we utilize the light of God's revelation, guidance and knowledge. Light and enlightenment cannot be over emphasized.

Night-time is a period that is void of sunlight and is called "darkness." The Lord uses the absence of the earthly *"sun"* to give a representation of the difficulty of working without light, which is vitally important to life. Likewise the absence of the heavenly *"Son"* causes difficulty in accomplishing the work of the Lord on Earth. There isn't a person reading this book that doesn't understand the difficulty of working without light. Our military forces have understood the difficulty of fighting battles at "night" and have developed ways to get around in the dark using night vision goggles and other devices. If we're in dark environments, either naturally or spiritually, we need the best technology available to overcome the darkness. We have a supernatural spiritual technology of light and enlightenment through Jesus Christ.

"We have also a more sure word of prophecy; whereunto ye take heed, AS UNTO A LIGHT THAT SHINETH IN A DARK PLACE, UNTIL THE DAY DAWN, AND THE DAYSTAR ARISE IN YOUR HEARTS."

(2 Pet. 1:19, KJV, emphasis added)

Christ, also known as the **"Daystar,"** dawns in our hearts and we are aware of much more of God's intent and plans for us. The term "daystar" actually refers to the star of the day, known as the "sun" which gives us daylight. Its preeminence is so great that no other star can be seen in the daylight hours except the sun. Likewise, no other source of light is greater than the Son of God. In the beginning of this chapter, we quoted Deut. 11:20-21 in which the people were instructed to write the words of the Lord on their doorposts and on their gates, to give them a constant experience of enlightenment through God's Word.

True kingdom conversions can never be fully accomplished without the Word of the Lord or without proper light and revelation. **John 1:1, 5** says, *"In the beginning was the Word, and the Word was with God and the Word was God... And the light shineth in darkness; and the darkness comprehended it not."* This text describes Jesus Christ Himself as both the Word of God and the Light, so the technology of empowerment through enlightenment has remained constant over time from Deuteronomy until the writing of the Gospel of John. We simply have a greater revelation of it today.

Another significant point in unpacking the mystery of the days of heaven on Earth is to examine how **"Days"** are defined in Deut. 11:20-21. This word comes from the Hebrew term **"Yowm,"** meaning: The hot part of the day, the time between sunrise and sunset, are the daylight hours which is the time of the greatest amount of visible light. Many New Testament texts relating to light or to "Glory" use the Greek term **"Doxa,"** meaning: **Very apparent.** This also relates to the term **"Dokeo,"** meaning: **To think.** This is why we need ever increasing levels of God's glory in our lives. Our thinking or understanding is directly related to how much light we experience in our relationship with God. The enlightenment of our minds is a very important aspect to spiritual awakening and the discovery of new revelations. It is difficult to "work" in a season of darkness, obscurity and befuddlement attempting to solve the problems of life. The "day" of the Lord is a time of great enlightenment and fresh focus.

> **"Heaven on Earth" is not a state of Euphoria,**
> **but a state of governance and awareness on how**
> **to apply the power of God to this planet.**

RELEASING A RENAISSANCE

The *"days of heaven on earth"* don't come because flowers begin to bloom in the middle of asphalt roadways or pretty birds begin to come to our windowsills to sing beautiful songs. Heaven on earth is a new state of enlightenment, where we begin to think and see like God! These are the times of our greatest enlightenment and wisdom and the greatest times of discovery ever experienced by man. This is indeed a **"Renaissance"** period that we are in! That word is very important to me because there is a story behind it. I'll never forget when I went to Phoenix, Arizona in September of 2012 to conduct a crusade and perform the wedding ceremony for my covenant brother, Dr. Francis Myles and his wife. God told me days before the trip that I was to minister on the word "Renaissance," which was part of a teaching series that I had been doing in Chicago a few months earlier. I didn't tell Dr. Myles what my message would be, but when I arrived, Dr. Myles took me to the *"Renaissance Hotel,"* believe or not!

When I arrived to minister in the service, I presented the "Renaissance" message and Dr. Myles' wife was ecstatic! She said, "Dr. Bradshaw, for months God has been showing me the numbers "909" and I wasn't sure what it was for until today. The "Renaissance" message is for us! Today is the 9th day of the 9th month! It's 9- 09! After that day the church and leaders began to experience a surge in supernatural power. It was truly a renaissance for them! It's a time of new discoveries and inventiveness for all of us now. It's a time of fresh creativity and supernatural encounters! These are the times where we can get the most **"work"** done for the transition of the kingdoms of this world into the Kingdoms of our Lord and Christ.

> **The eyes of our understanding are wide open according to Eph. 1:17-19. We can see more than we've ever seen before!**

"...I remember you in my prayers and ask the God of our Lord Jesus Christ, the glorious Father, to give you the Spirit, who will make you wise and reveal God to you, so that you will know him. I ask that your minds may be opened to see his light, so that you will know what is the hope to which he has called you, how rich are the wonderful blessings he promises his people, and how very great is his power at work in us who believe..."

(Eph. 1:16-19, GNB)

Light gives us an understanding of how to apply the power of God that is in us as the text above shows us. The spirit of wisdom and revelation in the knowledge of Christ is essential to become bold and courageous enough to confront challenges. If the eyes of our understanding are enlightened, we go on to know the realistic expectations of our calling and the richness of our inheritance. Our inheritance is fully saturated with the glory or light of God. Light and glory share the same spiritual DNA. Often, when you find one, you will find the other.

CASE STUDY – BROKEN BUT BLESSED

One day I was thinking deeply, pondering the process of how believers forge ahead toward our destiny and purpose, walking by faith and not by sight, and often, not seeing things materialize the way we wanted. I thought about the sometimes, "fragmented" inventory of experiences that people have, with many of them wondering if any of the pieces will ever fit together. I was standing near a demolition site looking at the twisted metal, dust and fragments, and was amazed at the damage, and wondered how it all could have fitted together at one time. I heard the Lord ask, *"Can these pieces of glass, metal, brick and dust come together after being wrecked like this?"* I replied like the prophet Ezekiel when God asked him if the bones in the dry valley could live again! I said, "Only you know the answer to that one, Lord." He replied, *"Yes, I do. Now watch this."*

Suddenly I had a vision of what looked like reverse video footage of the dust, fragments, brick and metal begin to reform into the shape of the original building. God said, *"I know where everything is... every single particle, of every single piece of this building. I never lose track of anything, and I keep track of every part of your lives even when things seem disconnected or lost or victory is out of your line of sight!"* I was astonished because the principle was so simple. God is eternal and nothing escapes His eyesight or divine oversight. He reminded me that life is that way when it comes to our assignments. We receive promises from heaven and we often feel so far away from heaven, here on earth and we sometimes feel like things are not coming together. But God hasn't misplaced one single particle of destiny and purpose. He still "remembers" what "the original plan looks like" and He hasn't lost track of anything. And to that, we decree... **"Shanah!"**

OUR DUAL CITIZENSHIP

We have dual citizenship in the sense that we are citizens of both heaven and Earth simultaneously, meaning we are coexistent in both dimensions or locations. In the spirit we are citizens of heaven, according to Phil. 3:20 and in our mortal bodies we are citizens of one or more nations on planet Earth. What this means is that the realm of heaven is available to us on a daily basis, not just after we die in a physical sense in the flesh. Our passport is the passover blood of the Lamb of God, Jesus.

Ecclesiastes 3:11 (NIV) states: *"He has also set eternity in the human heart; yet no one can fathom what God has done from beginning to end."* The NLT says: *"He has planted eternity in the human heart, but even so, people cannot see the whole scope of God's work from beginning to end."*

As Dr. Bruce Cook has noted so eloquently in his Foreword, "We see the Lord constantly before us and at our right hand when we are seated with Him in heavenly places. That can only happen when our spirit rules our flesh, and not the other way around, so there is a price we must pay to follow Jesus and be His disciples, and to access our throne. We must be willing to take up our cross daily and to die daily, as the Scriptures teach, exhort and admonish us. Jesus must become Lord of our lives in every area, and not just our Savior. This is part of what it means to rule and reign with Christ, not just in the age to come, in the sweet by and by, but also in the here and now, in the nitty gritty of life on planet Earth."

MY DECREE

I am a kingdom citizen of heaven and Earth. I live in both places equally well. My dual citizenship is a help and not a hindrance. I am not confused about my identity. The heavens work on my behalf and I walk in authority in the Earth. People, place and things are lined up to meet me and I will contribute to the progress of this planet. I will not strive unlawfully for the prize. What God has ordained for me is mine. I will be faithful to the purpose that God has ordered for my life. The foreknowledge of God has set my course. I will walk in agreement with God and with my destiny and purpose!

I will conduct my life with honor, integrity and civility toward all. I will seek wisdom daily according to James 1:5. I decree "Shanah" over people, places and things in my life. The spirit of Babylon is defeated and I will triumph over that spirit in every area of my assignment! I am the battle-axe of God and I am mighty in His hand! I am victorious in heaven and in Earth! Earth looks like heaven more each day! I decree "Shanah!"

I SEE *Thrones*!

FOREKNOWLEDGE
- THE FRAMEWORK
OF FAITH

"And we know that all things work together for good to them that love
God, to them who are the called according to his purpose. For whom
he did foreknow, he also did predestinate to be conformed to the image
of his Son, that he might be the firstborn among many brethren."

(Rom. 8:28-29, KJV)

Foreknowledge is the framework of faith toward God. His
foreknowledge is what creates and places all things in order. The
term **"Foreknowledge"** comes from the Greek word **"Proginosko,"**
meaning: To know beforehand. We are able to claim great victories
through our understanding of God's foreknowledge, which is
His predetermined and predestinated purposes for us. The term
"Predestinate," comes from the Greek word **"Proorizo,"** meaning:
To limit in advance, look out for beforehand, predetermine, or ordain.

The foreknowledge of God provides patterns and templates for our lives and assignments. God, through the counsel of His own will, positions us for success. I'm not implying that God is using predestination to condemn anyone to hell or to choose them to go to heaven in an arbitrary fashion. He gives every human being a free moral choice to receive or reject Him. However, God applies a considerable amount of influence to help us arrive at our destinations.

"Through faith we understand that the WORLDS WERE FRAMED BY THE WORD OF GOD, so that things which are seen were not made of things which do appear."

(Heb. 11:3, KJV, emphasis added)

The worlds were framed by the word of God! The term **"Worlds,"** which comes from the Greek work **"Aion,"** means: Perpetuity, the age, the beginning and ending, eternity and course. Everything in creation was formed by the eternal and sovereign intelligence of God and has a DNA pattern and a predetermined design and function. In essence, "worlds" are the eternal patterns by which everything exists. The word **"Framed"** comes from the Greek term **"Katartizo,"** meaning: To complete thoroughly, repair, adjust, restore, mend, perfect, and join together.

> **Nothing was created by God with an "open ended" assignment. Everything has an end design and purpose.**

Everything was created to bring forth, as God said to the Prophet Jeremiah, *"An expected end"* (Jer. 29:11). When something has been "framed," it's in anticipation of an eventual finished product. Carpenters don't frame out a building and leave it abandoned. In many places, they aren't even allowed to legally begin the work of framing out a building unless the complete blueprints are drawn and are approved by the appropriate authorities who need to know what the end results will look like. Plans and blueprints are provided at the beginning of the project. Every measurement and configuration of the structure is taken into account beforehand. Likewise, mankind and the Earth are designed to operate in covenant and unity with one another and with God and He has invested enough in both to expect a return on His investment (ROI).

"If one of you is planning to build a tower, you sit down first and work out what it will cost, to see if you have enough money to finish the job. If you don't, you will not be able to finish the tower after laying the foundation; and all who see what happened will laugh at you."

(Luke 14:28-30, GNB)

"I alone know the plans I have for you, plans to bring you prosperity and not disaster, plans to bring about the future you hope for."

(Jer. 29:11, GNB)

God plans to:

- ℘ Complete the process of fulfilled destinies – Fully utilize the eternal purpose of each human life

- ℘ Repair our thinking – Abolish the old mental perspectives of limitation and dis-function

- ℘ Adjust our posture – Realign our self-image and adjust how we process the journey

ఴ Restore our authority and governance – Educate redeemed mankind to the king/priest identity

ఴ Mend the rift between the earth and mankind – Return the keys of authority over terra firma

ఴ Perfect man's positions of governance – Place each person in the assigned seat of power

ఴ Join heaven and earth together as one – Reclaim the "days of heaven on earth"

Foreknowledge of divine assignments helps us to better utilize resources and relationships along the way. It helps us to take inventory of what we presently look like and what our destiny-based image looks like. The two images must be reconciled. There are key things that believers can do to accelerate the process.

ఴ Learn what the Bible says about foreknowledge, predetermination and predestination

ఴ Apply the language of the scriptures in prayer, intercession and declaration

ఴ Receive prophetic support that emphasizes assignments

ఴ Give quality time to musing over destiny-based prophetic words

ఴ Study and prepare to act on the prophecies and texts about assignments

ఴ Develop healthy covenants with likeminded people who can give constructive support

ఴ Frequent environments that nourish the assignments and make self-development a priority

   ᔓ Exercise hunger and thirst for more enlightenment and wisdom from God

Heaven and Earth share a desire to bring the will of God to pass. Even when we don't realize it, there is a bridge between the two, with God and the angels standing ready to manifest the joint contract between them. When we don't have this revelation, we'll lack the confidence and assertiveness to step out into the assignment that God has given us. We don't want to be like Jacob, who didn't know he was in the right place and time to become a catalyst for change!

THE FOUNDATION OF FOREKNOWLEDGE

Faith is a very important aspect of our ability to ascend to thrones of assignment. Without a clear understanding of faith, it becomes easy to "believe" for things that are completely beyond the scope of assignment that God has for us, simply because they are "good ideas." Since our "thrones" are given strictly for the fulfillment of assignments, we cannot afford to just "take a seat" any and everywhere that opportunity knocks. There is a very distinct difference between opportunity and assignment and our faith has to be on target so we arrive in the right place at the right time.

We know that *"...Without faith it is impossible to please Him..."* We mustn't avoid the possibility that there is more to learn about it and we can benefit from broadening our perspective on faith and see the more powerful technologies hidden within it. What is faith, and what type of faith pleases God? What type of faith steers us into a more precise direction as it relates to assignments and thrones? Should we assume that God will grant answers simply because we believe that we're on track?

One of the more common Greek interpretations for **"Faith"** is the word **"Pistis,"** which means: The truthfulness of God, or simply, that which God knows or believes to be the truth. Using a few more definitions from Strong's Exhaustive Concordance, I will add, that faith is also the **credence, constancy and assurance** [of God's beliefs.] This describes what can safely be called **"the foreknowledge of God."** Every one of the Pauline epistles uses the Greek word **"Pistis"** to describe the kind of faith that God or Christ used in dealing with mankind in the exercise of providence and sovereignty. It is the kind of faith that we are encouraged to build.

"Foreknowledge" is the foundation and true framework of faith.

It is not enough to simply believe that "foreknowledge" is real. We need a real experiential connection with it, so it becomes a real-time technology that's a part of our life's journey. It's available to change how we walk out our assignments and destinies and it's there to bring us into **"agreement"** with God. It creates the kind of faith that pleases God. A faith that *"pleases"* God is defined as **"Euaresteo"** in Greek, meaning: To gratify entirely. This is related to the Greek term **"Euarestos"** which means: To be fully agreeable. To be fully agreeable with God we must believe that "He is," meaning that He is the sovereign, unlimited source of all intelligence and order in the universe, the originator of all good things and what He believes is the template for all other positive belief systems.

It brings us into agreement with God, which is essential for knowing and applying the will of God to our lives. **"Can two walk together except they be agreed?"** Amos 3:3, to which I add, **"Can two agree, except**

they walk together?" What we agree with sets the tone for whether or not we can actually expect results. When we agree together with one another for something that we are praying about, it doesn't necessarily mean that we'll get the answers we desire, unless we are in line with God's ordained purposes. Foreknowledge reinforces the probability of being in agreement with God.

FACTS ABOUT FOREKNOWLEDGE

- Foreknowledge is as supernatural as healing and other signs and wonders because it originates from the substance of God's sovereign mind and purposes. His sovereignty is what created everything and keeps the supernatural patterns of creation in order.

- It contains immeasurable levels of truth, supernatural intelligence, creativity, providence, wisdom, love and commitment to divine purpose. It is relevant to every believer and not just those who are seeking the "deeper" things of God. Foreknowledge should be one of the most basic principles that we use in our walk with God.

- It is eternal but God introduces it to us in "segments" that are relative to our assignments and purposes according to natural time frames.

"For I know the thoughts that I think toward you, says the Lord, thoughts of peace and not of evil, to give you a future and a hope. Then you will call upon Me and go and pray to Me, and I will listen to you. And you will seek Me and find Me, when you search for me with all your heart."

(Jer. 29:11-13, NKJV)

"**Machashebeth,**" or "thoughts/plans" is a Hebrew word that means: Imagination, invented, means, purpose, or thought. It also means: A plan, texture, and cunning. The thoughts of God contain a perfectly-devised overview of life and everything in creation, both visible and invisible. The heavenly throne room, or *"mind of the Lord"* is where all things originate. The **"Mind"** of the Lord is **"Kowe"** in Greek, which means: To hold together, a cup [as a container] (1 Cor. 2:16). This *"container"* is the framework of divine order. Notice how the text suggests that knowing God's "thoughts" increases our accuracy in prayer. "**Then** you will call upon me... and I will listen to you."

After we have repeated God's divine plan back to Him in prayer, we are assured of a positive response! This all happens because of foreknowledge.

This is why the prophetic ministry is vital to the advancement of the kingdom, and for possession of the Seven Mountains of Culture. It's not just for personal life issues but for the "bigger picture." The "expected end" that we look forward to, is the divine design that He planned for us to walk in – a design of victory and strength and of abundant life and success.

FINDING FOREKNOWLEDGE

Foreknowledge is found in a place that directly relates to thrones and divine governance. It's found in the **GLORY** of God! In scripture, and in historical literature, kings and queens are described as having a sense of glory and majesty that is depicted by precious stones, royal robes, precious metals and the splendor and regalia of the palace and its ceremonialism. Even today, governmental figures, corporate leaders, entertainers, sports heroes and other key figures of the Seven Mountain Culture carry a high level of prestige, recognition and prominence in their lives. The "glory" of their positions is evident in a number of ways and influences people, places and things in their respective industries.

As kings and priests we also have a **glory** attached to us. It carries enlightenment, knowledge and wisdom from the throne of the King of kings and Lord of lords. We have the **Glory of the Foreknowledge of God!** We are empowered to accelerate the conversion of kingdoms because we are becoming fully exposed to the glory of His foreknowledge!

"... From Jesus Christ, who is the faithful witness, and the first begotten of the dead, and the prince of the kings of the earth. Unto him that loved us, and washed us from our sins in his own blood, and hath made us kings and priests unto God and his father; to him be glory and dominion for ever and ever. Amen."

(Rev. 1:5-7, KJV)

But, when kings misbehave, God often deposes them and they lose their glory.

"But when his heart was lifted up, and his mind was hardened in pride, he was deposed from his kingly throne, and they took his glory from him."

(Dan. 5:20, KJV)

> The glory of God is not a "novelty" experience used to impress people with our gifting and popularity. It is a kingdom technology that reveals the sovereign presence of the Lord.

According to Prov. 25:2-3, **"Kings"** should have a proclivity and sensitivity toward the hidden wisdom of God. Secrets are hidden inside of the glory of the Lord, but kings have the ability to draw it out for the good of the kingdom.

"We honor God for what he conceals; we honor kings for what they explain. You never know what a king is thinking; his thoughts are beyond us, like the heights of the sky or the depths of the ocean."

(Prov. 25:2-3, GNB)

"It is the glory of God to conceal a thing, but the glory of kings to search out a thing. As the heavens for height and the earth for depth, so the hearts and minds of kings are unsearchable."

(Prov. 25:2-3, AMP)

Since we are now kings and priests, the Glory of God begins to shine light upon things that were, beforehand, hidden from our view. We are able to ascertain **"the heights of the sky or the depths of the ocean!"** God has hidden many things from mankind in general, but He doesn't hide them from kings! God intentionally hid solutions and answers to weighty matters from people who are not "kings," but we are kings and are given to know these things! Imagine knowing that there are people all over the globe who are working like crazy to figure out the solutions to problems in the world and we serve the infinite, sovereign Creator of all things who already knows the answers! They travail and they labor continuously! But, God has planted a solution within the hearts of His people that can only be unlocked by **"KINGS!"** **"No man"** can find out the work that God made from the beginning to the end of eternity unless he or she becomes a king, who serves the ultimate King of kings! (Eccl. 3:11). **Only kings have the keys to the eternal foreknowledge of God.**

A STAIRWAY TO HEAVEN

God chose the patriarch Jacob to become the forerunner of His holy nation. But, Jacob was totally unaware of "who and where" he was. He didn't realize that heaven and earth were already connected to manifest his destiny.

"At sunset he came to a holy place and camped there. He lay down to sleep, resting his head on a stone. He dreamt that he saw a stairway reaching from earth to heaven, with angels going up and down on it. And there was the Lord standing beside him. 'I am the Lord, the God of Abraham and Isaac,' he said. 'I will give to you and to your descendants this land on which you are laying. They will be as numerous as the specks of dust on the earth. They will extend their territory in all directions, and through your descendants I will bless all the nations. Remember, I will be with you and protect you wherever you go, and I will bring you back to this land. I will not leave you until I have done all that I have promised you.' Jacob woke up and said, 'The Lord is here! He is in this place, and I didn't know it!' He was afraid and said, 'What a terrifying place this is! It must be the house of God; it must be the gate that opens into heaven.'"

(Gen. 28:11-17, GNB)

Jacob finally realized that he was in the "House of God" and at the "Gate of heaven!" God introduced Jacob to His foreknowledge and told him the plan that was to make him a part of Israel's legacy and history and promised to bring all of it to pass with a sovereign vow. By hearing the plan of God's foreknowledge, Jacob had an expectation of how to process his walk with God. I'm sure he began to have faith for the plan to unfold. This knowledge changed everything for Jacob, even as it does for us today when we receive strong prophetic words about our destinies, assignments and purpose. Jacob literally experienced "heaven on Earth" when he saw God standing at the top of the stairway, and the angels of the Lord traversing between two dimensions.

A NEW "FRAME" OF MIND

"Through faith we understand that the worlds were FRAMED by the word of God, so that things which are seen were not made of things which do appear."

(Heb. 11:3, KJV, emphasis added)

Through the type of faith that foreknowledge provides, we understand that the worlds were framed by the Word of God. The word **"Framed"** is very important to the idea of sovereign knowledge, plans, providence, foreknowledge, creativity, predestination and purpose. It comes from the Greek term **"Katargeo,"** which is actually a compound word from **"Kata,"** meaning: Pertaining to place or time, and **"Argeo,"** meaning: To be idle [still]. In other words, God keeps things still, properly formed, arranged and in place, according to His divine timing and will. How then, how do things become chaotic and out of place?

The opportunity for disruption emerges when demonic forces converge with the free will and fallen nature of unregenerate individuals. Together, they corrupt atmospheres, usurp authority, disrupt order and serve as vehicles for the darkness that opposes God's authority in mankind. Ambition, lust, greed, fear, pride, seduction, weakness, anxiety, doubt, lack of knowledge, and other works of the flesh and unregenerate human soul contribute to the unbalanced decisions of mankind. Demonic interference disrupts the affairs of mankind and makes people insensitive to the will and purpose of God. God is more than willing to supply us with wisdom and directions on how to fulfill His ultimate plans for our destinies. We are instruments in His hands and His desire is to make us successful at what we are called to do.

"And be not conformed to this world: but be ye transformed by the renewing of your mind, that ye may prove what is that good, and acceptable, and perfect will of God."

(Rom. 12:2, KJV)

A WEED IN THE WORKS

"Yet I had planted thee a noble vine, wholly a right seed: how then art thou turned into the degenerate plant of a strange vine unto me?"

(Jer. 2:21, KJV)

The plan is perfect and lacks nothing in the mind of God. Everything and everyone is a pure "original." But once sin is introduced, the nature begins to change. Things begin to degenerate or de -**"gene"**- erate, meaning the original **"gene"** or seed and creative design of God is taking a back seat to the "bootleg" version introduced by the adversary. When we degenerate, we take on a different identity than the one God created for us. We become a *"strange vine"* to God. God's question is, **"How did this happen?"**

God deals with everything from the perspective of being the "Creator" who takes custodial responsibility for creation. He provides an orderly context and pattern for the universe, ensuring that spiritual and natural laws are put in place to structure and "govern" creation. He reminds us in the text above that He has NOT forgotten His original intent.

"The Lord said to me, 'I chose you before I gave you life, and before you were born I selected you to be a prophet to the nations.' I answered, 'Sovereign Lord, I don't know how to speak; I am too young.' But the Lord said to me, 'Do not say that you are too young, but go to the people I send you to, and tell them everything I command you to say. Do not be afraid of them, for I will be with you to protect you. I, the Lord, have spoken!'"

(Jer. 1:4-8, GNB)

In speaking to the Prophet Jeremiah, God set a precedence on how destinies are formed. God's original plans are the "thoughts" that He had for Jeremiah before he was conceived. God introduces what He "thinks" to supersede thoughts that come to us from other places of influence. Thoughts generate in the mind and in the various levels of consciousness. There are many things that influence the mind, since it is a part of the soul. Our environments and demonically-engineered influences affect us through our souls, which contain the intellect, emotions, will, imagination and the content of our character.

Since man is a tri-partite being, he has a spirit and a body also, but the soul is the "leverage" or hinge-point between the spirit and the body and determines how a person processes information or other stimuli. If there is an unbalanced or unhealthy spiritual life, the soul will suffer by being influenced by the desires of the flesh and its entrapments. But, there is a way to *"spiritualize"* the mind and prepare it for making kingdom-level decisions. The thoughts of God are able to bathe the human mind in spirituality only if the believer submits to the process of refreshing and transformation. Having the foreknowledge of God helps us in this way.

The **renewing of the mind**, or **"Anakainosis"** (Greek) **is a renovation of the mind.**

"Do not conform yourselves to the standards of this world, but let God transform you inwardly by a complete change of your mind. Then you will be able to know the will of God – what is good and pleasing to him and is perfect."

(Rom. 12:2, GNB)

> **Transformation of our minds comes through saturation with the truth of God, until we become totally kingdom conscious with a new mentality. We are transformed by the renewing of our minds.**

The truth of God becomes a reality and we are able to *"prove the good, and acceptable, and perfect will of God."* Resistance to the truth is weakened and eventually disarmed when the mind of the Lord is present in us. We are reminded in the scriptures that having a renewed mind is essential to understanding and processing the thoughts of God in our lives:

&ero; *"…But we have the mind of Christ."* (1 Cor. 2:16, KJV)

&ero; *"And be renewed in the spirit of your mind."* (Eph. 4:23, KJV)

&ero; *"Let this mind be in you, which was also in Christ Jesus."* (Phil. 2:5, KJV)

Dr. Francis Myles has written an incredible book entitled, *"The Consciousness of Now – (The New Order of Wisdom) ...Living a Spirit Controlled Stress-Free Life in a Chaotic World."* It's an amazing book filled with wisdom on how to renew one's mind and begin to master the situations of life. It is a stark contrast to "new age" material because it totally invites Christ to be the master of one's spirit, soul and body. It's a must read!

Similarly, Dr. Gayle Rogers has written a seminal work titled *The Whole Soul: Rescripting Your Life for Personal Transformation* (Kingdom House Publishing, 2014). In it she teaches how to take control of your thoughts and change your life. I commend both of these excellent resources to you the reader.

"My thoughts, says the Lord, 'are not like yours, and my ways are different from yours. As the heavens are high above the earth, so high are my ways and thoughts above yours."

(Isa. 55:8-9, GNB)

Unrenewed minds have a difficult time processing higher heavenly thoughts, and developing the faith to walk out the process of seeing His will come to pass, so it's to our advantage to renew our minds as often as possible with the Word of God relating to "throne-room thoughts." It sharpens our discernment and it will be far easier then, to grasp the eternal patterns from heaven as we carry out our assignments on earth.

> **The "Throne Room" of God is where He generates supernatural commands, strategies and instructions to our "renewed minds."**

"A king who sits on the throne of judgment winnows out all evil [like chaff] with his eyes."

(Prov. 20:8, AMP)

THE POWER OF PROTOTYPES AND PATTERNS

"Those whom God had already chosen he also set apart to become like his Son, so that the Son would be the eldest brother in a large family. And so these whom God has set apart, he called; and those he called, he put right with himself, and he shared his glory with them."

(Rom. 8:29-30, GNB)

God's plan of predestination for us to become sons of God would be all but impossible if we had no heavenly prototype to bridge the divide between heaven and Earth. Jesus Christ became that "bridge" to make redemption a reality. Being **"Firstborn"** among many brethren says a lot about prototypes and patterns. It's from the Greek term **"Prototokos,"** which is a compound term. We get the English term **"Prototype"** from it. It comes from the word **"Protos,"** meaning: Foremost in time, place, order or importance, before, at the beginning and first of all; and **"Teko,"** meaning: To produce from a seed, a mother, a plant or the earth.

"This charge I commit to you, son Timothy, ACCORDING TO THE PROPHECIES PREVIOUSLY MADE CONCERNING YOU, THAT BY THEM YOU MAY WAR A GOOD WARFARE."

(1 Tim. 1:18, NKJV emphasis added)

Prophetic words are a part of the foreknowledge of God. When we receive accurate words from reliable sources, we can build courage and have a point of reference by which to defend ourselves and our assignments against the circumstances and lies of the enemy. Paul told Timothy to *"war a good warfare"* with the prophecies. Defend your place of victory by decreeing what the prophecies say and begin binding and loosing things accordingly. Prophecies are a pattern of God's will for us.

A great example of heavenly architecture as a pattern for earth is found in Heb. 8:5 GNB. When God instructed Moses to build the tabernacle, He didn't leave Moses to figure out what to do on his own. He took Moses to a high place on the mountain and exposed Moses to His glory. When Moses returned, his face was shining with the brightness of God's glory and he had instructions on how to build the tabernacle according to God's heavenly pattern. God gave Moses the principle of **"Divine Duplication."** He told Moses, *"Be sure to make everything according to the pattern you were shown on the mountain."* **Moses saw the patterns of the tabernacle on Mount Sinai, which is the forerunner of Mount Zion, the 8ᵀʰ Mountain.** As we maintain our **8ᵗʰ Mountain Mentality**, we will continue to see supernatural patterns that we'll present to the world as we reign on our thrones.

"Every High Priest is appointed to present offerings and animal sacrifices to God, and so our High Priest must also have something to offer. If he were on earth, he would not be a priest at all, since there are priests who offer the gifts required by Jewish Law. THE WORK THEY DO AS PRIESTS IS REALLY ONLY A COPY AND A SHADOW OF WHAT IS IN HEAVEN. It is the same as it was with Moses. When he was about to build the Sacred Tent, God said to him, 'BE SURE TO MAKE EVERYTHING ACCORDING TO THE PATTERN YOU WERE SHOWN ON THE MOUNTAIN.'"

(Heb. 8:3-5, GNB, emphasis added)

Here is Moses, the Hebrew child who was given up for adoption because of the harsh conditions of slavery and the genocidal edict of Pharaoh. The Egyptian king ordered all male babies to be slain because he feared that a "redeemer" was coming to free the Hebrew slaves. The baby was taken into the courts of Pharaoh to be raised as an Egyptian. He grew in fame and wealth as a member of the royal court, but that was not the sum of his destiny and purpose.

Indeed, he was the redeemer of Israel, as it had been prophesied, but he was to go through a process that would take him back to his people, Israel, then receive instructions from God on how to free them from bondage. We know the story. He frees them from Egypt and begins the journey to the promised-land. The text above shows an important time in his assignment when he was to bring *"heaven to earth."* When he constructed the tabernacle, God gave him instructions on how to mirror the images he saw in heavenly places so the people of God would have a pattern of heaven as their worshipping place.

By earthly standards, Moses was hardly priestly material. He was the most unlikely candidate to be a priest for God since his earthly experiences in Egypt as a member of the royal family were essentially pagan. He wasn't raised nor mentored by a priest and there was no priestly lineage for him to follow, after the order of his natural birth. **Moses' qualifications came from the destiny and assignment that God created.** Heaven's design trumps the disorder of Earth. God raised up Moses, and in spite of all of the drama of his life, made sure that he rose to his proper assignment. He received instructions directly from God. God infused Moses' thoughts with the pattern of heavenly designs so he could replicate on earth what he saw in "heaven."

The tabernacle was the place where God manifested Himself for Israel in those days, and today, we as believers are the tabernacle of God, the dwelling place of the Holy Spirit. Today, God reveals the patterns of how we should be "built" through revelation knowledge of His written and spoken prophetic words, and through relationships, experiences and sovereign activities.

GOD – BOTH COUNSELOR AND CUSTOMER

How does God untangle the mess caused by sin and the fall of mankind and still bring about good results? Many times when humans are faced with a challenge, we seek the advice of a person or organization that is skilled in solving the type of problems we are facing. In the case of the conflicts that exist within creation, God actually seeks counsel to solve problems too! He has a great counselor... **HIMSELF!** *"For I am the Lord, I change not..."* (Mal. 3:6, KJV). God is the only counselor that *"He"* trusts and the only one that *"He"* uses! He comes highly recommended by Himself to Himself! **Therefore, He is both Counselor and Customer throughout eternity!**

"For when God made promise to Abraham, BECAUSE HE COULD SWEAR BY NO GREATER, HE SWARE BY HIMSELF."

(Heb. 6:13, KJV, emphasis added).

He has to be His own counselor and customer for this reason... *"For who hath known the mind of the Lord, that he may instruct him?"* (1 Cor. 2:16, KJV). In other words, there is no higher intellect or power or sovereignty in existence above God, so He can't seek the counsel of anyone else. God becomes His own covenant partner in determining the outcome of conflicts through sovereign intent.

"For by him were all things created, that are in heaven, and that are in earth, visible and invisible, whether they be THRONES, or dominions, or principalities, or powers: ALL THINGS WERE CREATED BY

HIM AND FOR HIM: AND HE IS BEFORE ALL THINGS, AND BY HIM ALL THINGS CONSIST."

(Col. 1:16-17, KJV, emphasis Added)

"Our Lord and God! You are worthy to receive glory, honour, and power. For you created all things, and by your will they were given existence and life."

(Rev. 4:11, GNB)

In essence, everything is designed with God's pleasure in mind. What is the **pleasure** of God? It is defined as **"Thelema"** in the Greek language, meaning: Determination, choice, volition, purpose, decree, inclination and pleasure. In other words, God is completely driven by the supernatural intelligence that's within Him, an intelligence that is mostly beyond our ability to comprehend. But He's not a God who is hiding from His people and He wishes to share His knowledge with us. But we can only perceive and receive the greatness of His glory and power in measurements that we are able to absorb and apply to our daily lives. As we discover our true destinies, assignments and **"thrones"** in life, we'll be able to assert our rights as the legitimate occupants of those positions and we'll take advantage of the wonderful relationship that we share with our Father.

ALIGNMENT AND ALLOWANCES

I have attempted to be diligent in mapping out how the sovereignty of God, the substance of His foreknowledge and His counsel produce the destinies that believers walk in and ultimately fulfill. Needless to say, we all have questions about the *"possibilities and probabilities"* and the variances that happen when we make decisions outside of the will of God, or the adversary is allowed to gain ground without being apprehended and without being made to adhere to the mandates of *Prov.*

6:31 which says, *"But if he* [a thief] *be found, he shall restore sevenfold; he shall give all the substance of his house."* We must be careful to not allow guilt, condemnation, anxiety or regret to cloud our minds over things that happened in the past. We don't have the power to go back into our past to undo things, but we can be very encouraged and excited about the days to come, knowing that the foreknowledge of God and His sovereignty have factored in every event, leading to great fulfillment.

> *"From the beginning I predicted the outcome; long ago I foretold what would happen. I said that my plans would never fail, that I would do everything I intended to do."*
>
> *(Isa. 46:10, GNB)*

I have reason to believe in the power of an omnipotent, omnipresent and omniscient Father, who watches over His word to perform it. I don't believe that our destinies are so **"fragile"** as to be thrown completely off course by all of our issues of human frailty, and if so, even the shed blood of Christ was not enough to buy back our dominion in the earth or the value of our souls. On the contrary, the blood of Jesus Christ is more than enough to bring redemption to us, and in times of discouragement and despair we have to remember that the sovereignty of God is just that… **SOVEREIGN!** It supersedes the *"interruptions"* of satan, sin and self that often appear to derail our destinies!

I am not suggesting that we are allowed to live in sin with no regard for our actions and without concern for the consequences of them. Neither am I implying that we should avoid discipline, correction, self-control, self-improvement, consecration or dedication toward God. We owe ourselves and everyone whom we know, a better version of ourselves as we journey through life. I am simply saying, that we are redeemed to be able to **"finish"** what God began in us! Only God can truly judge each individual issue that troubles us or how each person reacts or responds to the circumstances they face in life. But, I will say that God is wise enough to judge things in a completely just manner. His decisions are final and I thank Him for that! He tempers His choices with mercy, love and kindness! Of course, we have to do our due diligence as part of the covenant of a kingdom relationship. If we *"love God"* and are *"the called according to His purpose"* and if we *"walk not after the flesh but after the spirit,"* we will be able to claim the truth of God and His evidence-driven faith as the substance of our destinies (Rom. 8:28).

"And so I am sure that God, who began this good work in you will carry it on until it is finished on the Day of Christ Jesus."

(Phil. 1:6, GNB)

GOD'S PREEMPTIVE STRATEGIES

I happen to believe that **"GPS"** is a great thing! Where would we be today without it. It's amazing that we found our way around before it was invented! **GPS** *(Global Positioning Satellite)* technology was invented in the heavens and put to use long before the invention of any electronic technology. Before sin interrupted the destiny of mankind, God knew where mankind was going and how many interruptions he would experience on the trip. God took everything into consideration and launched **"Godly Pre-emptive Strategies"** to disarm sin of its power over mankind! Just as Christ was *"the Lamb slain from the foundation of the world,"* and just as sin was *"interrupted"* in its course before Lucifer became Satan, God sees where everything is at all times in the course of eternity and makes provision for our victories through His foreknowledge.

Natural GPS systems work in our phones and automobiles through satellite technology, keeping track of our devices. If you program an address into the system, it will find the address, navigating you turn by turn in the proper direction. If you happen to miss a turn, the system will **NOT** discard the address and reply *"Oh well, you missed it!"* It will simply **re-configure** and **re-align** the patterns to compensate for the error! Before you know it, you'll be *"back on track"* and on your way. As long as you don't tamper with the **"ORIGINAL ADDRESS"** placed in the system when you began your journey, you won't be completely lost. It may take you longer to arrive and you may face traffic jams, obstacles and delays, but you will eventually arrive because reassessment, reassignment and realignment technology is built into the system!

> *"It shall come to pass that before they call, I will answer; and while they are still speaking, I will hear."*

(Isa. 65:24, NKJV)

CASE STUDY – FAITH THROUGH FOREKNOWLEDGE

> *"Then Jesus went to Nazareth, where he had been brought up, and on the Sabbath he went as usual to the synagogue. He stood up to read the Scriptures and was handed the book of the prophet Isaiah. He unrolled the scroll and found the place where it was written: 'The Spirit of the Lord is upon me, because he has chosen me to bring good news to the poor. He has sent me to proclaim liberty to the captives and recovery of sight to the blind; to set free the oppressed and announce that the time has come when the Lord will save his people.' Jesus rolled up the scroll, gave it back to the attendant, and sat down. All the people in the synagogue had their eyes fixed on him, as he said to them, 'This passage of scripture has come true today, as you heard it being read.'"*

(Luke 4:16-21, GNB)

The power of God's foreknowledge was truly demonstrated on that day! The fact that Jesus read a prophetic scripture, written hundreds of years earlier, about what He presently stood in the synagogue doing, was a powerful event. He made no attempt to convince the onlookers that He was the Messiah, the chosen one and the Savior of the world. He relied on the power of scriptures from the book of Isaiah, proving that the foreknowledge of God had already set events in motion for that historical moment. We can do the same with the written Word of God, prophetic words, dreams, visions and prophetic acts that reveal God's will and purpose in advance.

CASE STUDY – FOREKNOWLEDGE AND THE FUTURE

"One night Joseph had a dream, and when he told his brothers about it, they hated him even more. He said, 'Listen to the dream I had. We were all in the field tying up sheaves of wheat, when my sheaf got up and stood up straight. Yours formed a circle round mine and bowed down to it.' 'Do you think you are going to be a king and rule over us?' His brothers asked. So they hated him even more because of his dreams and because of what he said about them. Then Joseph had another dream and said to his brothers, 'I had another dream, in which I saw the sun, the moon, and eleven stars bowing down to me.' He also told the dream to his father, and his father scolded him: 'What kind of a dream is that? Do you think that your mother, your brothers, and I are going to come and bow down to you?' Joseph's brothers were jealous of him, but his father kept thinking about the whole matter."

(Gen. 37:5-11, GNB)

This was a prophetic dream about events that were still many years in the future and by which Joseph would come through many hardships and eventually become responsible for saving Egypt and other nations from famine through his prophetic dreams. By the time he saw his brothers again, he was a man of great power who lived in the palace of Pharaoh. His brothers had to come before him, not knowing who he really was, and would be forced to bow in honor before him, just as the dream predicted.

"Although Joseph recognized his brothers, they didn't recognize him. He remembered the dreams he had dreamt about them and said, 'You are spies; you have come to find out where our country is weak.' 'No, sir,' they answered. 'We have come as your slaves to buy food. We are all brothers. We are not spies, sir, we are honest men.'"

(Gen. 42:8-10, GNB)

As the account evolves, the brothers were in fear of their lives, knowing that this man possessed the power of the court of Pharaoh and could do with them as he pleased. He tricked them by asking them to bring their youngest brother to him to prove their honesty. They agreed, secretly knowing that their deceit had caught up with them after all these years and they grew remorseful. Because of the terrible hardships that Joseph faced in his life, I believe the dream served to encourage him and gave him hope, waiting for his day of redemption, not so much that his brothers would really bow to him, but for the fulfillment of God's ultimate purpose.

"Then his brothers came and bowed down before him. 'Here we are before as your slaves,' they said. But Joseph said to them, 'Don't be afraid; I can't put myself in the place of God. You plotted evil against me, but God turned it into good, in order to preserve the lives of many people who are alive today because of what happened. You have nothing to fear. I will take care of you and your children.' So he reassured them with kind words that touched their hearts."

(Gen. 50:18-21, GNB)

As the account ends, Joseph reveals his true identity to his brothers and reconciles with the family, sending them home with provisions for their journey. But, because he was providentially placed in Egypt, although it was through his brothers and their unrighteous deeds, God used his gift of interpreting dreams to reveal a plan to save Egypt from famine. All of these events were in the foreknowledge of God, who brought a valuable ending to the story.

MY DECREE

My God is sovereign, trustworthy and strong. There is no instability in Him. Because of this, I am poised and very purposeful in my walk of destiny. I have strong faith because I feast on the foreknowledge of God. I am not wandering in my beliefs. God created me as a noble vine and a right seed and I will not veer from the course that He has determined for me. This plan was created before I was formed in my mother's womb. Like Joseph, I will overcome obstacles and rise to the throne God has prepared and destined for me. I am valuable to myself and those around me. I have been created for this day and this assignment and I am victorious because God planned it all along. The foreknowledge of God has given me strength!

I SEE *Thrones*!

I SEE *Thrones!*

WHEN KINGS
GO TO WAR

"Or what king, going out to engage in conflict with another king, will not first sit down and consider and take counsel whether he is able with ten thousand [men] to meet him who comes against him with twenty thousand? And if he cannot [do so], when the other king is still a great way off, he sends an envoy and asks the terms of peace."

(Luke 14:31-32, AMP)

"So don't go to war without wise guidance; victory depends on having many advisers."

(Prov. 20:18, NLT)

I t is the nature of kings and kingdoms to search for other kingdoms and territories to subdue. Kings and their territories are highly exposed and constantly subject to invasions by other kings who want to enlarge their own realms. When kings go to war they assess and survey everything before them and they count the "cost" of invading another kingdom. If a king estimates that his resources are insufficient, he will take a more diplomatic approach to survival, and instead of attacking his enemy, he'll send an ambassador to reach terms of agreement with the opposing king. Prevailing through peace should always be our primary strategy in the kingdom of God since we have the government (Misrah) of Christ and *"Of the increase of his government and peace there shall be no end."*

Rom. 12:18, NIV, says, *"If it is possible, as far as it depends on you, live at peace with everyone."* The NAS translation says, *"So far as it depends on you, be at peace with all men."* We have great potential for gaining victory through godly and peaceful influences. Obviously, not everyone will willfully submit to the order of God, or choose to live in peace, but by increasing the number of godly "kings" in the earth, government will increase, peace will increase and God's people will be able to reduce the amount of conflict and opposition that others have toward kingdom values. Warfare, like in times past, will not be as frequent. For kings today, **"Going to War"** is more about leveraging the supernatural wisdom and power of God than overpowering our adversaries with brute strength.

We demonstrate the power of God through:

- *Prayers*

- *Decrees*

- *Prophetic words*

- *Reassignment, repurposing and rededication of resources*

- *Spiritual "redistricting and re-mapping" of territories for kingdom purposes*

- *Breaking territorial curses and pulling down strongholds*

- *Re-educating constituents and allies on kingdom culture and values*

&ᴏ *Reforming culture and terminology and developing "tribes" with shared goals and values*

&ᴏ *Positioning ambassadors and kingdom strategists who can advance the mission and expand the influence*

&ᴏ *Being fruitful*

&ᴏ *Loving one another*

&ᴏ *Words of knowledge*

&ᴏ *Divine wisdom*

&ᴏ *Divine healings*

&ᴏ *Mighty exploits*

&ᴏ *Raising the dead, or being raised from the dead*

&ᴏ *Signs, wonders and miracles*

A SOVEREIGN STATE OF MIND – THE CONSCIOUSNESS OF KINGS

"You will keep him in perfect peace, whose mind is stayed on You, because he trusts in You. Trust in the Lord forever, for in YAH, the Lord, is everlasting strength."

(Isa. 26:3-4, NKJV)

When kings go to war, they need the proper governmental mentality for engaging forces of opposition and they need the stabilizing power of supernatural peace to be ensured that God will bring victory, no matter what the circumstances may be. We rely on the sovereign and supernatural presence, power and peace of God to undergird and stabilize us in conflicts. As kings of the Earth we can only ensure victory if we think like the King of kings and if we bathe our consciousness with His life-giving perspectives, principles and precepts.

> *"But thanks be to God, who gives us the victory through our Lord Jesus Christ. Therefore, my beloved brethren, be steadfast, immovable, always abounding in the work of the Lord, knowing that your labor is not in vain in the Lord."*
>
> (1 Cor. 15:57-58, NKJV)

> *"Now thanks be to God who always leads us in triumph in Christ, and through us diffuses the fragrance of His knowledge in every place."*
>
> (2 Cor. 2:14, NKJV)

God is Sovereign and we don't rule independently of Him. The Father has designed our kingdom experience to be a direct extension of the one He shares with His Son and he is pleased to give us the kingdom through Jesus. Along with the kingdom comes the supernaturally-enhanced mind of Christ Jesus, an indispensable resource of power and light.

> *"But he who is spiritual judges all things, yet he himself is judged of no one. 'For who has known the mind of the Lord that he may instruct him?' BUT WE HAVE THE MIND OF CHRIST."*
>
> (1 Cor. 2:15-16, NKJV, emphasis added)

We have the mind of Christ, which I call **"The Consciousness of Kings."** The word **"Mind"** is from the Greek term **"Nous,"** meaning: Intellect, thought, feeling or will, mind or understanding. It comes from the base of the word **"Ginosko,"** meaning: To know, allow, be aware of, have knowledge, perceive, to be sure and to understand. The knowledge and counsel of God is vitally important because God as creator of all things has set the course for what He knows will provide the best and most favorable outcomes and the accomplishment of His sovereign purposes. If we "think" like Him, we are ensured of a far better experience during the process.

> **"Every purpose is established by counsel: and with good advice make war." (Prov. 20:18, KJV)**

"If any of you lacks wisdom, let him ask of God, who gives to all liberally and without reproach, and it will be given to him. But let him ask in faith, with no doubting, for he who doubts is like a wave of the sea driven and tossed by wind. For let not that man suppose that he will receive anything from the Lord; he is a DOUBLE MINDED MAN, unstable in all his ways."

(Jas. 1:5-8, KJV, emphasis added)

The word **Double** or **"Dipsuchos"** is a Greek term meaning: Two-spirited, vacillating in opinion or purpose. Bathing our minds in the Word of the Lord through study, worship and proper fellowship allows us to gain victory over the double mindedness that often comes to plague us during challenges.

"And I will give them SINGLENESS OF HEART AND ACTION, so that they will always fear me and that all will then go well for them and for their children after them."

(Jer. 32:39, NIV, emphasis added)

When we seek God and ask for His wisdom for our lives, we are empowered to do things we would never have the capacity to do using human reasoning and intellect.

"And Solomon said: You have shown great mercy to Your servant David my father, because he walked before you in truth, in righteousness, and in uprightness of heart with You; You have continued this great kindness for him, and You have given him a son to sit on his throne, as it is this day. Now, O Lord my God, You have made Your servant king instead of my father David, but I am a little child; I do not know how to go out or come in. And Your servant is in the midst of Your people whom You have chosen, a great people, too numerous to be numbered or counted. THEREFORE GIVE YOUR SERVANT AN UNDERSTANDING HEART TO JUDGE YOUR PEOPLE, THAT I MAY DISCERN BETWEEN GOOD AND EVIL. FOR WHO IS ABLE TO JUDGE THIS GREAT PEOPLE OF YOURS? The speech pleased the Lord, that Solomon had asked this thing."

(1 Kings 3:3-10, NKJV, emphasis added)

"Then God said to him: 'Because you have asked this thing, and have not asked long life for yourself, nor long life for yourself, nor have asked the life of your enemies, but have asked for yourself understanding to DISCERN JUSTICE, behold, I have done according to your words; see, I have given you A WISE AND UNDERSTANDING HEART, so that there has not been anyone like you before you, nor shall any like you arise after you. And I have also given you what you have not asked: both riches and honor, so that there shall not be anyone like you among the kings all your days. So if you walk in My ways, to keep My statutes and My commandments, as your father David walked, then I will lengthen your days.'"

(1 Kings 3:11-14, NKJV, emphasis added)

Solomon asked for an **UNDERSTANDING HEART.** The word **"Shamah"** is a Hebrew term meaning: To hear intelligently and attentively, to perceive, proclaim, publish and report. This meaning is a parallel to the Greek term **"Nous"** which is used to describe the mind of Christ. This consciousness or state of mind is further expressed in the following text.

"The Spirit of the Lord shall rest upon Him, The Spirit of wisdom and understanding, The Spirit of counsel and might, The Spirit of knowledge and of the fear of the Lord. His delight is in the fear of the Lord, And he shall not judge by the sight of his eyes, Nor decide by the hearing of his ears; But with righteousness he shall judge the poor, and decide with equity for the meek of the earth..."

(Isa. 11:3-4, NKJV)

This level of "kingdom consciousness" allows us to not only behave properly but have the ability to speak words of life and wisdom that are virtually irrefutable. We don't just randomly ramble on in our language as kings but we express a deliberate, intentional, targeted, purposeful and distinctive language that brings results.

WAGING WAR WITH YOUR WORDS

"Where the word of a king is, there is power: And who may say to him, 'What are you doing?'"

(Eccl. 8:4, NKJV)

"This charge I commit to you, son Timothy, ACCORDING TO THE PROPHECIES PREVIOUSLY MADE CONCERNING YOU, THAT BY THEM YOU MAY WAR A GOOD WARFARE."

(1 Tim. 1:18, NKJV, emphasis added)

Prophecies are composed primarily of "words." Since kings have such powerful words, why not take advantage of this technology and **"wage war"** with your prophecies? When you repeat a prophetic decree that you know to be authentic, it reflects the plans of God and the entire atmosphere begins "buzzing" with the original creative DNA of God's purpose. Everything that exists "remembers" the day it was created by God. When we war with prophecy, we are re-engaging every molecule, every atom and every cell in existence, to bring them under **"The Law of Sovereign Attraction."** (See Chapter 2)

"But seek ye first the kingdom of God and His righteousness, and all these things shall be added unto you."

(Matt. 6:33, NKJV)

When we speak "kingdom language" it attracts every provision and protection that we need. This is a direct affront to what the enemy attempts to do. It challenges his lies by leveraging the truth of God's plans for us. It provides light that defeats the darkness.

"And take… the sword of the Spirit; which is the word of God; praying always with all prayer and supplication in the Spirit, being watchful to this end with all perseverance and supplication for all the saints."

(Eph. 6:17-18, NKJV)

Keep a good **"supply"** of prophetic decrees and scripture texts handy, so you'll be able to bring down the enemy's defenses and go on the offensive. That's what supplication, *("supply-cation")* is about. It's literally the "supply" of words that you use to defend your case! Tell the enemy, *"I have victory, and you can mark my words!"*

WINNING THROUGH WISDOM

We will reign through wisdom, the technology that God gave to Solomon. Wisdom is a powerful type of **"governance."** Let's look at the prayer of King Solomon who was promised to have peace all of his days on the throne, in contrast to the kingly career of his father, David, a man of war who could not build the temple for God because he had shed too much blood. Solomon, in his prayer, makes a very significant point for kings who are going into battle for the kingdom of God. What he suggests is very much like the strategy of the 8th Mountain Mentality, in which we stand on Zion, the mountain that is higher than all other mountains. When we are *conscious* of the promises that are attached to Zion and the "oversight" that we have from that vantage point, we come into a new state of victory and prevailing power.

"When you command your people to go into battle against their enemies and they pray to you, wherever they are, facing this city which you have chosen and this temple which I have built for you, listen to their prayers. Hear them in heaven and give them victory."

(2 Chron. 6:34, GNB)

"Homes are built on the foundation of wisdom and understanding. Where there is knowledge, the rooms are furnished with valuable, beautiful things. BEING WISE IS BETTER THAN BEING STRONG; YES, KNOWLEDGE IS MORE IMPORTANT THAN STRENGTH. AFTER ALL, YOU MUST MAKE CAREFUL PLANS BEFORE YOU FIGHT A BATTLE, AND THE MORE GOOD ADVICE YOU GET, THE MORE LIKELY YOU ARE TO WIN."

(Prov. 24: 4-5, GNB, emphasis added)

The following text of Prov. 8:12-16 is a quote from the spirit of wisdom, one of our greatest assets of war. Let's bathe ourselves in the wisdom that comes through the Spirit of the Lord and the Word of God. Let's live by James 1:5 GNB. *"But if any of you lack wisdom, you should pray to God, who will give it to you; because God gives generously and graciously to all. But when you pray, you must believe and not doubt at all. Whoever doubts is like a wave in the sea that is driven about by the wind."*

"I am Wisdom, and I have insight; I have knowledge and sound judgment. To honour the Lord is to hate evil; I hate pride and arrogance, evil ways and false words. I make plans and carry them out. I have understanding, and I am strong. I help kings to govern and rulers to make good laws. Every ruler on earth governs with my help, officials and nobles alike."

(Prov. 8:12-16, GNB)

POWER AND PEACE

"He sent for his son Solomon and commanded him to build a temple for the Lord, the God of Israel. David said to him, 'My son, I wanted to build a temple to honour the Lord my God. But the Lord told me that I had killed too many people and fought too many wars. And so, because of all the bloodshed I have caused, he would not let me build a temple for him. He did, however, make a promise. He said, 'You will have a son who will rule in peace, because I will give him peace from all his enemies. His name will be Solomon, because during his reign I will give Israel peace and security.'"

(1 Chron. 22:6-9, GNB)

Isaiah 9:7 KJV tells us, *"Of the increase of his [Christ's] government and peace there will be no end."* The eventual establishment of godly, influential forces on the Seven Mountains will result in reduced conflict in the Earth. The souls, systems and societies that emerge under a willful relationship with God and His kingdom will reshape the climate of life. As we take our places upon thrones of the Seven Mountain Spheres we need wisdom in copious amounts to avoid the ambition of enlarging our kingdoms at any cost without regard to the risk and conflicts it may cause. There are times when we will be faced with stern opposition and we'll need tenacity, faith, boldness, courage and focus to engage the other kings and kingdoms. But, there are times when we are to recognize the strategy of the battle and use a more peaceful tactic. Peace, after all, is the "fruit" of the Spirit and Christ is called the Prince of Peace. As we ascend in power, prestige and purpose, remember to ascend in humility, grace and wisdom.

"The Lord says, 'The time is coming when I will choose as king a righteous descendant of David. That king will rule wisely and do what is right and just throughout the land. When he is king, the people of Judah will be safe, and the people of Israel will live in peace. He will be called The Lord Our Salvation.'"

(Jer. 23:5-6, GNB)

"He that is slow to anger is better than the mighty; and he that ruleth his own spirit, than he that taketh a city."

(Prov. 16:32-32, ASV)

It may be more advantageous to be ambassadorial according to Luke 14:21-32. God will often take one point of agreement between a believer and the powers that be, to form an alliance because they share a common interest. There is more than one way to win a war!

> "Agreement is the DNA of relationships." Being wise is often better than being strong and we need to be ambassadors and find a common thread of agreement to form useful alliances.

A VALIANT SPIRIT

"The angel of the Lord appeared to him and said to him, 'The Lord is with you, O valiant warrior.' Then Gideon said to him, 'O my lord, if the Lord is with us, why then has all this happened to us? And where are all His miracles which our fathers told us about, saying, Did not the Lord bring us up from Egypt. But now the Lord has abandoned us and given us into the hand of Midian.' The Lord looked at him and said, 'Go in this your strength and deliver Israel from the hand of Midian. Have I not sent you?' He said to Him. 'O Lord, how shall I deliver Israel? Behold, my family is the least in Manasseh, and I am the youngest in my father's house.' But the Lord said to him, 'Surely I will be with you, and you shall defeat Midian as one man.'"

(Judg. 6:12-16, NASB)

Gideon felt he wasn't sufficiently able to lead an attack against the army of the Midianites because he didn't have the "seniority" or social status to do it. Often, we feel the same way when we look at our backgrounds or look back at our past failures and shortcomings. No doubt, he considered the size of the opposition and thought, "No way are we going to win this." But God has a way of "balancing the playing field," even when the odds

194

are against us. We all know the story of Gideon and how God reduced his own army from about 32,000 soldiers to only 300 to give everyone a view of how powerful we can be when God stands with us.

But, God gave Gideon a powerful trait that every king needs. He gave him a *valiant spirit*. In the art of war, *"power respects power,"* even between enemies. In many of the wars that were fought throughout history, there was an "honor" attached to those who fought bravely and strongly and fought well. Sometimes superior opposing forces would offer an honorable defeat to a true champion because they honored his power and valiant spirit. If the "powers that be" detected weakness or a lack of courage in an opponent, no honor would be given during subjugation and the loser often suffered a humiliating death. The word **"Valiant"** means: Brave, courageous, intrepid, gallant, lion-hearted, bold, fearless, daring and audacious. When believers are valiant because they are confident in what God has equipped them to do, there will be results. The power of God, the Gifts of the Spirit and Misrah make us more than conquerors!

CASE STUDY – KINGS AND COUNSELORS

King Belshazzar was perplexed over a dream and no other person could interpret it and give him peace of mind. But God enabled Daniel to interpret the dream, causing him to increase in influence with the king.

"All of King Belshazzar's highest officials came in but not one of them could read the writing or tell what it meant, and they were completely puzzled. Now the king was more afraid than ever before, and his face turned white as a ghost. When the queen heard the king and his officials talking, she came in and said, 'Your majesty, I hope you live forever! Don't be afraid or look so pale. In your kingdom

there is a man who has been given special powers by the holy gods.
When your father Nebuchadnezzar was king, this man was known
to be smart, intelligent, and wise as the gods themselves. Your father
put him in charge of all who could talk with the spirits or understand
the meanings in the stars or tell the future. He also changed the
man's name from Daniel to Belteshazzar. NOT ONLY IS HE WISE
AND INTELLIGENT, BUT HE CAN EXPLAIN DREAMS AND
RIDDLES AND SOLVE PROBLEMS. Send for Daniel, and he will
tell you what the writing means.'"

(Dan. 5:8-12, CEVD, emphasis added)

The king summoned Daniel and told him, *"I've heard of you and you*
have great power. I need your help, and if you are successful, I'll promote you
in my kingdom and make you great!" Daniel was successful in interpreting
the dream and was promoted to President! The common thread that
Daniel and the king shared was the fact that Daniel had been brought
to Babylon to serve under the king's father. God had used him before to
interpret dreams before, and he was successful. His reputation preceded
him as he maintained an excellent spirit and valor in what he believed in.
Sometimes we are in dire circumstances, but the providence of God is still
in effect. We are placed there to become "the solution to a situation!" Like
Joseph, Daniel needed to be providentially positioned by God in a foreign
land, and serving under a foreign king to be in position to do the most
good. Likewise, God is positioning us as kings to be places where leaders
can receive godly counsel from us, even when it may seem like we've been
placed in harm's way.

CASE STUDY – DISTRACTED AND DISTRESSED

"The following spring, at the time of the year when kings usually go to war, David sent out Joab with his officers and the Israelite army; they defeated the Ammonites and besieged the city of Rabbah. But David himself stayed in Jerusalem. One day, late in the afternoon, David got up from his nap and went to the palace roof. As he walked about up there, he saw a woman having a bath. She was very beautiful. So he sent a messenger to find out who she was, and learnt that she was Bathsheba, the wife of Uriah the Hittite. David sent messengers to fetch her; they brought her to him and he made love to her. (She had just finished her monthly ritual of purification.) Then she went back home. Afterwards she discovered that she was pregnant and sent a message to David to tell him."

(2 Sam. 11:1-5, GNB)

Here's an account of a "distracted king" who created a set of difficult circumstances by his distraction. David should have gone to war with his army but he didn't and the situation resulted in David's act of adultery and his conspiracy in having Bathsheba's husband sent to the front line in battle in a clever ruse to get him to die as a hero. The ruse included bringing Uriah home from the front lines, to have time with his wife to cover up the fact that she'd had an affair with David. She became pregnant and a child was born. God was not pleased with this. The child became sick unto death, and despite David's pleas for change, the outcome was tragic, and the child died.

In short, David had an assignment as king and he failed to go to war at the appointed time. When "kings" are idle and they should be occupied with kingdom business, it has drastic results. If we fail to act

197

as kings and bring conversion to situations through asserting the power of our thrones, it allows something to be "birthed" that is not part of the original and sovereign plan of God. Like David, we'll end up with an "offspring" that cannot be sustained without God's approval. The child that David and Bathsheba conceived did not survive because it was a child born outside of God's divine order.

I am not implying that children born out of wedlock are cursed or worth less than those born to married parents. I'm just pointing out this was a very distinctive case where David operated out of divine order and there were *consequences.* In other words, there were *"contrasting sequences"* of events. Ironically, had David not interfered with the course of events that led to his affair with Bathsheba, he would have most likely eventually married her anyway because Uriah was probably going to die in battle! David and Bathsheba eventually did have another child, a boy name Solomon! This shows that his connection with her was always a part of God's plan but not the way David believed.

God was very displeased with David, and I'm sure this took a tremendous toll on the soul of the man known as "the apple of God's eye." There are times when God will instruct us to refrain from "going to war," but we have to be sure of it by seeking Him for a clear perspective on His timing and purpose. It's easy to become preoccupied with selfish motives such as greed, lust, fear, fatigue, and other distractions, but we have to guard our souls against them.

BREAKING THE BENCHMARKS OF BABYLON

We need to experience "Glory on Ground Level," a place where our kingly anointing from heaven manifests on the Earth. But, glory on ground level has enemies. One of the most prominent enemies is *"the spirit of Babylon."* The nation of Babylon no longer physically exists but the spirit of Babylon survives in the countless world systems that welcome its greed-fueled, ungodly, prideful, divisive and perverse nature. The spirits that drive many spheres of influence in the Seven Mountains of Culture are recruiting unsuspecting participants in the attempt to circumvent the kingdom order of God and lay waste to the momentum that the kingdom is gaining.

But, the kingdom of God cannot be stopped! It is a "sovereign system" that has eternal priority over every demonic and manmade system. Nonetheless, as kingdom citizens who believe that it's our rightful place to rule and reign on earth, we need to be educated about the *"satanic strategies"* behind Babylon. Historically, Babylon attempted to establish itself as a "benchmark" on society, making itself the standard of all things in the earth. A "Benchmark" is defined as: A mark on a permanent object serving as an elevation reference in topographical surveys, a point of reference for measurement; also, a standard. The motive and nature behind this attitude was the perversion of an originally noble and honorable craft... hunting. When the spirits of greed and pride entered in, the motives behind the skill of hunting changed from a means of survival to domination and control of systems; and amazingly, the idea of reaching and possibly controlling heaven itself!

Babylon attempted to establish their "benchmark" with the construction of the infamous "Tower of Babel." The implications of what they actually had in mind when they built it can be found in the meaning of the term **"Tower,"** as the Hebrews translated it. They used the word **"Migdallah,"** which means: Rostrum – a platform for speakers in the Roman forum decorated with beaks from captured ships. And according to Webster's New Explorer Dictionary it also means: To gnaw [To chew on]. In addition, it means: A stage or platform for public speaking. It becomes clear that Babylon's intention was to position itself with great influence in order to subjugate every other kingdom on Earth.

Since it's the nature of all kingdoms to enlarge themselves by absorbing smaller or weaker kingdoms, Babylon attempted to establish their tower as the icon that would give them stature and influence, leaving others awestruck at its magnitude. How Babylon got that way comes from a perversion of the gifting and nature of its original king, a man by the name of Nimrod. The study of roots and origins is indispensable when it comes to understanding how to challenge demonic systems and how to displace them with the righteous templates of God, restoring order in the Earth.

Today, the Tower of Babel is represented by overly ambitious projects and programs that are built by greed, avarice and the desire to become the "icons" that challenge God for influence in the hearts of mankind.

"And Cush begat Nimrod: he began to be a mighty one in the earth. He was a mighty hunter before the Lord: wherefore it is said, Even as Nimrod the mighty hunter before the Lord. And the beginning of his kingdom was Babel..."

(Gen. 10:8-10, KJV)

Nimrod, as a mighty hunter, had the ability to pursue and take down his prey. It was a noble and industrious skill, and one that would undoubtedly serve his family well. But, somewhere in his history, a satanic motive entered the picture. Wikipedia states that Nimrod was, *"According to the Book of Genesis and Books of Chronicles, the son of Cush and great grandson of Noah. He is depicted in the Tanakh as a man of power in the earth, and a mighty hunter. Extra-biblical traditions associating him with the Tower of Babel led to his reputation as a king who was rebellious against God."* This illustrates the roots and origins of a nation whose nature was driven by ungodly ambition.

"At first, the people of the whole world had only one language and used the same words. As they wandered about in the East, they came to a plain in Babylonia and settled there. They said to one another, 'Come on! Let's make brick and bake them hard.' So they had bricks to build with and tar to hold them together. They said, 'NOW LET'S BUILD A CITY WITH A TOWER THAT REACHES THE SKY, SO THAT WE CAN MAKE A NAME FOR OURSELVES AND NOT BE SACATTERED ALL OVER THE EARTH.' Then the Lord came down to see the city and the tower which those men had built, and he said, 'Now then, these are all one people and they speak one language; this is just the beginning of what they are going to do. Soon they will be able to do anything they want! Let us go down and mix up their language so that they will not understand one another.' So the Lord scattered them all over the earth, and they stopped building the city. The city was called Babylon, because there the Lord mixed up the language of all the people, and from there he scattered them over all the earth."

(Gen. 11:1-9, GNB, emphasis added)

The Babylonians grew in pride and felt that they were to be the premier nation on the planet. They were going to use their inherent *"hunting DNA"* to eventually prospect the entire earth and bring it under their command. God stopped them and confounded their language, crippling their diabolical plan of conquest. Babylon's history doesn't end there. God stopped the people themselves, but the spirit continued to operate in willing recipients. Later, throughout biblical history, from Genesis to Revelation, Babylon stands as the negative image of the kingdom of God's most formidable enemy. The righteous "kings" of the Seven Mountains of Culture are God's special operations team that's deployed against the spirit of Babylon.

"The Lord says, 'I am bringing a destructive wind against Babylonia and its people. I will send foreigners to destroy Babylonia like a wind that blows straw away. When that day of destruction comes, they will attack from every side and leave the land bare."

(Jer. 51:1-2, GNB)

As a play on words, instead of "foreigners," I'll say God has sent **"Fore-Runners,"** who are His special agents to defeat Babylonian culture in the world. We will break the spirit of Babylon and restore the structure of the Seven Mountains to godly proportions!

"The Lord says, 'Attack the people of Merathaim and of Pekod. Kill and destroy them. Do everything I command you. I, the Lord, have spoken. The noise of the battle is heard in the land, and there is great destruction. BABYLONIA HAMMERED THE WORLD TO PIECES, AND NOW THAT HAMMER IS SHATTERED! All the nations are shocked at what has happened to that country. Babylonia, you fought against me, and you have been caught in the trap I set for you, even though you did not know it. I HAVE OPENED THE PLACE WHERE MY WEAPONS ARE STORED, AND IN MY ANGER I HAVE TAKEN THEM OUT, BECAUSE I, THE SOVEREIGN LORD ALMIGHTY, HAVE WORK TO DO IN BABYLONIA. Attack it from every side and break open the places where its grain is stored. Pile up the loot like piles of grain! Destroy the country! Leave nothing at all.'"

(Jer. 50:21-26, GNB, emphasis added)

202

God shattered the "hammer" of Babylon and opened His arsenal, where He has reserved us for times like this! We are released to finish the assignment of Rev. 11:15. Babylon has fallen according to Rev. 14:8 and 18:2! God has a serious attitude against Babylon and the spirits that enforce the Babylonian structure and strategies in the earth! He has launched "kings" as the **"Naphats"** (Hebrew) in the earth, the **"Breakers"** or **"Those who scatter."** "The Mantle of Misrah," God's governmental authority, equips believers to dismantle and destroy the influence and effects of the spirit of Babylon today! Don't think for one minute that God will allow this inferior force to take over His earth. *"The earth is the Lord's and the fullness thereof; the world and they that dwell therein!"* (Ps. 24:1) It all belongs to God and He has reconciled all things back to Himself!

CROWNS AND CONVERSIONS

Things are changing, even as you read this book! Step by step, level by level, and day by day, things are changing!

"But we all, with open face BEHOLDING AS IN A GLASS THE GLORY OF THE LORD ARE CHANGED INTO THE SAME IMAGE FROM GLORY TO GLORY, EVEN AS BY THE SPIRIT OF THE LORD!"

(2 Cor. 3:18, KJV, emphasis added)

The only way to truly experience "heaven on earth" is for something to change! Long ago, the world and the religious systems of the day were "in limbo." The Old Testament law had run its course and wasn't able to change the hearts of men and the way that society functioned. Earthly kings had reached a limit in how they could affect the planet for good. Christ, the King of kings came to "reinstate" the glory of the Lord on Earth and reverse the state of Ichabod that existed. Actually, it wasn't a new plan to God since He chose Christ to be the Lamb slain from the foundation of the world. But, it was new to mankind and it brought about the foundational changes that restored our lives, even today. It took a "King" to convert the falling status of Earth and its populations.

"WHERE THE WORD OF A KING IS, THERE IS POWER: AND WHO MAY SAY UNTO HIM, WHAT DOEST THOU?"

(Eccl. 8:4, KJV, emphasis added)

> **Christ served a dual role as both "Word" and "King," giving Him a unique status of "Power" and the ability to bring about phenomenal transformations in people, places and things.**

Everything yields to Him for this reason. Jesus said, *"All power is given unto me, in Heaven and in Earth."* It is clear in the following text that all crowns are subordinate to the crown of God and every other authority figure is subject to His omnipotent glory and authority. Everything was created for His pleasure and yields to Him. As we, the "kings" of culture, leverage the power of our *"crowns and thrones"* as a privilege granted by God, all other ruling forces, whether good or evil, are required to "cast their crowns" before God.

"The four and twenty elders fall down before him that sat on the throne, and worship him that liveth forever and ever, and CAST THEIR CROWNS BEFORE THE THRONE saying, Thou art worthy, O

Lord, to receive glory and honour and power: for thou hast created all things, and for thy pleasure they are and were created."

(Rev. 4:10-11, KJV, emphasis added)

The presentation of **"the crown,"** which is a term used by monarchies to indicate their authority, brings all other forces into subjection or allegiance. Herein, is the meaning of the phrase that Christ is, "King of kings, and Lord of lords." Some of our "warfare" in this season will be a type of the "Cold War" of the 20th Century. When governments showed tremendous amounts of weaponry and armament, they often didn't need to fire a single shot to prove their strength. The display of weapons was enough to convince certain other governments to avoid conflicts. Very often, the display of majesty will deter an active war. Jesus met with a hoard of demons in Mark 1:23-26. The demons said, **"We know who you are Jesus of Nazareth. Don't destroy us; just send us away!"** Jesus didn't even exert much energy, because His presence and majesty alone, were a show of power. The situation was converted.

CROWNS, CONSCIOUSNESS AND CONFIDENCE

Life on earth takes on an entirely new meaning when we are fully persuaded that God has chosen us, not only as born again sons and daughters but for specific assignments. Every role that we are chosen for has a certain mentality that equips us for successful service in that role. The "crowns" that we wear are representative of the mindsets that enable us to be the conquerors that he chose us to be. Many things that we do are affected by our confidence or the lack thereof. When God establishes a believer on a throne, a **"diadem or crown"** comes with the earthly assignment to empower the person to be successful in the assignment. The signature text of this book's theme (Ezek. 21:26), describes the displacement of the wicked prince of Israel, and how he is commanded by God to remove the diadem and crown as a sign that he was being officially defrocked.

Diadems and crowns are outward symbols of authority, but they also relate to the **"mindset"** that comes with governance. Likewise, when God raises one to a throne, a spiritual type of the diadem and crown are added to the believer's stature, equipping them for service on the throne, changing their mindset and increasing their ability to receive instructions and wisdom from God. The diadem and crown become part of the earthly "standard equipment" for governance, not as visible or physical symbols of authority since most positions of authority today don't require a crown like those worn in times past, but in the consciousness, sensitivity and awareness that come from being on assignment.

The word **"Crown,"** in Hebrew is **"Atarah,"** or **"Atar,"** meaning: **Circle** (for attack or protection), implying that traditionally every crown is given for the purpose of advancing kingdoms and for protecting the gains of territories and assets and resources. Since all kingdoms exercise dominion of some kind, it becomes evident that there will be offensive and defensive measures taken to protect and preserve gains and to provide for future success. Wearing the diadems and crowns of a kingdom assignment result in knowing and being able to properly "process" the plans of protection, preservation and provision that God translates to believers through the Word of the Lord, the Gifts of the Spirit, the mind of Christ and the guidance of the Holy Spirit. We'll experience incredible downloads of supernatural knowledge for problem solving.

When the supernatural crown is worn and when the believer is conscious of the dynamic empowerment that comes to the wearer, powerful things begin to happen. The revelation of heaven comes to earth, unrestricted, unrestrained and unhindered, from the mind of God to mankind. *Luke 11:2, KJV says, "...Thy kingdom come. Thy will be done, AS IN HEAVEN, SO IN EARTH."* (emphasis added) The believer begins to have a clear perspective of the "will" of God in fresh new ways. This affects how we "translate" the language of God from the spirit realm into the natural realm. As we well know, every plan and gift of God is perfect.

"Every good gift and every perfect gift is from above, and cometh down from the Father of lights, with whom is no variableness, neither shadow of turning."

(Jas. 1:17, KJV)

There is perfection in all that God does. His light and glory make all things clear and there is no loss in content regarding His purposes. Sometimes, we experience various "losses" during our "downloads" of what God is saying to us. We lose "consciousness" much like a person who experiences a hard blow to the head. The legs grow weak and the person "blacks out." During a blackout, there is no light! During a blackout, someone could go through our pockets and steal everything. We need to stay spiritually conscious and "keep the lights on" to keep abreast of every good and perfect gift from our Father above. The crowns and consciousness that we can experience now have a built in "translator" that helps us "decode" the intent of His will and purpose and doesn't allow the misinformation and misrepresentations of the past. Now, there is more consistency in our understanding because we are more conscious of the assignments that we sense in the spirit.

Because we are **"assignment conscious"** we will be more likely to hold on to things that supplement and augment our ability to fulfill the assignments and more likely to deprioritize things of lesser value or importance or things of obvious non-importance. There will be a supernaturally empowered **"Transcription"** of events and information from the mind of God to us. Transcription is defined as: An act or process of transcribing [making a copy of something], an arrangement of a musical composition for some instrument or voice other than the original, the process of constructing a messenger RNA molecule using a

207

DNA molecule as a template. In other words, it's the ability to reproduce in earth what has been formulated in heaven. It's a **"Divine Duplication"** process and provides…

- A decreased loss of **Transmission** – Receiving the pure and original intent of God

- A decreased loss of **Translation** – Understanding and articulating the assignment

- A decreased loss of **Transition** – Accepting an increase of consciousness for the assignment

- A decreased loss of **Transformation** – Manifesting the results of the assignment

I intentionally use the term "decreased loss" because each person may respond to the challenge of transcription in a different way. How much clarity is gained will depend on an individual's level of absorption and how much they invest in the process. One thing is for sure, with the download of God's supernatural plans in our hearts, we are ensured of greater success and victory along the way. We are ensured of a greater level of confidence in the long run, giving us an increase in boldness and assertiveness as it relates to the fulfillment of assignments. We'll become as bold as lions, and unafraid to move forward in taking back the kingdoms that were lost.

THE KINGS HAVE THE KEYS!

"And I saw in the right hand of Him who sat on the throne a scroll written inside and on the back, sealed with seven seals. Then I saw a strong angel proclaiming with a loud voice, 'Who is worthy to open the scroll and loose its seals?' And no one in heaven or on earth was able to open the scroll, or to look at it. So I wept much, because no one was

found worthy to open and read the scroll, or to look at it. But one of the elders said to me, 'Do not weep. Behold, the Lion of the tribe of Judah, the Root of David, has PREVAILED to open the scroll and to loose its seven seals."

(Rev. 5:1-5, NKJV, emphasis added)

The King of kings and the Lion of the tribe of Judah **"prevailed"** to open the book! He possessed **"Misrah,"** which is a Hebrew word that relates to the name **"Sarah,"** and means: **"To Prevail!"** We can open what could never be opened before and we can shut what could never be shut before. As the leading King, He passed this power down to His king/priests so that we could restore the Earth to proper order using heaven's resources.

"I will give you the KEYS to the kingdom of heaven, and God in heaven will allow whatever you allow on earth. But he will not allow anything you don't allow."

(Matt. 16:19, CEVD, emphasis added)

The kings have keys to unlock mysteries relating to their crafts, skill sets and Seven Mountain assignments. We can access eternity to discover how to bring the planet into order.

We can **"command"** things to open or close because we are kings! As priests we **"petition and pray"** to God or ask for His blessings, but as kings, we **"command and commandeer"** things into place.

"Thus saith the Lord, the Holy One of Israel, and his Maker, ASK ME of things to come concerning my sons, [Priesthood function] and of the work of my hands COMMAND YE ME. [Kingly function]

(Isa. 45:11, KJV, emphasis added)

"He hath made everything beautiful in HIS TIME: also he hath set THE WORLD in their heart, so that no man can find out the work that God maketh from the beginning to the end."

(Eccl. 3:10-11, KJV, emphasis added)

Where is this powerful place inside of the Glory of God where the foreknowledge of God is hidden? Let's begin first by establishing one important foundational fact... *"God has made everything beautiful... in HIS TIME,* which is **ETERNITY**, or **"Eth,"** as the Hebrews define it. God's time is eternal and doesn't require centuries, decades, years, months, weeks, days, hours, minutes or seconds. His foreknowledge has a complete picture of eternity. This place is called **"Owlam"** which is Strong's translation of the Hebrew word for **"World,"** as found in the KJV Bible. It means: Something properly concealed, i.e., the vanishing point, generally, time out of mind, (past or future), i.e., (practically eternity) and among other things, perpetual, without end, any time...

Our **INTERNAL** being is more **ETERNAL** than our **EXTERNAL** being, and we've been looking all "around us" to discover what has been "in" us all along! God knows that He can hide the mysteries of creation in His Spirit, which is now inside of believers. We have been so determined to "set out in search of destiny" that we forgot to look inside! This inward look requires a type of personal spiritual fellowship with God that only those who love His presence will enjoy. It requires covenant, agreement, obedience, patience, shared values with God and others and the death of self-serving motives, greed, avarice and tyranny.

> **Finding "Eternity" inside of us requires us to make God our *"first resort"* and not our *"last resort"* when solving the issues of life.**

I thank God for Jesus and His most obvious sacrifice that He performed for us, in that He innocently suffered at the hand of His accusers and died for us, rising from the grave to declare that all power was now His both in heaven and on Earth. But, I also appreciate an often under-emphasized benefit of His life, and that is, He showed us all how to be "sons" of God. He showed us how to put the Father's desires above our own and to seek to fulfill the Father's purposes. In doing so, we see the kingdom arise in and around us. He showed us how true "kings" act under pressure and how they treat humanity with dignity, civility, kindness and love. We learned a lot from this King of kings and received the **"Keys of the Kingdom"** from Him, not realizing just how much we would soon be able to unlock with them!

We didn't realize that much of what we would unlock would be found inside of us and that God would keep it under strong security until we gained the maturity and sense of purpose that would enable us to administer this newfound grace and power without ambition or a thirst for personal power. Prov. 25:2-3, shows that **"Kings"** have a proclivity toward sensitivity to the hidden wisdom of God.

"We honor God for what he conceals; we honor kings for what they explain. You never know what a king is thinking; his thoughts are beyond us, like the heights of the sky or the depths of the ocean."

(Prov. 25:2-3, GNB)

"It is the glory of God to conceal a thing, but the glory of kings to search out a thing. As the heavens for height and the earth for depth, so the hearts and minds of kings are unsearchable."

(Prov. 25:2-3, AMP)

CASE STUDY - SPOILING THE SPOILERS

David had the **Mantle of Misrah** upon him when he deposed other kings and took spoils of their substance. We are equipped to do the same as we gather the substance of the earth and realign and repurpose it for the kingdom. There are many who believe that the exploits that we read about in the Bible were only for the people of the past and we can't expect to operate so powerfully. Some say the kingdom is for another time and season. The kingdom is now!

"And David gathered all the people together, and went to Rabbah, and fought against it, and took it. And he took their king's crown from off his head, the weight thereof was a talent of gold with the precious stones: and it was set on David's head. AND HE BROUGHT FORTH THE SPOIL OF THE CITY IN GREAT ABUNDANCE."

(2 Sam. 12:29-30, KJV, emphasis added)

King David took the crown of king **Molech**, whose name means: To reign and to ascend to the throne, in Hebrew. David not only defeated the army of the opposing king, but he removed the crown, a figure of authority, and placed it on his own head. The power to reverse the authority of an enemy was now in David's hands. The Mantle of Misrah is on our shoulders and it relates to the power of David's throne, which enables us to depose unrighteous ruler-ship at God's command. We triumph over the enemy! **The spoilers have been spoiled!**

"And having spoiled principalities and powers, he made a shew of them openly, triumphing over them in it."

(Col. 2:15, KJV)

David is a **"spoiler of spoilers."** The Amalekites attacked and raided Ziklag, burned it with fire, took women and children captive and also took David's wives. It was a time of great distress for him because his own tribesmen intended to stone him in their displeasure. Nevertheless, he prevailed.

"David asked the Lord, 'Shall I go after those raiders? And will I catch them?' He answered, 'Go after them; you will catch them and rescue the captives.' So David and his 600 men started out, and when they arrived at the brook of Besor, some of them stayed there... David rescued everyone and everything the Amalekites had taken, including his two wives; nothing at all was missing. David got back all his men's sons and daughters, and all the loot the Amalekites had taken."

(1 Sam. 30:8-9, 18-20, GNB)

MY DECREE

I am a King in the kingdom of Jesus Christ, who sits on the throne with God, our Father. If necessary, I am anointed for war and I'm also anointed for peace. I am valiant and I have courage and boldness. I wear a crown of wisdom and righteousness and my government and peace will never come to an end in Christ. Babylon is broken and cannot thrive in my presence. I have the keys to eternity and the kingdom of God within me. Whatever I prohibit on earth, is prohibited in heaven and what I permit on earth is permitted in heaven. I rule from my assigned throne according to God's plan! I will overtake my enemy and gather the spoils of the battle. I will recover all that has been stolen from me!

I SEE *Thrones*!

RESTORING
SOULS, SYSTEMS
AND SOCIETIES

"For the Son of man came to seek and to save that which was lost."

(Luke 19:10, AMP)

This is a very broad statement and it challenges us to ask the question, **"What has been lost?"** Once this question is answered, we can focus on what has to be recovered. We lost the power of healthy **souls, systems and societies.** Sin affected everything on this planet and because the entire spiritual ecosystem was off balance, the natural systems were affected as well. Both the natural and spiritual "ecosystems" of the earth are in a state of imbalance. An Ecosystem is a community of living organisms in conjunction with the nonliving components of their environment (things like air, water and mineral soil), interacting as a system. (Wikipedia)

Mankind's stewardship and custodial ability over the planet were weakened by sin, and since man is a part of his environment, everything on the planet, both natural and spiritual is affected. By Jesus Christ's sacrifice on Calvary, man is redeemed from sin and the curse of the law, and his authority is restored as the legal and lawful custodian of earthly things. The law of the spirit of life in Christ Jesus, has made us free from the law of sin and death. Our sins are forgiven and our souls are redeemed. But, since mankind is part of this "ecosystem," simply restoring his soul from sin but neglecting everything else that he interacts with would be shortsighted and problematic. We must go further. But, we can never manifest a change in the systems and societies of the world unless we are aware of our power. It's time to become fully **enlightened**.

"I ask that your minds may be opened to see his light, so that you will know what is the hope to which he has called you, how rich are the wonderful blessings he has promised his people, and how very great is his power at work in us who believe. This power working in us is the same mighty strength which he used when he raised Christ from death and seated him [enthroned him] at his right side in the heavenly world. Christ rules there above all heavenly rulers, authorities, powers, and lords; he has a title superior to all titles of authority in this world and in the next. God put all things under Christ's feet and gave him to the church as supreme Lord over all things."

(Eph. 1:18-22, GNB emphasis added)

"For by him were all things created, that are in heaven, and that are in earth, visible and invisible, whether they be THRONES, or dominions, or principalities, or powers: all things were created by him, and for him."

(Col. 1:16, KJV, emphasis added)

"All things" includes all souls, systems and societies, which are all embedded within the Seven Mountains of Culture. God has already released powerful insights and revelations through believers who are active on the forefront of the recovery and restoration of the seven mountains, bringing them under the full influence of the kingdom of God. I offer this book as a technical manual on mantles, thrones, kingdom citizenship, sovereignty, kingdom principles, and empowerment and not as replacements to what has been taught. I offer this book to augment the incredible truths that our "Seven Mountain Mentors" have been revealed over the years. My assignment is to gather the scripture texts, reference points, case studies, revelation and practical truth into one package, enabling the readers to have, at their disposal, a reasonable reference to ruler-ship and to empower the believer to know that he or she sits on thrones that are powered by God Himself! Our eyes are constantly being enlightened and God is working to convince principalities and powers in heavenly places of His sovereign intentions toward restoring us and the planet we live on! (Eph. 3:10-11)

TAKING BACK TERRITORY

"And He said to me, 'Son of man, THIS IS THE PLACE OF MY THRONE AND THE PLACE OF THE SOLES OF MY FEET, WHERE I WILL DWELL IN THE MIDST OF THE CHILDREN OF ISRAEL FOREVER...'"

(Ezek. 43:7, NKJV, emphasis added)

The Lord marks the places where He desires to establish His kingdom by His **words**. Likewise, we do the same. The example found in this text refers to Israel but it becomes a template or pattern for how the throne of God marks locations that are expressly designed to reflect His presence, glory and divine purposes. When God chooses a nation to become His "throne," it raises the conduct and activities of that nation to a higher standard and causes many new developments and advancements. He causes the people to become "conscious" of His divine presence, mandates and motives and activates their moral conscience, bringing them to a higher level of witness and function for Him. In spite of the presence of unbelief or opposition, God begins to accomplish powerful things through His "remnant" people.

"If My people who are called by my name will humble themselves, and pray and seek My face, and turn from their wicked ways, then I will hear from heaven, and will forgive their sin and heal their land. Now My eyes will be open and My ears attentive to the prayer made in this place. FOR NOW I HAVE CHOSEN AND SANCTIFIED THIS HOUSE, THAT MY NAME MAY BE THERE FOREVER; AND MY EYES AND MY HEART WILL BE THERE PERPETUALLY."

(2 Chron. 7:14-16, NKJV, emphasis added)

"Kings" are beginning to arise to war, contending with the powers that be, both natural and spiritual, to detect, design, develop and defend the thrones of purpose that God establishes in the places that He has chosen. The word **"Chosen"** is from the Hebrew term **"Bachar,"** meaning: Desired, choicest, preferred, selected and required. What God has "chosen" is for His will to be done in planet Earth and in its people. It is like the mandate of the prayer in Luke 11:2. *"They kingdom come. Thy will be done, as in heaven, so in earth."* The will of God is arriving along with the power of the kingdom of God and of heaven. God highlights areas of special assignment for His "kings" to raise the standards of His will in nations, communities, corporations, organizations and every other entity found in the Seven Mountain spheres.

Territory is regained and the will of God is established through the release of new information, ideas and activities regarding:

ᏏᏜ **Methodology** – The ways and means of accomplishing end results

ᏏᏜ **Apology** – The acknowledgement of social injustice or acts of injury or wrongdoing

ᏏᏜ **Technology** – The techniques, processes and methods of production or productivity

ᏏᏜ **Ideology** – The system of beliefs that decide economic and political policy and theory

ᏏᏜ **Soteriology** – The science of promoting and preserving health

ᏏᏜ **Terminology** – Nomenclature or use of words to define people, places and things

ᏏᏜ **Etymology** – The development of language, terms and words relating to pertinent subjects

ᏏᏜ **Sociology** – The study of human behavior and interactions

ᏏᏜ **Ecology** – The science of the preservation of Earth and its resources

ᏏᏜ **Urbanology** – A study dealing with specialized problems of cities

ᏏᏜ **Missiology** – The study of the mandates, message and mission of the Christian Church

EDITOR'S NOTE: The author is fully aware that several of these terms have variant meanings and multiple definitions and usage.

"All the earth honors the Lord; all the earth's inhabitants stand in awe of him. Because when he spoke, it happened! When he commanded, there it was! The Lord overrules what the nations plan; he frustrates

what the peoples intend to do. But the Lord's plan stands forever; what he intends to do lasts from one generation to the next. THE NATION WHOSE GOD IS THE LORD, THE PEOPLE WHOM GOD HAS CHOSEN AS HIS POSSESION, IS TRULY HAPPY! THE LORD LOOKS DOWN FROM HEAVEN; HE SEES EVERY HUMAN BEING. FROM HIS DWELLING PLACE GOD OBSERVES ALL WHO LIVE ON EARTH. GOD IS THE ONE WHO KNOWS EVERYTHING THEY DO."

(Ps. 33:8-15, CEB, emphasis added)

The sovereignty of God is being transposed upon the affairs of mankind through the establishment of "thrones" in the Earth. His "kings" are reintroducing the planet to their maker and God! The territories are already marked for change! Thrones may be established virtually anywhere that God has mandated, so one need not be a head of a nation to qualify for divinely-inspired leadership over a "marked" territory. Neither do they have to be individuals who engage a great public display of resistance or rebellion against the status quo.

> **"I press toward the mark for the prize of the high calling of God in Christ Jesus" (Phil. 3:14). There are "marks" along the way that let us know where to focus our energies. They also let us know that we are on track and are headed straight for victory!**

Brand new, Spirit-led strategies are arising in the hearts of the kings who are especially assigned for the issues of our day and for the future. Wisdom will be the greatest weapon of our day and we'll win a great number of "wars" without some of the counterproductive activities of our past. Kings who gain influence in the Seven Mountain spheres are not necessarily looking for a "fight" but often depend on a different strategy to gain victory. We *"pray"* and know what to *"say"* the right things when others would rather fight and *"slay."*

Through prophetic words, revelation knowledge and other supernatural references we have a more clearly-defined picture of the areas where we can *"war a good warfare"* and go after things that are already on God's radar. These are territories that He has *"marked"* with His will, intent and purpose. We have types and shadows from scripture such as Mount Zion, the "temple," Israel, "the Promised Land," The Churches of Asia Minor and many others which serve as an example of right and wrong societal models. God can easily highlight examples from history to stimulate our consciousness of what we should be focusing on today. When we leverage the power of reference points or marks, it ignites our consciousness of plans that come from God's sovereignty, foreknowledge and supernatural power. It's a "wisdom" strategy designed to win conflicts and it came from a king who was credited as the wisest man of his day. Words can win wars.

"FOR I WILL GIVE YOU A MOUTH AND WISDOM WHICH ALL YOUR ADVERSARIES WILL NOT BE ABLE TO GAINSAY NOR RESIST."

(Luke 21:15, NKJV, emphasis added)

Remember that power in the hands of an immature believer can be trouble. An unwise person can't handle this magnitude of responsibility; so wisdom is essential in the exercise of high authority. The wisdom of God gives us the power to **"bind"** the strategies of opposing kings and people of influence, but we can be wise and choose not to engage in an open conflict. It takes wisdom for kings to go to war against other kings. It is not a venture for the unlearned nor the unwise. Again, our ability to leverage this kind of power and authority comes by being extremely *"conscious"* of the energizing effect of Zion, the 8th Mountain, and our relationship with the King of kings. Notice the energizing **"marks"** (words) in the following text.

> *"Let Israel rejoice in him that made him: LET THE CHILDREN OF ZION BE JOYFUL IN THEIR KING. Let them praise his name in the dance: let them sing praises unto him with the timbrel and harp. For the Lord taketh pleasure in his people: he will beautify the meek with salvation. Let the saints be joyful in glory: let them sing aloud upon their beds. LET THE HIGH PRAISES OF GOD BE IN THEIR MOUTH, AND A TWO EDGED SWORD IN THEIR HAND; TO EXECUTE VENGEANCE UPON THE HEATHEN, AND PUNISHMENTS UPON THE PEOPLE; TO BIND THEIR KINGS WITH CHAINS AND THEIR NOBLES WITH FETTERS OF IRON; TO EXECUTE UPON THEM THE JUDGMENT WRITTEN: THIS HONOUR HAVE ALL HIS SAINTS. Praise ye the Lord."*

(Ps. 149:2-9, KJV, emphasis added)

Here are some of the key points or "marks" that we can leverage...

- ∞ We are children of Zion and dwell in God's "household" and lineage

- ∞ We have a personal relationship with our king and are authorized to act on His behalf

- ∞ We rejoice in His presence and power which gives us strength and assurance

- ∞ We recognize His pleasure in us and we are bold and confident in our assignments

- ৪১ We use our mouths as instruments to transmit power that transforms situations

- ৪১ We deploy the two-edged sword of the Kingdom of Heaven and the Kingdom of God

- ৪১ We execute the vengeance of God which is about "vindication" rather than "vindictiveness"

- ৪১ We judge situations and render righteous verdicts in accordance with God's purposes

- ৪১ We have the power to alter, minimize or terminate the authority of opposing kings in the spirit realm, rendering them ineffective in the physical realm

- ৪১ We promote "righteous alliance" and we command "demonic compliance"

- ৪১ We have "honor" ("Hada" – Hebrew) or majesty and greatness resting upon us

RENEWED BY RECONCILIATION

"But all things are from God, Who through Jesus Christ reconciled us to Himself [received into favor, brought us into harmony with Himself] and gave us THE MINISTRY OF RECONCILIATION [that by word and deed we might aim to bring others into harmony with Him]."

(2 Cor. 5:18-20, AMP, emphasis added)

In order to experience full restoration, we begin with **Reconciliation.** Mankind is a social being and societies are a vital part of man's interaction with others. The word **"Reconciliation"** comes from the Greek term **"Katallasso,"** meaning: To change mutually. This suggests that mankind and his world are mutually attached to each other and restoration for man means restoration of the systems that he interacts with. The word "Reconcile" also means: To cause to be friendly or harmonious again; to adjust, settle (differences), to bring to submission or acceptance. In addition, it means: To conform, accommodate, harmonize and coordinate. (*Webster's New World Dictionary and Thesaurus*) This is what creates healthy societies.

There's no way we could live up to the lofty expectations of God without reconciliation. As fallen souls, we couldn't possibly work our way back into right standing with God through laws and ordinances and commandments. Something more was needed. God made a decision to give us something we couldn't have provided for ourselves. His wonderful loving and sovereign plan of redemption defeated sin and the penalties that it brought to our world.

A **Human Society** is defined as: A group of people involved in persistent interpersonal relationships, or a large social grouping sharing the same geographical or social territory, typically subject to the same political authority and dominant cultural expectations. (Wikipedia). When societies erode, order and structure dissolve and life becomes difficult. Chaos would over-run the planet. We would constantly struggle to survive and our environments would destroy us. Societies would erode and the social structure of nations would crumble. Redeemed man is now *"coordinating"* the repair of systems and societies to bring them into righteous order. We rely on the supernatural reconciliation process to take place for us, through us and by us. As we take our seats on the thrones of the Seven Mountains, we'll will begin to exercise wisdom and skills that we did not have before. **Souls will be saved, systems will be streamlined and societies will be salvaged.**

THE TOOLS OF OUR "TRADE"

"I am telling you the truth: those who believe in me will do what I do - yes, they will do even greater things, because I am going to the Father. And I will do whatever you ask for in my name, so that the Father's glory will be shown through the Son. If you ask me for anything in my name, I will do it."

(John 14:12-14, GNB)

The word **Reconcile** is translated from the Greek word **"Katallage,"** meaning: Exchange, adjustment and restoration to divine favor. In a play on words, our **"trade"** is also our spiritual and natural occupations blended together to change circumstances. In other words, it's about a **tradeoff** or exchange of conditions. This offers us the opportunity to really understand the depth of God's love for us and His desire to return the earth and its inhabitants to a state of divine order. Provision was made when Christ became the Lamb slain from the foundation of the world, long before the fall of Adam and Eve in the Garden of Eden. In order for the earth to improve, the highest life form on the planet (mankind) has to return to a relationship with the highest life form in existence (God).

In so doing, God gives us the tools necessary for producing change. He gave us **"the ministry of reconciliation,"** which is the on-going technology of divine change. Through Christ, God placed the entire world, the planet and all of its various systems, in a potential pattern of exchange. When spiritual "change agents" enter the picture with the ministry of reconciliation and the word of reconciliation, change is imminent. It is a ministry, or the ability to dispense and deploy the assets of reconciliation and to impart all of the elements that initiate change.

225

God reconciled us to Himself, which is the
first step in the process of the reformation
of Earth and all of its systems.

God also gave us a valuable technology called **"the word of reconciliation."** The Greek term **"Logos"** is used to describe the **"word"** of reconciliation as: A computation, divine expression, motive, utterance, word or work. We are able, through the sovereign wisdom and word of God to influence an "exchange" of the conditions of ownership regarding the elements of the earth. The world's systems are exposed to both divine and demonic influences. Satan or the "god of this world" (2 Cor. 4:4) desires to claim the lion's share of this planet and its resources. While we live on this planet, we are a part of the "world," or the operational systems of the Earth. The term "World," is from the word "Kosmos" in Greek, meaning: Orderly arrangement, decoration, and the world in a wide or narrow sense, including its inhabitants, literally or figuratively. These operating systems govern the castes, cultures, climates, conflicts, customs, communities and commercial interests of humanity. Every human system is subjected to their influence. They become part of the "kingdoms" or societal spheres of activity.

The spirit of reconciliation is the transferring agency behind the restructuring and reassignment of kingdoms. *"...The kingdoms of this WORLD are BECOME the kingdoms of our Lord and of his Christ; and he shall reign for ever and ever." (Rev. 11:15, KJV, emphasis added)* The implication here, is that a trade, transference or transition is possible. The more preeminent and sovereign kingdom of God is able to influence lesser, man-made kingdoms and to embrace and enhance the positive aspects of those kingdoms while stripping or subdueing the negative aspects.

"For God so loved THE WORLD, that he gave his only begotten Son that whosoever believeth in him should not perish, but have everlasting life."

(John 3:16, KJV, emphasis added)

God loves the "systems" as He created them in His original plans but He doesn't love the corrupted, Babylonian image they have taken on. He loves the inherent efficiency, effectiveness and energy that the systems have and how they are driven to be productive. After all, He created them in His own heart to be that way. A perfect example is the marijuana plant. It's not evil in its own right, and as long as it grows quietly somewhere in a field and isn't harvested by someone intending to turn it into an "illegal drug" it's harmless. In fact, pickles would become contraband if someone found a way to process them into mind altering drugs! It's the intent behind harvesting the plant and using it as contraband that gives it a bad name. Systems in themselves are not evil. Sin has perverted them.

Satan, sin and self are the elements that either initiate perversion or enhance it. The adversary, the devil doesn't have a single creative bone in his body. Only God has the power to create. Demonic forces can only make things "different" through perverting their original intent and purpose. **That's why God still "loves" the world.** He still sees the systems as they were created by His supernatural intelligent mind and how they were formed for His original plans. But He doesn't love the greed, corruption, seduction and sin that have become their nature. Likewise, He loves every person on this planet, knowing full well that many of them lead corrupt lives. But in His eternal mind He looks back at the original destiny, plan and purpose that He has for each one of us and this is what He focuses on bringing out. This is what every experience of instruction, correction, chastisement, and adjustment are about. They reflect God's efforts to realign us with His

227

original pattern for our lives. He doesn't love our sin, but He loves us and knows our great potential.

"ENVISION HIS VERSION"

"He hath made everything beautiful in his time... That which hath been is now; and that which is to be hath already been; and God requireth that which is past."

(Eccl. 3:11(a), 15, KJV)

The world we now live in is a far cry from the version that God maintains in His mind. From the moment He thought of what to do, a perfect template for creation was established. God created the Garden of Eden and placed mankind in the garden as His chosen custodians of planet Earth. Sin entered the picture and the fall of mankind became "front page news."

The text above shows God's version of His own vision for Earth and mankind. It was seemingly placed on hold while God reformatted the ideologies of fallen man, giving him tutorials on how to come to know Him as the true and living God, and all the while dealing with mankind's fallen nature and the propensity to do wrong. This process took thousands of years and finally yielded the fruit of God's patience, Jesus Christ, the Son of God and Savior of the world. The text of Gen. 1:27-28 shows us a pattern of creativity, process and results that only an eternal God could envision. He made everything *"Beautiful"* in His time.

In the mind of God things are *"beautiful"* or they still maintain the original purpose and pattern which He intended, although it only takes a moment to look around and see disruption and corruption in the earth. That's the physical result of sin. But, God is not affected by sin and is able to maintain His pure view of things. The word **"Time,"** in this text is from the Hebrew word **"Eth,"** which means: **Eternity.** Everything is beautiful in God's eternity which contains the past, present and future and no time frame within that sphere of eternity has the authority nor the technology to completely alter the course of God's sovereign design.

"Be glad then, you children of Zion, And rejoice in the Lord your God; For he has given you the former rain faithfully, And he will cause the rain to come down for you – The former rain, And the latter rain in the first month. The threshing floors shall be full of wheat, And the vats shall overflow with new wine and oil. SO I WILL RESTORE TO YOU THE YEARS THAT THE SWARMING LOCUST HAS EATEN..."

(Joel 2:23-25, NKJV, emphasis added)

KEEP YOUR EYES ON THE PRIZE

"For we fix our attention, not on things that are seen, but on things that are unseen. What can be seen only lasts for a time, but what cannot be seen lasts forever."

(2 Cor. 4:18, GNB)

We are encouraged by the Apostle Paul not to focus too much on the corrupted version of creation we now see but to remember that we have been advised and empowered by God to take another approach. We remember that there is an invisible dimension far more powerful than the one we see with our natural eyes. We must exercise the disciplines of study, worship, praise and proper fellowship to even accept, believe and practice such a belief system because the visible world and its pitfalls are constantly vying for superiority in our hearts. The devil is doing all he can to make the visible world the pattern for life. We are constantly exercising our beliefs to focus on what God has to say about life and everything within it.

"Do not love the world or anything that belongs to the world."

(1 John 2:15, GNB)

We now have what appears to be a contradiction between the texts of *John 3:16* which says *"For God so loved the world..."* and the text above which tells us *"Do not love the world..."* We need to examine the context of the latter to understand the best way to digest both texts in the light of God's will. Why does God love something that He instructs us not to love? The beginning of this chapter explains that God loves the righteous intent and creativity behind the systems of the world as they were originally created by Him, but not the corrupt and unrighteous results that come from the "hijacked" versions that sin produced. He simply doesn't want us to "love" or become entangled with the corrupt processes that are being used today.

People lie, cheat, steal, misappropriate, alter, dilute, misrepresent, and embellish the simpler and more innocent elements of Earth's systems, turning them into corrupt machines of demonic conquest. In other words, it's alright to love it as God made it and originally intended it to be, and made *"beautiful in His time,"* but don't love the contaminated version it has become and don't depend on it to further our positions in life. God offers us a powerful alternative to the methods of a corrupted system.

"By his divine power the Lord has given us everything we need for life and godliness through the knowledge of the one who called us by his own honor and glory. Through his honor and glory he has given us his precious and wonderful promises, that you may share the divine nature and escape from the world's immorality that sinful craving produces."

(2 Pet. 1:3-4, CEB)

How can we experience the conversion of the systems of the world and see transformation the way God wants? We can learn to *"love"* what God loves and to *"hate"* what God hates. As we grow in our quest to *"envision His version"* we'll become more effective in transforming and translocating the systems and kingdoms of the world. God will continue to save souls and more present truth will be released in the earth, motivated by the urgency to transform and translocate the kingdoms of this world into the kingdoms of God according to Rev. 11:15.

Listed below are verses that will enhance our ability to **"envision His version"** of world systems.

- *"Don't be conformed to the patterns of this world, but be transformed by the renewing of your minds so that you can figure out what God's good will is — what is good, pleasing and mature." (Rom. 12:2, CEB)*

- *"Adopt the attitude that was in Christ Jesus." (Phil. 2:5, CEB)*

- *"We know that God works all things together for good for the ones who love God, for those who are called according to his purpose." (Rom. 8:28, CEB)*

- *"We haven't received the world's spirit but God's Spirit so that we can know the things we are talking about — not with words taught by human wisdom but with words taught by the Spirit — we are interpreting spiritual things to spiritual people." (1 Cor. 2:12, CEB)*

- *"But thank God, who is always leading us around through Christ as if we were in a parade. He releases the fragrance of the knowledge of him everywhere through us. We smell like the aroma of Christ's offering to God, both to those who are being saved and to those who are on a road to destruction." (2 Cor. 2:14-15, CEB)*

- *"Through faith they conquered kingdoms, brought about justice, realized promises, shut the mouths of lions, put out raging fires, escaped from the edge of the sword, found strength in weakness, were mighty in war, and routed foreign armies." (Heb. 11:33-34, CEB)*

> ᔆ *"Declaring the end from the beginning, and from ancient times the things that are not yet done, saying, My counsel shall stand, and I will do all my pleasure." (Isa. 46:10, KJV)*

TRIUMPHANT IN TRUTH

People everywhere are searching for "answers" but we can't focus on answers alone. Answers are a part of a bigger design called "solutions." Simple answers alone may or may not solve the *"systemic issues"* within world systems. We need the "truth" because it's the foundation for providing "solutions." The "truth" is far more than exciting facts or powerful declarations. It's the way God sees things!

"However, when the Spirit of Truth comes, he will guide you in all truth."

(John 16:13, CEB)

The revelation of truth by the Holy Spirit is one of the driving forces behind the sovereign solutions that God is offering us. Truth is an instrument of supernatural technology that God uses to refute the lying images of satan. When God made mankind, He made us in His own "image." "Image" is everything to God because it represents a pattern. The true image of things the way God sees them is being restored. Without a truth like this one, we'll continue to look at ourselves and to ourselves for solutions and won't find any, and we'll have very little hope for transformation.

> **"For the word of the Lord is right; and all his works are done in truth." (Ps. 33:4, KJV)**

Everything that God does contains the supernatural DNA of truth. Keep referring back to what God says and don't "reinvent the wheel." In forensic science, nearly everything is about cause and effect. Evidence at a crime scene didn't just appear there out of nowhere. Nothing is there by accident and there is always a cause for why things are as they are. Criminologists and forensic pathologists make their cases by "tracing" things back to their origins through deductive reasoning and scientific process. God created the technology and methodology for natural science to make discoveries and develop processes. *"That which is to be hath already been." (Eccl. 3:11, KJV)*

Natural DNA can be recovered from the most minute and seemingly insignificant particles at a crime scene. The accuracy of how those tiny traces of evidence point to a person, place or thing is astounding! If natural DNA can trace a path and pattern back to its original source, do we think it's beyond God's ability or desire to do this? Now is the time to step out in faith and expect to begin receiving brand new truth! The word **"Truth"** in the text above is **"Aletheia"** in Greek, which means: Truth, or truly. It also relates to the word **"Alethes,"** meaning: True or not concealing. God is not concealing truth; He's revealing truth!

FOCUSING ON THE FUTURE

"It's not that I have already reached this goal or have already been perfected, but I pursue it, so that I may grab hold of it because Christ grabbed hold of me for just this purpose."

(Phil. 3:12, CEB)

There is a "mark" in time that we all press toward. It's the time of accomplishment and fulfillment and the time of manifestation that we've looked for. We've spent days, weeks, months, years and decades looking for it. We've said that we are "waiting on our change to come," to quote Job from the Old Testament. But we're not actually "waiting," considering that a person can't "wait" for something that is actually in front of him. One can only wait for something that's behind him. We can't wait for the future because it hasn't come yet. In reality, the future is waiting on us! Paul the Apostle emphasized the importance of getting a true positional perspective and to look ahead at what is to come rather than behind you or at what is "following" you. We're taking on a new perspective or point of view. This is called **"Parallax,"** or: The difference in apparent direction of an object as seen from two different points.

In order to truly understand what God is doing, we have to observe things from a different position. We have faith for what we believe God is going to do, but the "answer" actually manifests at a particular day, time and place. While we are believing and using faith, at some point, it is "the present time" but it gives way to a future event that eventually become our "present time." If June 15th 2012 is the date that God chooses to release a certain blessing to us, then that date is **"marked for manifestation."** The future is more important to us than the past. The future actually contains the time of manifestations that we look for. This is why Paul "pressed" toward the future and gave it his best effort. It's not always easy and requires tenacity and a heavenly point of view, but when the Holy Spirit shows us "things to come," He is giving us insight to how God really wants things to be. It gives us energy and encouragement to keep moving forward.

"When you pray, I will answer you. When you call to me, I will respond. If you put an end to oppression, to every gesture of contempt, and to every evil word; if you give food to satisfy those who are in need, then the darkness around you will turn to the brightness of noon. And I will always guide you and satisfy you with good things. I will keep you strong and well. You will be like a garden that has plenty of water that never runs dry. YOUR PEPLE WILL REBUILD WHAT

*HAS LONG BEEN IN RUINS, BUILDING AGAIN THE OLD
FOUNDATIONS. YOU WILL BE KNOWN AS THE PEOPLE
WHO REBUILD THE WALL, WHO RESTORED THE RUINED
HOUSES."*

(*Isa. 58: 9-12, GNB, emphasis added*)

The Amplified version of verse 12 calls us "**Repairers of the Breach, and Restorers of Streets to Dwell In.**" The Hebrew word for **"Restore"** is the term: **"Shuwb,"** meaning: To turn back, literally or figuratively (not necessarily with the idea of returning to the starting point). It also means: To recover, refresh, relieve, rescue, restore, return, and retrieve, (among other things). Restoration, then, is the return to a place that is unhindered by sin and demonic strategies. This doesn't mean that there won't be any adversaries to contend with but it does support the technology of *Isaiah 54: 17 NKJV*, which says, *"No weapon formed against you shall prosper."* There is no denying that weapons will form, but it is clear that they will not prosper!

A restoration of streets or paths to dwell in reminds me of Jacob's "stairway to heaven" experience. He stood at the foot of an expressway to heaven where angels traversed up and down and where God Himself stood at the top. Jacob called this "the gate of heaven" and was awestruck by its magnificence. I believe that pathways to the heavens are steadily manifesting to us as we, like Jacob, awaken to the "places" that God has positioned us. Our thrones sit right in the pathways of those "open heaven gateways." Angels move for us, as the God of angel armies, the Lord of Hosts stands guard over us. We return to the place where God, by supernatural dictation, reveals His originals plans and purposes. This may require us to become more spiritual than we've been, not in a "spooky" way, but in the sense of "sensitivity" itself and the ability to move at His unction with immediacy.

235

New paths mean supernatural new ways of doing things. If we deny that supernatural change has come, and is continuing to come to this planet, then we deny the entire premise of the Gospel of Christ. He was and is a King, and if we are His Body, then we are preparing to do what he called **"Greater Works!**

"Incline your ear, and come to Me. Hear, and your soul shall live; and I will make an everlasting covenant with you – The sure mercies of David. Indeed I have given him as a witness to the people, A leader and commander for the people. SURELY YOU SHALL CALL A NATION YOU DO NOT KNOW. AND NATIONS WHO DO NOT KNOW YOU SHALL RUN TO YOU, BECAUSE THE LORD YOUR GOD, AND THE HOLY ONE OF ISRAEL; FOR HE HAS GLORIFIED YOU."

(Isa. 55:3-5, NKJV, emphasis added)

"Thus says the Lord: The labor of Egypt and merchandise of Cush and the Sabeans, men of stature, shall come over to you, AND THEY SHALL BE YOURS; THEY SHALL WALK BEHIND YOU, THEY SHALL COME OVER IN CHAINS; AND THEY SHALL BOW DOWN TO YOU. THEY WILL MAKE SUPPLICATION TO YOU, SAYING, 'SURELY GOD IS IN YOU, AND THERE IS NO OTHER; THERE IS NO OTHER GOD.'"

(Isa. 45:14, NKJV, emphasis added)

It is clear, there is no other God, and we will serve Him as we "SEE THRONES!" "MISRAH!"

CASE STUDY

The leader of an important community organization was faced with a dilemma. He had tremendous credentials, social connections, education and experience but he had an idea that he shared with other influential people and organizations only to be met with indifference. He knew the community needed his idea but couldn't seem to find the right people to launch it. There was a committee in his organization that would have been the right one to launch the idea but the members of that committee didn't seem to have the energy, mindset or concern to do anything. In fact, the committee eventually dissolved with no accomplishments on record. In other words, there was an "empty throne" on the committee that needed to be filled! The leader knew the idea had great potential but he also knew that he couldn't go at it alone, so after resolving within himself that he would push forward to do good things for his community whether he had support or not, he simply kept forging ahead with other endeavors.

Soon, he reconnected with a friend who was doing similar work in other areas and wanted to partner with him. They formed an alliance and reinstated the committee, with the long-lost friend at the helm. The friend took the empty committee chairmanship or "throne" and brought valuable ideas, resources and materials that fed into the leader's original idea and it now had the "legs" that it needed to stand on its own! The committee grew within one week and there was a "renaissance" within the organization. The idea was reborn and suddenly the idea took off and became a major community project. The growth of the initiative and the amount of "sudden support" and resources that materialized was astounding. The initiative grew and became a major force for community peace-making and social reform.

The mountains of media and government virtually adopted the initiative and took it abroad to influence the other mountains of culture.

237

Community leaders, legislators, corporations, family support groups, city councils, major corporations, ministries, marketplace organizations, newspaper publishers, radio and television stations and others came onboard this initiative and it had great results. The entire panorama of the Seven Mountain Spheres was exposed to this initiative in record time and it continues to grow with positive effects. It affected souls, systems and societies because it was an idea from the heart and mind of God and it produced efforts that embraced the good of humankind and encouraged each person to respect his fellow man and create peaceful environments in which to live, work and play.

MY DECREE

I am on assignment from God! I am not drifting about, looking for a place to dwell in. I am not a wanderer. I am an instrument of reconciliation. I am attached to people, places and things that need my natural and spiritual skill-sets. My assignments are preordained by God. I have the right tools to work with and I have courage to do the job. I will feast on the Word of the Lord so that I am strong in Him! I'm not led by my own ambitions. I submit my limitations to God so that I will have grace to go beyond my weaknesses. I am led by the Spirit of God. I want the truth and I love the truth! I am marked for manifestations! I contribute to the reconciliation of souls, systems and societies. I am a repairer of the breach and a restorer of streets to dwell in!

I SEE *Thrones*!

GOD SAVE THE KING! THRONE TESTIMONIES

*"Then they brought out the king's son, and put upon him the crown, and gave him the **testimony**, and made him king. And Jehoiada and his sons anointed him, and said, GOD SAVE THE KING."*

(2 Chr. 23:11, KJV, emphasis added)

H istorically when one was elevated to the throne there was a coronation and there were laws or testimonies given to affirm his office and help him rule well. The word **"Testimony"** is from the Hebrew term **"Eduwth,"** meaning: **Witness**. It comes from the word **"Ed,"** meaning: A recorder, or a witness. *"In the mouth of two or three witnesses shall every word be established."* *(2 Cor. 13:1, KJV)*. People of the royal court served as witnesses to the elevation so that it could be legitimized and placed into law. The benefit of this ceremony was further expressed as the witnesses sealed the event with the words **"God save**

the king!" This phrase literally meant, "May the king live a long and prosperous life at the hands of God."

It's a decree that entreats the favor and blessings of God so that the king is successful. This decree is still legitimate for us today as we take our rightful places upon thrones. Sons and daughters of God who believe in the office of the king/priest according to the Order of Melchizedek and see thrones as legitimate expressions of God's order for the kingdom are standing as witnesses in support of every "king" that rises to a throne in the Seven Mountain spheres. Since you are reading this book, it too serves as a testimony to your legitimacy as a king.

> **The testimonial decree – "God Save the King!" – produces a spiritual law that gives the king testimonies of great victories!**

The testimony of "God save the king!" is literally spoken over every king today by virtue of our present-truth prayers, prophecies and proclamations according to *Luke 11:2, "Thy kingdom come. Thy will be done, as in heaven, so in earth."* It is the will of God to bring the kingdom to us and for His will to be manifested through us. When we accept the office of king today, we accept the *testimony* and it produces a new reality. God WILL save the king and bring great victories into manifestation!

A HISTORY OF VICTORY

The Bible is full of great victories that God's people have experienced. We find people who faced insurmountable odds and who, according to the laws of physics and the art and strategies of war, should never have come out alive! They not only survived these conflicts but gave us supernatural testimonials of what happens when God chooses someone to fulfill an assignment for Him. From Genesis to Revelation we find victorious "kings" in the Bible. The following is not an exhaustive list but it gives great examples of men and women who were legitimately chosen by God for great victory.

"Now the valley of Siddim was full of asphalt pits; and the kings of Sodom and Gomorrah fled; some fell there, and the remainder fled to the mountains. Then they took all the goods of Sodom and Gomorrah, and all their provisions, and went their way. They also took Lot, Abrams brother's son who dwelt in Sodom, and his goods, and departed. Then one who had escaped came and told Abram the Hebrew, for he dwelt by the terebinth trees of mamre the Amorite, brother of Aner; and they were allies with Abram.

> *"Now when Abram heard that his nephew was taken captive, he armed his three hundred and eighteen trained servants who were born in his own house, and went in pursuit as far as Dan. He divided his forces against them by night, and he and his servants attacked them and pursued them as far as Hobah, which is north of Damascus. So he brought back all the goods, and also brought back his brother Lot and his goods, as well as the women and people."*
>
> (Gen. 14:10-16, NKJV)

> *"And Melchizedek king of Salem brought forth bread and wine: and he was the priest of the most high God. And he blessed him, and said, Blessed be Abram of the most high God, possessor of heaven and earth: And blessed be the most high God, which hath delivered thine enemies into thy hand. And he gave him tithes of all."*
>
> (Gen. 14:18-20, KJV)

Abram was a man who was led by God to depart from his home land and take a journey of faith into new territory. God promised him divine favor, and the blessing of an innumerable company of descendants. He was challenged along the way to the fulfillment of that promise and became the man who believed God in spite of circumstances of conflict and old age, eventually giving rise to the nation of Israel. In the text of Gen. 14:18-20, Abram faced tremendous odds against armies larger than his group of men but he was victorious. He later met Melchizedek who intercepted his meeting with the King of Sodom who would attempt to bribe him. Melchizedek, the king/priest of Salem, gave a "king's blessing" or "testimony" to Abram, thus affecting his entire future and that of his posterity. This is a foundational part of how we are able to be kings and priests today. Because the Order of Melchizedek is restored to us through Christ, we now have the full blessings of Abraham and are made kings and priests. (See Ps. 110:1-7, Heb. 5:5-6)

"The king and his officials approved this plan, [of Joseph] and he said to them, 'We will never find a better man than Joseph, a man who has God's Spirit in him.' The king said to Joseph, 'God has shown you all this, so that it is obvious that you have greater wisdom and insight than anyone else. I will put you in charge of my country, and all my people will obey your orders. YOUR AUTHORITY WILL BE SECOND ONLY TO MINE. I NOW APPOINT YOU GOVERNOR OVER ALL EGYPT.' The king removed from his finger the ring engraved with the royal seal and put it on Joseph's finger. He put a fine linen robe on him, and placed a gold chain round his neck. He gave him the second chariot to ride in, and his guard of honour went ahead of him and cried 'Make way! Make Way!' And so Joseph was appointed governor over all Egypt. The king said to him, 'I am the king - and no one shall so much as lift a hand or foot without your permission.'"

(Gen. 41:37-44, GNB, emphasis added)

> ## Supernatural promotions and favor come to "kings" in the exercise of divine assignments!

Joseph, the great grandson of Abraham is an example of a man who had a dream from God about being exalted. He wasn't completely sure of the purpose of that dream as a child, but he knew he was destined for greatness. He angered his many brothers by sharing the dream and was eventually assaulted by his brothers and thrown into a hole to be eaten by animals. As the story goes, he was eventually rescued only to be sold into slavery in Egypt. Under the providence of God, he was still able to provide an interpretation for a dream of Pharaoh, and received great favor for his deed. He eventually interpreted another dream that resulted in Egypt and surrounding nations having grain to eat and not being consumed by famine. He was promoted and became second only to Pharaoh himself. As time passed he met his brothers again and was reconciled to his family.

"One day while Moses was taking care of the sheep and goats of his father-in-law Jethro, the priest of Midian, he led the flock across the desert and came to Sinai, the holy mountain. There the angel of the Lord appeared to him as a flame coming from the middle of a bush. Moses saw that the bush was not burning up. 'This is strange,' he thought. 'Why isn't the bush burning up? I will go closer and see.' When the Lord saw that Moses was coming closer, he called him from the middle of the bush and said, 'Moses! Moses!' He answered, 'Yes, here I am.' God said, 'Do not come any closer. Take off your sandals, because you are standing on holy ground. I am the God of your ancestors, the

God of Abraham, Isaac and Jacob.' So Moses covered his face, because he was afraid to look at God.

"Then the Lord said, 'I have seen how cruelly my people are being treated in Egypt; I have heard them cry out to be rescued from their slave-drivers. I know all about their sufferings, and so I have come down to rescue them from the Egyptians and to bring them out of Egypt to a spacious land, one which is rich and fertile and in which the Canaanites, the Hittites, the Amorites, the Perizzites, the Hivites, and the Jebusites now live. I have indeed heard the cry of my people, and I see how the Egyptians are oppressing them. NOW I AM SENDING YOU TO THE KING OF EGYPT SO THAT YOU CAN LEAD MY PEOPLE OUT OF HIS COUNTRY. But Moses said to God, 'I am nobody. How can I go to the king and bring the Israelites out of Egypt?' God answered, 'I WILL BE WITH YOU, AND WHEN YOU BRING THE PEOPLE OUT OF EGYPT, YOU WILL WORSHIP ME ON THIS MOUNTAIN. THAT WILL BE THE PROOF THAT I HAVE SENT YOU.'"

(Ex. 3:1-12, GNB, emphasis added)

Here is another example of a person with humble beginnings who was rescued from adversity and taken to the court of Pharaoh to be raised as one of his own. There, he was educated and trained in the ways of Egypt and got the opportunity to see the plight of the Israelites first hand. Unknown to him, this was all God's plan. Moses eventually learned of his Hebrew heritage and left the riches and ambiance of the palace of Pharaoh, eventually marrying and taking a job as a shepherd in Midian. While there, he experienced his high calling to become God's ambassador for Israel.

Moses had a place of secular authority when he was in Egypt, but now he had the highest authority of any man on Earth at that time. He went on to confront Pharaoh, a powerful leader, and released the judgments of God against him. He spoke to God again, receiving the Ten Commandments on Mount Sinai. Moses' "throne" was shown by his rise from slavery to rulership as the first leader of a free-Israel and as the man who spoke directly to God to receive the Ten Commandments.

Moses was allowed to ascend the holy mountain and stand in the presence and glory of God where no other man had gone before and speak with Him "face to face." In so doing he was **"seated in heavenly places"** where God showed him the pattern of heavenly things that he would bring back to Earth to use as a template in building the tabernacle. This is a prototype of the glorious pattern that Christ would reveal and superimpose upon those who would become His Body in the Earth. We are now the temple of God (1 Cor. 3:16).

"The work they do as priests is really only a copy and a shadow of what is in heaven. It is the same as it was with Moses. When he was about to build the Sacred Tent, God said to him, 'be sure to make everything according to the pattern you were shown on the mountain. But now, Jesus has been given priestly work which is superior to theirs, just as the covenant which he arranged between God and his people is a better one, because it is based on promises of better things.'"

(Heb. 8:5-6, GNB)

And in the same way that Moses was a savior and shepherd to the children of Israel to lead them out of bondage and oppression in Israel, Jesus was a savior and shepherd to His generation and beyond through the church and the word of God for all eternity.

"For every house is built by someone, but the builder of all things is God. Now Moses was faithful in all His house as a servant, for a testimony of those things which were to be spoken later; but Christ was faithful as a Son over His house—whose house we are, if we hold fast our confidence and the boast of our hope firm until the end."

(Heb. 3:4-6, NAS)

WHEN LESS IS MORE

"The Lord said to Gideon, 'I will rescue you and give you victory over the Midianites with the 300 men who lapped the water. Tell everyone else to go home.' So Gideon sent all the Israelites home, except the 300, who kept all the supplies and trumpets. The Midianite camp was below them in the valley. That night the Lord commanded Gideon, 'GET UP AND ATTACK THE CAMP; I AM GIVING YOU VICTORY OVER IT. But if you are afraid to attack. Go down to the camp with your servant Purah. You will hear what they are saying, and then you will have the courage to attack.' So Gideon and his servant Purah went down to the edge of the enemy camp. The Midianites, the Amalekites, and the desert tribesmen were spread out in the valley like a swarm of locusts, and they had as many camels as there were grains of sand on the seashore.

"When Gideon arrived, he heard a man telling a friend about a dream. He was saying, 'I dreamt that a loaf of barley bread rolled into our camp and hit a tent. The tent collapsed and lay flat on the ground.' His friend replied, 'IT'S THE SWORD OF THE ISRAELITE, GIDEON SON OF JOASH! IT CAN'T MEAN ANYTHING ELSE! GOD HAS GIVEN HIM VICTORY OVER MIDIAN AND OUR WHOLE ARMY!' When Gideon heard about the man's dream and

246

what it meant, he fell to his knees and worshipped the Lord. Then he went back to the Israelite camp and said, 'GET UP! THE LORD IS GIVING YOU VICTORY OVER THE MIDIANITE ARMY!'"

(Judg. 7:7-15, GNB, emphasis added)

Gideon is a great example of how God gives "thrones" and victories to the underdog, the one who is outnumbered, and in this case, intentionally outnumbered by the hand of God. The power of God makes a person more capable than one could ever be by reason of personal strength. *"You will chase your enemies, and they shall fall by the sword before you. Five of you shall chase a hundred, and a hundred of you shall put ten thousand to flight; your enemies shall fall by the sword before you."* (Lev. 26:7-8, NKJV).

"Then Nebuchadnezzar lost his temper, and his face turned red with anger at Shadrach, Meshach, and Abednego. So he ordered the furnace to be heated seven times hotter than usual. And he commanded the strongest men in his army to tie the three men up and throw them into the blazing furnace. So they tied them up, fully dressed – shirts, robes, caps, and all – and threw them into the blazing furnace. Now because the king had given strict orders for the furnace to be made extremely hot, the flames burnt the guards who took the men to the furnace. Then Shadrach, Meshach, and Abednego, still tied up, fell into the heart of the blazing fire. Suddenly Nebuchadnezzar leapt to his feet in amazement. He asked his officials, 'DIDN'T WE TIE UP THREE MEN AND THROW THEM INTO THE BLAZING FURNACE?' They answered, 'Yes, we did, Your Majesty.' 'THEN WHY DO I SEE FOUR MEN WALKING ABOUT IN THE FIRE?' he asked. 'THEY ARE NOT TIED UP, AND THEY SHOW NO SIGN OF BEING HURT – AND THE FOURTH ONE LOOKS LIKE AN ANGEL!'"

(Dan. 3:19-25, GNB, emphasis added)

Once again, when God has a "throne" for us to sit on and a divine purpose for our lives, we can face the fire and not be harmed by it. The Hebrew men may have been outnumbered by the authority of the king, the men who threw them into the flames, and the high temperature of the fire, but God added His angel to the mix and overcame every obstacle!

"'Your Majesty,' David said, 'I take care of my father's sheep. Whenever a lion or a bear carries off a lamb, I go after it, attack it, and rescue the lamb. And if the lion or bear turns on me, I grab it by the throat and beat it to death. I have killed lions and bears, AND I WILL DO THE SAME TO THIS HEATHEN PHILISTINE, WHO HAS DEFIED THE ARMY OF THE LIVING GOD. THE LORD HAS SAVED ME FROM LIONS AND BEARS; HE WILL SAVE ME FROM THIS PHILISTINE.'"

(I Sam. 17:34-37, GNB, emphasis added)

"Goliath started walking towards David again, and David ran quickly towards the Philistine battle line to fight him. He put his hand into his bag and took out a stone, which he slung at Goliath. It hit him in the forehead and broke his skull, and Goliath fell face downwards on the ground. AND SO, WITHOUT A SWORD, DAVID DEFEATED GOLIATH WITH A SLING AND A STONE! He ran to him, stood over him, took Goliath's sword out of its sheath, and cut off his head and killed him."

(I Sam. 17:48-51, GNB)

Nearly everyone is familiar with the story of the young man David, who stood against the Philistine giant, Goliath. Surely David was "outgunned" against such an enemy. Goliath is said to have been between nine and 11 feet tall, with armor weighing from 125 to 130 pounds. (bibleapologetics. wordpress.com). Certainly, no average person could stand against such a massive champion of war. However, David was chosen by God to become a king and an ancestor of Jesus Christ and his "throne" was clearly in his sight as he gained victory over the giant.

"The king of Syria was at war with Israel. He consulted his officers and chose a place to set up his camp. But Elisha sent word to the king of Israel, warning him not to go near that place, because the Syrians were waiting in ambush there. So the king of Israel warned the people who lived in that place, and they were on guard. This happened several times. The Syrian king became greatly upset over this; he called in his officers and asked them, 'Which of you is on the side of the king of Israel?' One of them answered, 'No one is, Your Majesty. THE PROPHET ELISHA TELLS THE KING OF ISRAEL WHAT YOU SAY EVEN IN THE PRIVACY OF YOUR OWN ROOM.' 'Find out where he is,' the king ordered, 'and I will capture him.' When he was told that Elisha was in Dothan, he sent a large force there with horses and chariots. They reached the town at night and surrounded it.

"Early the next morning Elisha's servant got up, went out of the house, and saw the Syrian troops with their horses and chariots surrounding the town. He went back to Elisha and exclaimed, 'We are doomed, sir! What shall we do?' 'DON'T BE AFRAID,' ELISHA ANSWERED. 'WE HAVE MORE ON OUR SIDE THAN THEY HAVE ON THEIRS.' THEN HE PRAYED, O LORD, OPEN HIS EYES AND LET HIM SEE! THE LORD ANSWERED HIS PRAYER, AND ELISHA'S SERVANT LOOKED UP AND SAW THE HILLSIDE COVERED WITH HORSES AND CHARIOTS OF FIRE ALL ROUND ELISHA. WHEN THE SYRIANS ATTACKED, ELISHA

PRAYED, 'O LORD, STRIKE THESE MEN BLIND!' THE LORD ANSWERED HIS PRAYER AND STRUCK THEM BLIND."

(2 Kings 6: 8-18, GNB, emphasis added)

Being supernaturally sensitive has great advantages. The average person will look at outward circumstances, much like Elisha's young colleague, and see the worst about to unfold. But Elisha was a seasoned and confident man of God and prayed a prayer that activated the visible manifestation of an army of angels! In the natural sense, it appeared as if the Syrian army outnumbered the men of God, but in reality the army of God was standing by to bring victory. Not only was this a supernatural event but the prophet Elisha exercised his authority to speak blindness over the enemy.

> **"...But you belong to God... the Spirit who is in you is more powerful than the spirit in those who belong to the world." (1 John 4:4, GNB)**

BUILDING BEYOND BARRICADES

"When Sanballat heard that we Jews had begun rebuilding the wall, he was furious and began to ridicule us. In front of his companions and the Samaritan troops he said, 'What do these miserable Jews think they're doing? Do they think that by offering sacrifices they can finish the work in one day? Can they make building stones out of heaps of burnt rubble?' Tobiah was standing there beside him, and he added, 'What kind of wall could they ever build? Even a fox could knock it down!' I prayed, 'Listen to them mocking us, O God! Let their ridicule fall on their own

heads. Let them be robbed of everything they have, and let them be taken as prisoners to a foreign land. Don't forgive the evil they do and don't forget their sins, for they have insulted us who are building.'

"So we went on rebuilding the wall, and soon it was half its full height, because the people were eager to work. Sanballat, Tobiah, and the people of Arabia, Ammon, and Ashdod heard that we were making progress in rebuilding the wall of Jerusalem and that the gaps in the wall were being closed, and they were very angry. So they all plotted together to come and attack Jerusalem and create confusion, but we prayed to our God and kept men on guard against them day and night."

(Neh. 4:1-9, GNB)

"I saw that the people were worried, so I said to them and to their leaders and officials, 'DON'T BE AFRAID OF OUR ENEMIES. REMEMBER HOW GREAT AND TERRIFYING THE LORD IS, AND FIGHT FOR YOUR FELLOW COUNTRYMEN, YOUR CHILDREN, YOUR WIVES, AND YOUR HOMES.' OUR ENEMIES HEARD THAT WE HAD FOUND OUT WHAT THEY WERE PLOTTING, AND THEY REALIZED THAT GOD HAD DEFEATED THEIR PLANS. THEN ALL OF US WENT BACK TO REBUILDING THE WALL."

(Neh. 4:14-15, GNB, emphasis added)

Just like Nehemiah and the Jews, we reform and rebuild what has been laid waste and decayed by the enemy. Even as we go forward to restore things, our adversaries may plot to interrupt our work and prevent progress. But when God has crowned us with a commission and enthroned us with an assignment, we are empowered to build beyond the blockades that our enemies construct. The supernatural power of

God is at work within us and He'll confuse and confound our enemies, thus giving us the victories we need!

> *"When the Israelites saw the king and his army marching against them, they were terrified and cried out to the Lord for help. They said to Moses, 'Weren't there any graves in Egypt? Did you have to bring us out here in the desert to die? Look what you have done by bringing us out of Egypt! Didn't we tell you before we left that this would happen? We told you to leave us alone and let us go on being slaves of the Egyptians. It would be better to be slaves there than to die here in the desert.' Moses answered, 'DON'T BE AFRAID! STAND YOUR GROUND, AND YOU WILL SEE WHAT THE LORD WILL DO TO SAVE YOU TODAY; YOU WILL NEVER SEE THESE EGYPTIANS AGAIN. THE LORD WILL FIGHT FOR YOU, AND THERE IS NO NEED FOR YOU TO DO ANYTHING."*

(Ex. 14:10-14, GNB, emphasis added)

> *"Moses held out his hand over the sea, and the Lord drove the sea back with a strong east wind. It blew all night and turned the sea into dry land. The water was divided, and the Israelites went through the sea on dry ground, with walls of water on both sides. The Egyptians pursued them and went after them into the sea with all their horses, chariots, and drivers... THE LORD SAID TO MOSES, 'HOLD OUT YOUR HAND OVER THE SEA, AND THE WATER WILL COME BACK OVER THE EGYPTIANS AND THEIR CHARIOTS AND DRIVERS."*

(Ex. 14:21-23, 26, GNB, emphasis added)

The Red Sea wasn't the only barricade that Moses faced. He was confronted with the stubborn, unbelieving attitude of some of the

Israelites. Moses stood on the Word of God, maintained his authority, held up the rod which symbolizes the scepter of a king and commanded the waters to open for Israel and close again upon the Egyptians. This was a great victory for God's people!

SUPERNATURAL SUPPORT

"Then Jesus made the disciples get into the boat and go on ahead to the other side of the lake, while he sent the people away. After sending the people away, he went up a hill by himself to pray. When evening came, Jesus was there alone; and by this time the boat was far out in the lake, tossed about by the waves, because the wind was blowing against it. Between three and six o'clock in the morning Jesus came to the disciples, walking on the water. When they saw him walking on the water, they were terrified. 'It's a ghost!' they said, and screamed with fear. Jesus spoke to them at once. 'Courage!' he said. 'It is I. Don't be afraid!' Then Peter spoke up. 'Lord, if it is really you, order me to come out on the water with you.' 'Come!' answered Jesus.' SO PETER GOT OUT OF THE BOAT AND STARTED WALKING ON THE WATER TO JESUS."

(Matt. 14:22-29, GNB, emphasis added)

The power that enabled Peter to walk on water was a supernatural support system initiated by the command of Jesus. At the Lord's word, Peter was able to walk on water, which would have been impossible under any other circumstances. When the King of kings gives us commands, it enables us to defy the laws of physics, and other restrictions and causes us to perform supernaturally. *"The king acts with authority, and no one can challenge what he does. As long as you obey his commands, you are safe, and a wise person knows how and when to do it." (Eccl. 8:4, GNB).*

The expression, "Walking on water" can apply to situations where God supernaturally enables us to do things that we couldn't normally do, but at His word, we obey and great results follow.

> **"...Greater is he that in in you, than he that is in the world." (1 John 4:4, KJV)**

"All of us who administer your empire—the supervisors, the governors, the lieutenant-governors, and the other officials—have agreed that Your Majesty should issue an order and enforce it strictly. Give orders that for thirty days no one be permitted to request anything from any god or from any human being except from Your Majesty. Anyone who violates this order is to be thrown into a pit filled with lions. So let Your Majesty issue this order and sign it, and it will be in force, a law of the Medes and Persians, which cannot be changed. And so King Darius signed the order. When Daniel learnt that the order had been signed, he went home. In an upstairs room of his house there were windows that faced towards Jerusalem. There, just as he had always done, he knelt down at the open windows and prayed to God three times a day."

(Dan. 6:7-13, GNB)

Conspirators rose up against God's faithful man Daniel by coercing the king into making a decree that would surely snare Daniel in the process. Daniel was unmoved and continued his dedication to God in prayer, as he had always done. Although the king honored and respected

Daniel, he was bound by his own law, thus having no choice but to have Daniel arrested.

"So the king gave orders for Daniel to be arrested and he was thrown into the pit filled with lions. He said to Daniel, 'May your God, whom you serve so loyally, rescue you." A stone was put over the mouth of the pit, and the king placed his own royal seal and the seal of his noblemen on the stone, so that no one could rescue Daniel. Then the king returned to the palace and spent a sleepless night, without food or any form of entertainment. At dawn the king got up and hurried to the pit. When he got there, he called anxiously, 'Daniel, servant of the living God! Was the God you serve so loyally able to save you from the lions?' Daniel answered, 'may Your Majesty live for ever! GOD SENT HIS ANGEL TO SHUT THE MOUTHS OF THE LIONS SO THAT THEY WOULD NOT HURT ME. HE DID THIS BECAUSE HE KNEW THAT I WAS INNOCENT AND BECAUSE I HAVE NOT WRONGED YOU, YOUR MAJESTY.'"

(Dan. 6:16-22, GNB, emphasis added)

Daniel was clothed with the majestic protection of the Most High God, who preserved His servant because he was a righteous man and was totally dedicated to His purposes. Daniel was bold in his steadfastness toward God even to the extent of defying the decrees and authority of the natural king. Only a man who was confident in his God and in his own place in God, could have survived such a thing. God gave him sovereign and supernatural protection.

"Then the Spirit led Jesus into the desert to be tempted by the Devil. After spending forty days and nights without food, Jesus was hungry. Then the Devil came to him and said, 'If you are the God's Son, order these stones to turn into bread.' But Jesus answered, 'The scripture

says, Human beings cannot live on bread alone, but need every word that God speaks.' Then the Devil took Jesus to Jerusalem, the Holy City, set him on the highest point of the Temple, and said to him, 'If you are God's Son, throw yourself down, for the scripture says: 'God will give orders to his angels about you; they will hold you up with their hands, so that not even your feet will be hurt on the stones.'

"Jesus answered, 'But the scripture also says, 'Do not put the Lord your God to the test.' Then the Devil took Jesus to a very high mountain and showed him all the kingdoms of the world in all their greatness. 'All this will I give you,' the Devil said, 'if you kneel down and worship me.' Then Jesus answered, 'Go away, Satan! The scripture says, 'Worship the Lord your God and serve only him!' THEN THE DEVIL LEFT JESUS; AND ANGELS CAME AND HELPED HIM."

(Matt. 4:1-11, GNB, emphasis added)

Jesus was confronted by the Devil face to face, making this a very serious issue indeed. He faced His adversary, not as God, but as a man, representing the entire human race and proving that mankind can stand against the enemy victoriously. His victory came because He relied on the Word of God as His defense. He didn't argue nor debate with His enemy; he simply presented the truth of the Word and it caused the adversary to leave Him. When we rely on the supernatural support of the Word of God, we are assured that God's power will be in it and victory will come if we hold fast to the truth and trust God. There are also angels on hand to minister to us when we make the Word of God our defense.

Daniel, who was known for his dedication to God, received the same response of angelic support when he chose the right words during challenging times. Angels will come and support effective spiritual language.

Then said he unto me, fear not Daniel: for from the first day that thou didst set thine heart to understand, and to chasten thyself before God, THY WORDS WERE HEARD AND I AM COME FOR THY WORDS."

(Dan. 10:12, KJV, emphasis added)

SUPERNATURAL SAFETY

"We sailed slowly with difficulty for several days and with great difficulty finally arrived off the town of Cnidus. The wind would not let us go any further in that direction, so we sailed down the sheltered side of the island of Crete, passing by Cape Salmone. We kept close to the coast and with great difficulty came to a place called Safe Harbours, not far from the town of Lasea. We spent a long time there, until it became dangerous to continue the voyage, for by now the Day of Atonement was already past. So Paul gave them this advice. 'Men, I see that our voyage from here on will be dangerous; there will be great damage to the cargo and to the ship, and the loss of life as well. But the army officer was convinced by what the captain and the owner of the ship said, and not by what Paul said...

"But soon a very strong wind-the one called 'North-easter' – blew down from the island. It hit the ship, and since it was impossible to keep the ship headed into the wind, we gave up trying and let it be carried along by the wind... 'Men, you should have listened to me and not have sailed from Crete; then we would have avoided all this damage and loss. BUT NOW I BEG YOU, TAKE HEART! NOT ONE OF YOU WILL LOSE YOUR LIFE; ONLY THE SHIP WILL BE LOST. FOR LAST NIGHT AN ANGEL OF THE GOD TO WHOM I BELONG AND WHOM I WORSHIP CAME TO ME

AND SAID, 'DON'T BE AFRAID, PAUL! You must stand before the Emperor. And God in his goodness to you has spared the lives of all those who are sailing with you.' So take heart, men! For I trust in God that it will be just as I was told.'"

(Acts 27: 7-11, 14-17, 21-25, GNB, emphasis added)

Paul was aboard a ship with an unwise captain, owner and crew. They, like many people today, didn't heed the obvious warning signs of "bad weather," or conditions that could be obviously unfavorable to everyone and to their investments. But, the presence of an anointed man of God gave unmerited favor to the crew of the ship when they faced a terrible storm. Paul had a sure and powerful word and it was further reinforced by the angelic visitation. Although the ship and precious cargo were lost, not one life was lost. Paul had divine favor upon him because he was on a mission from God to stand before the Emperor. This is a great example of how divine purpose preserves us.

As kings we have the power, purpose and peace of God upon us. We are protected by angels, supported by God's Word and profoundly blessed!

MY DECREE

GOD SAVE THE *King!*

EPILOGUE - RELEASE THE REFORMERS!

The time of reformation for the Seven Mountains of Culture has truly arrived. **Hebrews 9:10** is the only verse in the Bible that mentions the word **reformation**, but be assured, the culture of reformation is found throughout the Bible. God is consistently engaging the disorder that resulted from the fall of mankind in the Garden of Eden, overlaying kingdom order upon disruptive patterns. His first order of business in doing that was to place mankind back in the authoritative role that Adam was originally in, but without the weakness of being without redemption and being legally bound to submit to sin. In order to restore Earth, God had to raise the "standard" and give mankind supernatural ability and clear marks for the territories and assignments we are to undertake. Our authority isn't ambiguous, random or undefined. It is authority for assignment—specific and focused. We are empowered to "press into success" by re-"forming" planet Earth's cultures and spheres of influence.

The word **"Reformation"** is from the Greek term **"Diorthosis,"** from **"Dia"** or "channel," or "to go through," and **"Orthos,"** meaning: To rise and be erect. Collectively this means that God has released a channel or frequency of knowledge and revelation that causes the downtrodden nature of the world to arise to a higher and more perfect consciousness. This frequency is being transmitted through messages of kingdom culture, wherein believers hear a more intense and powerful word about who they are and can become in Christ. This frequency is invitational and its drawing all of us to hear things we might not have heard before. It stirs us and challenges us and makes us hungry and thirsty for greater dimensions of the demonstration of the Spirit and power, that the faith of people will not be in the wisdom of men but in the power of God. (I Cor. 2:4)

More than conflict, unrest, and a demand for change, reformation is more about the application of supernatural principles that encourage us to be better people, with better beliefs and better responses to crisis. It's about a change in how we view ourselves, how we view others and how we view life. It's about new alliances and partnerships—how talking about unity can bring great results. Reformers want what God wants!

> **We can raise the standard of behavior in the Seven Mountains of Culture by raising the standard of action!**

It may not all happen in our lifetimes, but we will see more positive changes than we ever have. We'll see distinctive parts of the wealth transfer take place as God shifts the balance of power, placing "kings" onto thrones to make those changes happen. God will place believers in seats of power and influence in every cultural pivot point in the world. Brilliant minds will appear in laboratories making some of the most profound discoveries of all

time. Financial geniuses will come on the scene with incredible solutions to the most pressing problems we now face in the marketplace. Inventors will discover the most practical and powerful solutions of all time. Statesmen with profound diplomatic and peacemaking skills will bring calm in the midst of severe conflict. People who spent many years on the bottom will rise to the tops of their mountains with great influence.

NEW REALMS OF REFORMATION

The spirit of Cyrus will arise, fresh in the Earth, to befriend and bolster the work of dedicated "kings." Even among nations that do not profess Christianity, you will see reduced animosity and antagonism toward kingdom culture. *"When you please the Lord, you can make your enemies your friends." (Prov. 16:7, GNB).* All of the kings in this new season will not be Christians but many of them will be allies.

> *"The Lord has chosen Cyrus to be king! He has appointed him to conquer nations; HE SENDS HIM TO STRIP KINGS OF THEIR POWER; THE LORD WILL OPEN THE GATES OF CITIES FOR HIM. To Cyrus the Lord says, 'I MYSELF WILL PREPARE YOUR WAY, LEVELLING MOUNTAINS AND HILLS. I will break down bronze gates and smash their iron bars. I will give you treasures from the dark, secret places; then you will know that I am the Lord, and that the God of Israel has called you by name. I appoint you to help my servant Israel, the people that I have chosen. I HAVE GIVEN YOU GREAT HONOR, ALTHOUGH YOU DO NOT KNOW ME.'"*

> *(Isa. 45:1-4, GNB, emphasis added)*

New alliances are rising from some of the oddest places. There are "kings" that we didn't know before, but who'll align themselves with us to reform the Earth! God will release them to **"strip** [other] **kings of**

their power and level mountains [errant authorities]!" They'll do some of the **"dirty work"** for us.

Since we have become the blessed seed of Abraham through our faith in Christ, we are able to share the turnabout that is promised to Israel. Whereas we struggled in times past to gain the stature and strength that was needed to face worldly powers, we will now see the roles reversed. This new state of reform, or **"Orthos,"** which means: To rise and be erect raises us to new levels. We are not demanding people or nations to serve us, but they will begin to recognize the power of our sovereign God. This new stature will result in a greater transfer of wealth, substance and resources, enabling us to bring much needed changes. Kingdom influence and resources will cause believers to gain the attention of world powers. We'll become the **"deal closers"**—finishing and locking up assignments—that represent God and bring true reform! We will do this successfully. We are in place to become "**game-changers**" and bring about the type of reformation that exalts the King of kings and brings the Seven Mountains of Culture back into divine alignment.

MY DECREE

I am more than a conqueror through Christ who has chosen me, prepared me and equipped me for my throne. I will arise in victory and be confident in the power of God, who sits on the throne of heaven. This is God's plan and has been, long before today. I am part of a perfect plan for the redemption of souls, systems and societies. I am open to new and effective partnerships with people who God has chosen for me. I am part of a winning team. My "team" and my "tribe" are heading my way. We will connect in divine intersections of life. I am a reformer! I am a king… and

I SEE *Thrones!*

ABOUT THE AUTHOR
DR. GORDON E. BRADSHAW

D r. Gordon E. Bradshaw is the Founder/President of Global Effect Movers & Shakers Network (GEMS) and the 3M Project Global Initiative-Merging Ministries, Marketplace and Municipalities for Community Transformation. Serving God for over 42 years, with 25 of them as an apostle, he has made a wide variety of contributions to the kingdom and the community. His assignment and mission are to empower, enlighten and encourage kingdom citizens to reach their full potential and purpose in life and to see the kingdoms of this world become the kingdoms of God.

In addition to church planting, mentoring, bridge-building, teaching and conducting conferences and seminars, he served in the U.S. Navy and Reserves for 16 years, and served in Public Safety and the Fire Service for over 30 years, rising to the rank of Chief Executive Officer

(Fire Chief). He was on the faculty of the Indiana Vocational Technical College and state fire service training staff; and is a consultant and advisor to public safety officials, mayors and corporate and community leaders. He serves as Senior Scholar of Spiritual Formation and Leadership for Hope Bible Institute and Seminary; and is the Founder/President of the Misrah Academy – Governmental Empowerment Center.

He is an Executive Board Member of the Southland Ministerial Health Network of Chicago-land, Founding Member of Pastors4PCOR (Patient Centered Outcomes Research Group), member - Board of Directors and Chairman of the Public Policy Committee with the Gary, Indiana Chamber of Commerce; member - Northwest Indiana World Trade Alliance, and former member of the International Fire Chief's Association. He is a member of the board of directors for KCIA (Kingdom Congressional International Alliance), Goodwill Ambassador for Golden Rule International; winner of the iChange Nations Human Conservation Solutionist Award, and the Distinguished Leadership Award.

Dr. Bradshaw holds a degree in Applied Fire Science and Technology and Ph.D., Th.D., and D.D. degrees in ministry and theology. He is the author of the acclaimed books - *The Technology of Apostolic Succession: Transferring the Purposes of God to the Next Generation of Kingdom Citizens*, and *Authority for Assignment: Releasing the Mantle of God's Government in the Marketplace.* He resides in a suburb of Chicago, Illinois with his family.

ALSO FROM DR. BRADSHAW
with Kingdom House Publishing

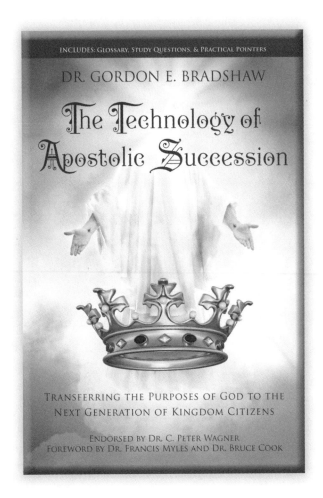

The Technology of Apostolic Succession
Transferring the Purposes of God to the Next Generation of Kingdom Citizens

ALSO FROM DR. BRADSHAW
with Kingdom House Publishing

Authority for Assignment
Releasing the Mantle of God's Government
in the Marketplace